MURDERS, MASSACRES, & MAYHEM

IN THE MID-ATLANTIC

Horrific Tales of Death & Destruction
& Information about the Graves of the Deceased

JOE FARRELL AND JOE FARLEY
with Lawrence Knorr

SUNBURY
PRESS ®
Mechanicsburg, PA USA

Published by Sunbury Press, Inc.
Mechanicsburg, Pennsylvania

SUNBURY
P R E S S ®
www.sunburypress.com

For information about special discounts for bulk purchases, please contact Sunbury Press Orders Dept. at (855) 338-8359 or orders@sunburypress.com.

To request one of our authors for speaking engagements or book signings, please contact Sunbury Press Publicity Dept. at publicity@sunburypress.com.

SECOND SUNBURY PRESS EDITION: January 2024

Set in Adobe Garamond | Interior design by Crystal Devine | Cover by Lawrence Knorr | Edited by the authors.

Publisher's Cataloging-in-Publication Data
Names: Farrell, Joe, author | Farley, Joe, author | Knorr, Lawrence, author.
Title: Murders, massacres, and mayhem in the mid-Atlantic : horrific tales of death & destruction & information about the graves of the deceased / Joe Farrell, Joe Farley, and Lawrence Knorr.
Description: Second trade paperback edition. | Mechanicsburg, PA : Sunbury Press, 2024. | Includes index.
Summary: The authors have combed the Mid-Atlantic region, including Pennsylvania, Maryland, New Jersey, New York, Delaware, and Washington, DC, to write about and visit the graves of some of the most horrendous murders, massacres, and calamities in our nation's history.
Identifiers: ISBN : 979-8-88819-178-1 (softcover) | ISBN : 979-8-88819-179-8 (ePub).
Subjects: BISAC: BIOGRAPHY & AUTOBIOGRAPHY / Rich & Famous. | HISTORY / US History / Mid-Atlantic.

Product of the United States of America
0 1 1 2 3 5 8 13 21 34 55

Continue the Enlightenment!

CONTENTS

INTRODUCTION

The three of us were talking on an early morning drive headed to the New York City area to visit some sites to include in the book Gotham Graves Volume Two. The conversation turned to topics we had covered in our series of Keystone Tombstone books. As we spoke we were all somewhat surprised by the number of our stories that included untimely deaths, executions, and tragedies that resulted in a massive loss of life. Larry gave voice to the idea first saying there's enough material there for a new book adding you could call it *Murders, Massacres, and Mayhem in the Mid-Atlantic*. The idea seemed to make a lot of sense. Not only could we share some of the stories we had already told but it opened up the opportunity to research and tell new tales that we could make available to our readers.

The first task was selecting chapters that had already been written that would be appropriate for this volume. Some were fairly obvious. After all, we had already told the story of Herman Mudgett who by now is widely recognized as the nation's first serial killer. Mudgett has been the subject of a History Channel series that included his exhumation to prove that he was indeed laid to rest in a cemetery outside Philadelphia. The story of the Molly Maguires that culminated in the largest mass execution in the history of the Commonwealth of Pennsylvania was another easy choice. The previously written chapters on Flight 93, the Titanic, and the Triangle Factory Fire also seemed logical choices for their inclusion.

Other stories are not nearly as well known or have been largely forgotten. The chapter on the "Babes in the Woods" covers a tragedy that made nationwide news in the Depression-era 1930s but is known by few today. The tale of Mary Mallon better known as Typhoid Mary is told. There is also a chapter on Harry Thaw whose Madison Square Garden rooftop murder of the building's architect has been the subject of two major motion pictures. Additionally, moving back to the Pennsylvania coalfields, the slaughter of Slavic miners in the 1890s that became known as the Lattimer massacre is brought to light. Finally, there is the story of Joseph Petrosino the crime-fighting New York City policeman who was killed in Italy while investigating crimes associated with a New York syndicate known as the Black Hand.

New stories include America's most famous duel that pitted the sitting Vice President of the United States against the former Secretary of the Treasury. There is also a chapter on the *General Slocum* disaster which until 9/11 was the incident that accounted for the greatest loss of life in the history of New York City. The murder of labor leader Jack Jablonski and his family is also detailed on the pages that follow.

As with our past works, the information contained in the chapters that follow is derived from a number of sources. These include public and our personal libraries, newspapers and of course the Internet.

With every book we've written we continue to uncover new stories, people, and events we were previously unaware of. It is our hope that the reader will have a similar experience as the pages in this volume are turned. It is after all to our readers that we are most indebted for the positive feedback they have given us that supplies us with the renewed energy to pursue these projects.

We would be remiss not to thank Lou Sauers and Jim Farley (Joe's brother) for their assistance as they accompanied on some of our trips to locate the graves and other important sites associated with these stories. We'd also like to thank our two sons Marc Farrell and James Farley for their technical and research assistance sorely needed by their fathers.

It goes without saying (though we'd never let it) that we more than appreciate the support we've received from our wives: Sharon Farley, Mary Farrell, and Tammi Knorr. Their solid support has made this and our other projects possible.

"America's First School Massacre"

ENOCH BROWN (1694-1764) AND RUTH HALE, RUTH HART, EBEN TAYLOR, GEORGE DUNSTAN, TWO DEAN BOYS, AND FOUR UNKNOWNS

County: Franklin County, Pennsylvania
City: Antrim Township
Cemetery: Enoch Brown Memorial Park
Address: 2730 Enoch Brown Road

In a bucolic wooded park in rural Antrim Township, Franklin County, Pennsylvania, northwest of Greencastle, stands a solitary gray granite obelisk honoring a deceased schoolmaster and ten of his pupils lost in a horrific mass murder committed by members of the Delaware tribe in the months after the French and Indian War during a conflict known as Pontiac's War. It was the first mass murder in a school in what would become the United States of America.

The French and Indian War had ended with the Treaty of Paris in February 1763. However, tensions remained high in Penn's colony between the natives and the white settlers, especially as the Scotch-Irish continued to settle into the western reaches of the commonwealth, outside of the territorial limits agreed to in treaties.

Later that year, in December, the infamous Paxton Boys massacred over twenty Conestoga Indians, including women and children, who had been living peacefully near Lancaster. This was in response to attacks occurring in the wilderness and a general lack of trust between the two sides.

William Henry, from Lancaster, witnessed the attack:

The horrific murder of the Conestogas by the Paxton Boys near Lancaster, Pennsylvania.

I saw a number of people running down the street towards the gaol, which enticed me and other lads to follow them. At about sixty or eighty yards from the gaol, we met from twenty-five to thirty men, well mounted on horses, and with rifles, tomahawks, and scalping knives, equipped for murder. I ran into the prison yard, and there, O what a horrid sight presented itself to my view! Near the back door of the prison, lay an old Indian and his women, particularly well-known and esteemed by the people of the town, on account of his placid and friendly conduct. His name was Will Sock; across him and his Native women lay two children, of about the age of three years, whose heads were split with the tomahawk, and their scalps all taken off. Towards the middle of the gaol yard, along the west side of the wall, lay a stout Indian, whom I particularly noticed to have been shot in the breast, his legs were chopped with the tomahawk, his hands cut off, and finally a rifle ball discharged in his mouth; so that his head was blown to atoms, and the brains were splashed against, and yet hanging to the wall, for three or four feet around. This man's hands and feet had also been chopped off with a tomahawk. In this manner lay the whole of them, men, women, and children, spread about the prison yard: shot-scalped-hacked-and cut to pieces.

The Paxton Boys march on Philadelphia to demand action and to attack Indians harbored there.

When 250 Paxton Boys marched on Philadelphia in January 1764 to demand action by the government and to attack over 150 Indians hiding there, Benjamin Franklin and other civic leaders met with them. Said Franklin at the time, ". . . the Conestoga would have been safe among any other people on earth, no matter how primitive, except white savages from Peckstang and Donegall!" Embarrassed, the Paxton Boys dispersed.

Throughout the year, tensions simmered and attacks flared on the edges of the wilderness. Finally bending to pressure from the settlers, on July 7, 1764, John Penn, the governor and grandson of William Penn, signed a decree offering a bounty for Indian scalps:

> For every male Indian enemy above ten years old, who shall be taken prisoner and delivered at any forts garrisoned by the troops in pay of this Province, or at any of the county towns, to the keeper of the common gaols there, the sum of one hundred & fifty Spanish dollars, or pieces of eight; for every female enemy taken prisoner and brought in as aforesaid, and for every male Indian enemy ten years old, or under, taken prisoner, and delivered as aforesaid, the sum of one hundred & thirty pieces of eight; for the scalp of every male Indian enemy above

the age of ten years, produced as evidence of their being killed, the sum of one hundred & thirty pieces of eight, and for the scalp of every female Indian enemy above the age of ten years, produced as evidence of their being killed, the sum of fifty pieces of eight; and that there shall be paid to every officer, or officers, soldier, or soldiers, as are or shall be in the pay of this Province, who shall take, bring in, and produce any Indian enemy prisoner, or scalp, as aforesaid, one half of said several and respective premiums & bounties.

The Pennsylvania Archives record "secret expeditions" following the decree that were "more effective than any sort of defensive operations."

Less than three weeks later, on July 26, 1764, a small war party of four or more Delawares approached the settlements in Antrim Township. They came upon Susan King Cunningham, on the road on her way to a neighbor's house. She was with child. The Indians beat her to death, scalped her, and cut the unborn baby from her body, setting it next to her.

The party then turned its attention to a log cabin in which Enoch Brown, the schoolmaster, was conducting a class for eleven of his students. Fortunately, several students did not attend that day for various reasons. Enoch, who had been born in Ireland and was approaching his 70th birthday, was a pious man and one of the few teachers in the region. When the war party entered the cabin, Brown offered himself provided the children would be spared. The Indians would hear none of it and while at least two guarded the door, the third proceeded to murder and scalp all present. From *Notes on Franklin County History* by John L. Finafrock:

One of the cherished traditions of the terrible tragedy is that Schoolmaster Brown was shot down with the Bible in his hand before he could make any resistance and on his knees begged only that the innocent children might be spared. Parkman, in describing the ghastly sight that met those who first entered the schoolhouse after the massacre says: 'In the center lay the master, scalped and lifeless, with a Bible clasped in his hands; while around the room were strew the bodies of

The obelisk marking the spot of the former Enoch Brown cabin where the massacre occurred.

SACRED TO THE MEMORY OF SCHOOLMASTER
ENOCH BROWN AND ELEVEN SCHOLARS, VIZ:
RUTH HART, RUTH HALE, EBEN TAYLOR, GEORGE
DUNSTAN, ARCHIE McCULLOUGH AND SIX OTHERS
(NAMES UNKNOWN) WHO WERE MASSACRED AND
SCALPED BY INDIANS ON THIS SPOT, JULY 26
1764, DURING THE PONTIAC WAR,
  TWO DEAN BOYS WERE AMONG THE VICTIMS HERE.
   TOFORE UNKNOWN. AUG. 4, 1898.

One of the four inscriptions on the obelisk.

his mangled pupils.' Another tradition says that Mr. Linn, while working in a meadow in the vicinity, heard the shot that killed Schoolmaster
Brown, and when he and others came to see what was the matter they
found little Archie McCullough, who survived the scalping, sitting
by the spring nearby washing the blood from his mangled head. He
told them that when the four Indians opened the door, Master Brown,
knowing well their object begged them to take him as their victim
and let the innocent children return to their homes. The same instant
he was shot down, and then he and the other children were quickly
tomahawked and scalped by two of the savages while the other two
stood with murderous weapons in the doorway.

The local farmers were horrified. The bodies of the children were
initially returned to their families and taken to their homes. Several days
later, Enoch Brown and his students were laid to rest together in a large
wooden box and buried near the schoolhouse. Most accounts say ten students were killed. Ruth Hale, Ruth Hart, Eben Taylor, George Dustan,
two Dean boys and four unknowns are listed among the dead. Some
accounts say one child other than Archie survived the scalping. One account adds that four additional children were captured.

When the war party returned home to their camp at Muskingum in the Ohio Country and showed-off their scalps, they were ostracized by their chief. John McCullough, a young settler and cousin of Archie who had been captured years before and was a prisoner, witnessed the arrival of the warriors and wrote in his diary:

I saw the Indians when they returned home with the scalps; some of the old Indians were very much displeased at them for killing so many children, especially Neep-paugh'-whese, or Night Walker, an old chief, or half king—he ascribed it to cowardice, which was the greatest affront he could offer them.

The nearby grave of Enoch Brown and ten schoolchildren.

According to tradition, some of the children had hesitated to go to school that day. Only eleven, two girls and nine boys, were present, representing ten families.

One of the absentees was Sarah "Sally" Brown, the daughter of George Brown of Brown's Mill. She remained home to assist the family with pulling flax. Later, she married Benjamin Chambers, the son of the founder of Chambersburg and a Lieutenant in the Revolutionary War.

Elenore Cochran, who was from Waynesboro, was living with the George Brown family to attend school with Sally. She also stayed home that day. She later married Captain Joseph Junkins who became a hero in the Revolution. Of their fourteen children, Elenore was the first wife of General Stonewall Jackson.

Elenore Pawling, whose father operated the Pawling Tavern, remained home that day. She ultimately married Dr. Robert Johnston, a distinguished surgeon during the Revolutionary War.

Mary Ramsey had a premonition that some evil was going to happen and stayed home. She later married into the Agnew family who were in

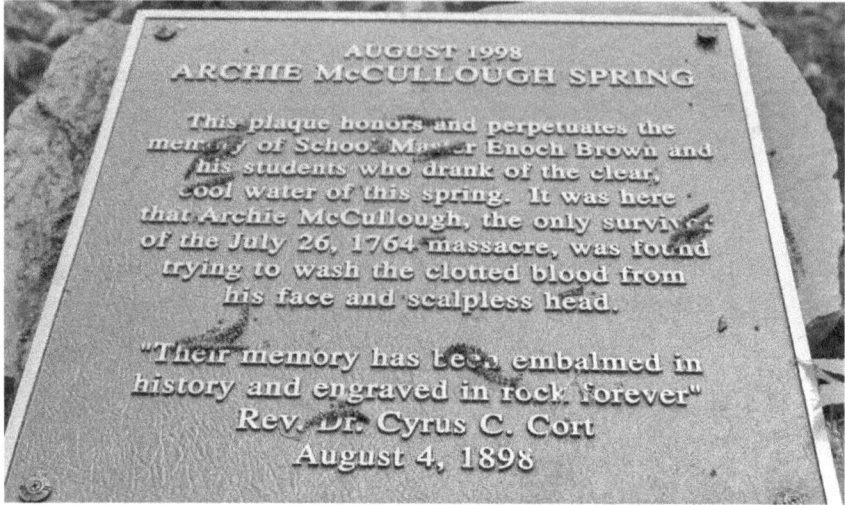

The plaque marking the spot where Archie McCullough washed his bloody head.

the medical profession. Her niece, Mary, married Archibald Irvin. One of their daughters, Jane, married the son of President William Henry Harrison. As a widow in 1841, she was the mistress of the White House during her father-in-law's brief administration. Jane's sister, Elizabeth, married John Scott Harrison, also a son of the president. They became the parents of Benjamin Harrison who was the twenty-third president of the United States.

James Poe played hooky that day. A neighbor, Mrs. Betty Hopkins, saw James climb a tree to watch a local farmer mow his hay. When he returned home, he lied about going to school and was punished. James later served in the militia and rose to captain during the Revolution. He was involved in local government and politics for many years.

For many years, this tale was thought to be legendary. The grave site was unmarked, and many of the families had moved away. Widow Betty Hopkins, who lived in a small house near the school had her windows covered with wooden boards giving the appearance that the house was abandoned. The war party passed her by that day, but she vividly recalled the burial of the unfortunates and repeated the story to David Detrich as a boy. He later became General David Detrich who laid Mrs. Hopkins to rest at the age of 104 in the 1840s. Detrich recalled the story of the schoolhouse scalpings and worked with community member Andrew Rankin to investigate it. Rankin and twenty citizens of the area dug at the location to try to rediscover the burial site. They were successful, unearthing the skeletons of one adult and ten children in a common grave. At the time, the landowner, Chrisitan Hoser, planted four locust trees to mark the site.

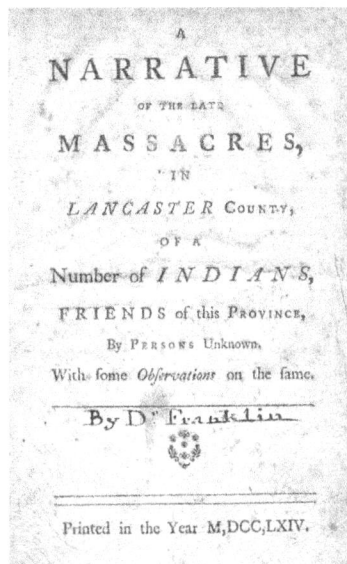

Ben Franklins pamphlet regarding the Paxton Boys.

When the trees were cut down in the spring of 1883, some locals felt the site would be forgotten if something wasn't done. The following year, the Franklin County Centennial Convention decided to raise money in order to honor Enoch Brown and the children with a park and a monument on the site of the former cabin. It was dedicated in 1885 inscribed with information about the fallen and the following:

The ground is holy where they fell
And where their mingled ashes lie,
Ye Christian people mark it well
With granite column strong and high;

And cherish well, forevermore,
The storied wealth of early years,
The sacred legacies of yore
The toils and trials of pioneers.

The nearby grave site was also marked with a monument inscribed: "The grave site of Enoch Brown and ten scholars massacred by the Indians July 26, 1764. In 1998, a third monument was erected by the creek, down the hill from the grave. It honors the Archie McCullough spring, where the children would go for water and where Archie washed his bloody scalp.

Remembrances have been held at the site over the years and a coin was struck by the Greencastle Rotary Club in 1964, upon the 200th anniversary.

Today, quaint little Enoch Brown park is tucked between residences along Enoch Brown Road. There is a children's playground on the site and a short hiking trail in addition to the monuments.

If You Go:

Greencastle, Pennsylvania, is just a few miles from the Mason-Dixon line, on the west side of Interstate 81. Prior to the Civil War, the Underground Railroad was prevalent in the area. During Lee's invasion of the North, before and after the Battle of Gettysburg, Confederate troops passed through.

There are several fine establishments at or near the quaint circle at the center of town, or venture a few blocks south on Route 11 to the John Allison Public House for a hearty meal and good spirits.

2

"Babes in the Woods"

NORMA SEDGWICK
ELMO NOAKES
DEWILLA NOAKES
WINIFRED PIERCE
CORDELIA NOAKES

County: Cumberland
Town: Carlisle
Cemetery: Westminster Memorial Gardens
Address: 1159 Newville Road

Sadly, the authors are old enough to have been raised by parents who lived during the Great Depression. I remember hearing lots of stories from my parents and grandparents about how tough times were and how much people suffered during the Depression. I think I was in high school before I learned that "depression" could be an economic term. Until then, I thought it was called "The Depression" because so many people were depressed emotionally as a result of the hard times. The story of the "Babes in the Woods" is perhaps illustrative of just how bad things were during that time.

On November 24, 1934, two men were in the woods near Carlisle intending to cut some firewood when they saw a mound covered with a green blanket. Clark Jardine and John Clark thought it was an odd thing to see in the woods and by the looks of it, it hadn't been there very long. They decided to check it out and were horrified at what they found. Under the blanket were the bodies of three young girls. The two men went in search of a telephone and called the police in Carlisle. The police arrived shortly and so did a crowd, some seeking children of their own who had gone missing.

The bodies of Norma, Dewilla, and Cordelia Noakes, collectively known as the "Babes in the Woods," were found Nov. 24, 1934. (Pennsylvania State Police)

The girls looked like they were almost certainly related to one another. The Carlisle chief of police speculated that they were probably sisters. They were dressed in nice outfits, including coats. No one knew or had any idea who the girls were. A Dickinson College professor analyzed pieces of their hair and corroborated the speculation that they were sisters. The bodies had no wounds or marks on them other than a small mark on the forehead of one girl. This mark launched police on a search for a possible secret society whose symbol might have been marked on the child. This led nowhere. The sad mystery of the three girls swept the nation.

The quest for the girls' identity started a nationwide media frenzy. The photographs of the children lying on a blanket at the site were printed in newspapers across the country. Thousands came to view the bodies in hopes of identifying them. Death masks were made before burial to continue the search. The media frenzy led to many false leads for the police.

Five days after the bodies were discovered, a black leather suitcase was found in brush about three miles from the point where the bodies had been located. A man named John Naugle, of New Cumberland, had found the suitcase. It contained clothing similar to that worn by the three small girls, as well as a notebook with the name "Norma" written on it, in what appeared to be a youngster's handwriting.

Brothers Robert and Elmo Noakes served in the U.S. Marine Corps during World War I.

Shortly after the girls' bodies surfaced, the bodies of a man and woman were found in an abandoned railroad flag stop about 100 miles away in Duncansville, Pa., just south of Altoona. The woman had been shot in the heart and the head, and the man had been shot in the head. A few days later a 1929 blue Pontiac sedan was found abandoned in a field near McVeytown, in Mifflin County. The car had no license plates and was out of gas. Its engine number had been intentionally obscured.

The car was traced to a man by the name of Elmo Noakes. The description of the car, the physical features of the bodies, and Elmo Noakes' fingerprints from U.S. Marine records led to identification of the bodies as being that of Noakes (31 years old at the time of his death) and Winifred Pierce (age 18), formerly of Roseville, California. Pierce was also identified from pictures and by the fact that she had a deformed left foot.

Elmo Noakes was born on January 8, 1903 in Springville, Utah. He and his brother Robert served in the Marines from 1920 to 1922. In July 1923, he married a woman named Mary Hayford. Mary had a daughter named Norma Sedgwick from a previous marriage. Mary and Elmo had two children together: daughters Dewilla (born May 2, 1924) and Cordelia (born June 2, 1926).

In 1932, Mary died from infection following a self-induced abortion in Salt Lake City, Utah. Subsequently, Elmo moved to Roseville, California, where his three sisters could help care for and raise Norma, Dewilla, and Cordelia. He was employed by Pacific Fruit Express, a railroad fruit shipping company.

Winifred "Winnie" Pierce was born on September 1, 1916, in Utah, to father Hugh Pierce and mother Pearl Noakes (Elmo's oldest sister, thus making Elmo Winifred's uncle, and she his niece). Winifred moved to

This tombstone marks the spot where the babes were laid to rest.

Roseville and attended high school there. After high school, she went to work as a housekeeper for Elmo. How she and Elmo and his three daughters wound up lying dead on Pennsylvania soil would prove to be an interesting challenge for investigators in the Keystone State, who were essentially left with no choice other than to start working backwards in the hopes of piecing together what may have transpired.

The girls' bodies were taken to the Ewing Funeral Home on South Hanover Street in Carlisle. An autopsy revealed that the children had had nothing to eat for at least 18 hours prior to their deaths. A pathologist at Harrisburg Hospital, George Moffitt, tested sections of the girls' organs and determined that they had not died of carbon monoxide poisoning, and that they had not been sexually assaulted. Another postmortem exam failed to find any indications of poison in the girls' systems.

If the girls could not be identified, they would be buried in a potter's field. State police asked the Pa. Board of Education to inquire about missing children of every school in Pennsylvania. Finally, three people came forward who claimed to have seen a man and a woman together with the three children in a restaurant in Philadelphia on November 19. The restaurant was the LaSalle Sandwich Shoppe on North Broad Street. The owner, Louis Ellis, remembered talking to Elmo Noakes about looking for work and Noakes saying he would take anything he could get. He mentioned his family was getting to be a "pretty big burden."

A waitress at the restaurant, Ann Gasparon, seated the party of five at two tables, and remembered that they ordered only one meal to be shared by all of them. A customer sitting nearby with her eight-year-old son heard this and felt sorry for the children. Anna LaFauvre invited the girls to join her and her son for a meal. The youngest Noakes child did, and they had a nice conversation. The girl told Mrs. LaFauvre they were from California and that she was in the third grade.

After the discovery of the bodies, all three adult witnesses from the restaurant were brought to Carlisle to assist in identifying the deceased children. Mrs. LaFauvre identified the bodies and fainted. Ellis and Gasparon also identified the girls as the ones they had seen in the restaurant. They were all driven to view the adult decedents and again recognized the bodies. As a result, the papers printed their identities on November 30, 1934, as:

Cordelia Noakes, age 8
Dewilla Noakes, age 10
Norma Sedgwick, age 13
Elmo Noakes, age 32
Winifred Pierce, age 18

On December 1, the funeral for the girls was held at Ewing Funeral Home. Hundreds of people attended, despite a heavy rain. The funeral/burial was paid for by the American Legion Post, apparently because Elmo Noakes had been a Marine. Boy scouts and girl scouts served as pallbearers. Presbyterian, Catholic, and Episcopal clergy all participated. The burial was in Westminster Cemetery. A stone monument marks their burial spot.

Days later, Elmo Noakes and Winifred Pierce were also buried in Westminster Cemetery, about 100 yards from the girls in separate graves. The American Legion provided for Elmo's funeral and a bugler played "Taps" over his grave. At that time, his role in the girls' deaths had not been established. Winnie's funeral was paid for by a sister.

Norma Sedgwick's father, Rowland, had tried to gain custody of his daughter after Mary Noakes died. He failed in his efforts and now he could not even afford to have her body transported to Utah where he lived. He was reportedly heartbroken.

In 1968, a group of Pennsylvania highway workers on their own time and initiative erected a blue and yellow keystone-shaped sign along Route 233 where the childrens' bodies were found. It reads:

ON   THIS   SPOT
WERE FOUND THREE
BABES IN THE WOODS
NOV. - 24 - 1934

We will never know for sure what happened. A State Police investigation concluded that Elmo Noakes left Roseville, California on November 11, 1934, with the three children and Winifred Pierce. Eleven days prior to their departure, on October 31, Noakes had purchased a blue 1929 Pontiac sedan for $46. Police theorized that he ran out of money and without prospects of employment killed the girls on November 21 rather than let them starve. It is generally believed that Noakes killed his daughters by suffocating them while they slept.

Then (the theory goes), after leaving the girls' bodies on blankets in the woods, Noakes and Pierce drove west, abandoned their car when it ran out of gas between McVeytown and Altoona, and hitchhiked to Altoona. On November 23, Pierce sold her coat, which was the couple's last possession except for the clothes they were wearing. Noakes bought a .22-caliber rifle from a second-hand store with the $2.55 Pierce got for her coat, and on November 24 used it to kill Pierce and then himself. The weapon was found lying between their bodies. They spent their last

This sign on a rural Pennsylvania road marks the spot where the bodies of the three young girls were found.

night together at the Congress Hotel at 118th Street in Altoona, where the woman who ran the hotel confirmed afterwards that she had indeed rented them a room for all the money they had on them: 48 cents.

By all accounts, Elmo Noakes had a good reputation, a job, loved and cared for the girls, and had a non-violent nature. There are many strange elements to this story—elements on which one can only speculate. For instance, the group left California three days before Noakes would have gotten a paycheck for two weeks' work—money that would have come in extremely handy for a group of people about to embark on a cross-country trip. The speculation is that family strife caused them to leave suddenly. News accounts report that Noakes' sisters cared for his daughters at first, that is up until the time Elmo hired his niece, Winnie, to be his housekeeper and take care of the girls. Winnie started by working at Elmo's house in the day and returning to her home at her mother's house in the evening. After about six months however, Winnie quit going home and moved in with Elmo.

The gossip in the community was that the relationship between uncle and niece had turned romantic, and two of Noakes' sisters strongly objected, even threatening to get the children removed from the household. Soon none of Elmo's sisters would speak to him. There was also acrimony between Winnie's mother, Pearl, and her husband, Hugh, over the situation. After the bodies were found, two of Noakes' sisters were found guilty of disturbing the peace stemming from

Here is the grave of Elmo Knoakes who took his own life after killing his three daughters.

their harassment of Pearl who they blamed for the deaths. Perhaps the turmoil reached a breaking point and led to impulsive, reckless behavior.

Also puzzling is the fact that—despite Elmo claiming to be looking for work—they traveled very fast across the country, and there were no reports of Noakes or Pierce actually asking for work. Their feeble attempts to avoid identification are also odd. The effacing of the car's VIN number, the discarding of the license plates, the use of aliases at places they stayed, the couples' manner of travel after leaving the bodies—these things all beg for explanations that won't ever be known for certain. Yet even after nearly 80 years, the memory of those beautiful young girls remains as haunting as ever.

If You Go:

Westminster Memorial Gardens is the final resting place for two American heroes:

John W. Minick, who was a staff sergeant in the United States Army when he was killed in action near Hurtgen, Germany, on November 21, 1944. On that day, he voluntarily led a small group of men through a minefield, single-handedly silenced two enemy machine gun emplacements, and engaged a company of German soldiers before he was killed while crossing a second minefield. For his actions he was awarded the Medal of Honor. His citation reads that he killed 22 enemy soldiers and captured 23 more. He was 36 years old.

Randall D. Shughart, who was a Special Forces soldier from Newville, Pennsylvania, and one of two soldiers (the other being Gary Gordon) who died trying to save the life of pilot Michael Durant, the only surviving member of a downed helicopter crew in Somalia on October 3, 1993. Shughart's actions—while costing him his own life—saved Durant's. For those actions, Shughart was awarded the Medal of Honor by President Clinton—the first soldier to be posthumously awarded the Medal of Honor since the Vietnam War. This incident was featured in the book and blockbuster Hollywood film *Black Hawk Down*. The movie won two Oscars and was nominated for two more.

Shughart has been memorialized in many ways. A United States Navy ship, a training facility in Fort Polk, Louisiana, and his hometown post office in Newville all bear his name. Twenty years after his death, his modest grave was enhanced with a monument in his memory.

Also in Carlisle is the Old Public Graveyard (South Bedford & East South Streets), where Molly Pitcher and a number of Revolutionary War figures are buried.

A very short distance from Westminster Memorial Gardens is the Rustic Tavern (823 Newville Road). We stopped in for lunch and were hoping the experience would pick up our spirits. It was a cold, gloomy day and the story of the "Babes in the Woods" had proven to be equally cold and gloomy. It worked! The food, service and ambiance were all great. We warmed ourselves by the fire, had a hearty lunch and some spirits, and left determined to live on.

3

"Dueling Founders"

AARON BURR

County: Essex
City: Princeton, New Jersey
Cemetery: Princeton Cemetery
Address: 29 Greenview Avenue

ALEXANDER HAMILTON

County: Manhattan
City: New York City
Cemetery: Trinity Churchyard
Address: 74 Trinity Place – Broadway and Wall Street

In the early morning hours of July 11, 1804, two small boats waited on the New York side of the Hudson River preparing to transport passengers to the Jersey side. The first two men to arrive near the village of Weehawken began clearing the grounds of tree limbs and brush on a grassy ledge. Sometime later the second boat arrived and two of its occupants made their way toward the outcropping where the original two passengers waited. Leaving a physician and his boatmen at the water's edge Alexander Hamilton, the former Secretary of the United States Treasury and Nathaniel Pendleton made their way to the newly cleared area where they were greeted as gentlemen by the sitting Vice President of the United States Aaron Burr and William P. Van Ness. Pendleton and Van Ness had agreed to act as seconds in what was to be the most famous duel in the history of the United States of America.

Hamilton and Burr had been political enemies for more than a decade yet they had much in common. Both had served the country well in the recently fought revolution. Both were lawyers who were widely considered to be the ablest legal minds in the city of New York. Both had

Alexander Hamilton

been instrumental in creating the first political parties formed in the new country. Both men were living beyond their means supporting large New York estates. Finally, both had political careers that were in decline on the day they met on the dueling grounds in New Jersey.

In the political world, Burr's star began its ascent when he was elected to the United States Senate in 1791. In doing so Burr bested Hamilton's father-in-law Phillip Schuyler. The Governor of New York was George Clinton, a man who Hamilton had accused of stealing the 1777 governor's race from the aforementioned Mr. Schuyler. Hamilton had also supported Clinton's opponent, Robert Yates, in the most recent governor's race. It was with Clinton's support that Burr unseated Schuyler. If anyone was responsible for Burr's rise and Schuyler's fall, it was Hamilton

Plaque at the site of America's most famous duel.

himself who, in addition to alienating the Clinton Family, had also managed to anger New York's powerful Livingston family by preventing them from receiving appointments from the Washington administration. It was with the backing of the Clinton and Livingston factions that Burr was elected, though Hamilton seemed to blame Burr for the outcome. Burr seemed to acknowledge the bitterness over the election confiding to one friend that "my election will be unpleasing to several persons now in Philadelphia."

In the presidential election of 1800, Burr once again bested Hamilton and, in doing so, provided the margin necessary to make Thomas Jefferson the third President of the United States. Unlike today, in 1800 the popular vote did not determine each state's electoral vote. In 1800 state legislators basically acted as middlemen who decided who would serve as presidential electors in the Electoral College.

Jefferson and Burr were both members of the Democratic-Republican Party that had been formed to oppose the Federalist party which, by 1800, was viewed as a party run by Hamilton even though the current president, John Adams, was a Federalist. Jefferson's party was championing him for the highest office in the land and Burr for the vice presidency.

An artists depiction of the duel which incorrectly shows Hamilton firing into the air. Hamilton's wayward shot actually struck a tree branch several feet above Burr's Head.

Burr had deduced that control of the New York electors would be in the hands of the party that elected the majority of Manhattan assemblymen. It appears that Jefferson agreed with Burr's view since he advised James Madison that "all depended on the city election."

Burr went to work assembling his list of candidates but did not announce them until after Hamilton's Federalists made public their candidates for office. The majority of men on the Federalist slate were not well-known while Burr's candidates included former Governor George Clinton and the hero of the Battle of Saratoga, General Horatio Gates. He rounded out his ticket with other Revolutionary War heroes while making sure that all three Republican party factions were represented; the Clintons, the Livingstons, and the vice presidential candidate's own supporters who were known as Burrites. When the votes were counted, the Republicans had won all thirteen of the contested seats in what was seen as a Burr victory over Hamilton.

A defeated Hamilton then wrote a letter to New York's governor John Jay urging the New York executive to call a special lame-duck session of the legislature to create a new process for naming presidential electors that would take that power away from the newly-elected assembly. Hamilton urged Jay to ignore the rule of law in dealing with what he described as a matter of "public safety." Hamilton viewed Jefferson's election to be a national emergency that could not go unchecked. The governor did not share Hamilton's views as he wrote on the bottom of Hamilton's missive, "Proposing a measure for party purposes which I think it would not become me to adopt." Needless to say, Jay did not act on Hamilton's request.

The New York vote, as it turned out, did not settle the election though that state's electoral vote did put Jefferson and Burr on top. When the final Electoral College votes were tabulated, Jefferson and Burr each received 73, besting their opponents Adams and Pinckney who received 65 and 64 votes respectively. The tie between Jefferson and Burr sent the election of the president to the House of Representatives.

With the election thrown to the House, where each state's vote counted as one and nine votes would elect the next President, members of Hamilton's party began considering other alternatives to deny Jefferson the presidency. Among the possibilities was throwing Federalist support behind Burr. The advantage here, as some Federalists saw it, was to create a division between Jefferson and Burr and their supporters. Some Federalists believed that such a schism would require Burr to seek the aid of their party if Burr wanted to achieve any success in administering the government. Indeed, many Federalist's preferred Burr to Jefferson. Gouverneur Morris reported that Federalists viewed Burr as a "vigorous practical man" who combined "courage" with "generosity." One article in the *Washington Federalist* used their service during the Revolution to compare the two men noting that Burr had risked his life and "gallantly exposed his life" in the fight for independence while Jefferson's only actions could be found in his writings. Burr was described as having risked his blood while Jefferson

Hamilton's likeness graces the country's ten dollar bill.

Bust of Hamilton near the New Jersey dueling site where he lost his life.

"has only hazarded his ink." One Federalist who did not prefer Burr to Jefferson was Hamilton. Hamilton accused Burr of being an unbalanced man who lacked moral values and political convictions. Many have viewed Hamilton's choice in the matter to reflect how unbiased he was. In making this choice, the reasoning was he must have had the interests of the nation at heart to prefer his longtime foe, Jefferson. This conclusion ignores one important possibility. If Federalists moved and elected Burr, might not Burr have replaced Hamilton as the most important leader and the man who had the most influence within his own party? Wouldn't Burr's election speed the erosion of Hamilton's waning political influence?

Eventually, Jefferson made a deal with the Federalists that elected him president. But all the rumors surrounding Burr had indeed planted doubts in Jefferson's mind relative to his vice president. The new chief executive refused to nominate those suggested by Burr for Federal posts and he began making his own friends among the powerful New York families, most notably the Clintons.

By 1804, New York's votes were no longer vital to Jefferson's reelection and his vice president was viewed as expendable. In addition, Jefferson was determined to be succeeded in office by another Virginian; his Secretary of State, James Madison. Seeing little future in Washington, Burr returned to New York to run for Governor. In many ways that decision set in motion the event that would end the political careers of both Hamilton and Burr.

The 1804 New York governor's campaign was as nasty as they come. The Clinton family backed John Lansing who accepted the Republican nomination. Just two days later on February 18th, Burr's supporters made known the Vice President's plan to seek the office. Not wanting to compete with Burr, Lansing withdrew and the Clintonians were forced to scramble to find another candidate. They settled on New York Supreme Court Justice Morgan Lewis. Hamilton had previously declared his support for Lansing and his exit from the race was seen as a positive sign for Burr. Though Burr narrowly carried New York City, he was soundly trounced outside of the city and lost the election.

On April 23, 1804, a Federalist, Dr. Charles D. Cooper, published a letter in the Albany newspaper. In the letter, Cooper reported that at a dinner Hamilton had referred to Burr as a "dangerous man" who was not to be trusted to run a government. The letter went on to state, "I could detail you a still more despicable opinion which General Hamilton has expressed of Mr. Burr." Burr did not learn about Dr. Cooper's letter until after the election. The Vice President did not take offense to being called a dangerous man and as a matter of fact, he was well aware that Hamilton had made similar statements about him in the past. It was the word despicable that concerned him. Burr viewed the use of that word as an insult to his private character.

This monument marks the final resting place of Alexander Hamilton. Based on it's location one would guess that Aaron Burr often passed it during his latter years in New York City.

Burr composed a letter that he had his friend, William P. Van Ness, deliver to Hamilton. The letter demanded that Hamilton "make the avowal or disavowal of the remark." Hamilton, in his written response, said he could not avow or disavow the statement. He wrote that the word "despicable" had various meanings and infinite shades "from very light to very dark." He also held that he could not be held accountable for remarks he might have made about a political opponent. Hamilton closed his letter saying, "I trust, on more reflection, you will see the matter in the same light as me. If not, I can only regret the circumstance, and must abide the consequence."

Hamilton's response only added fuel to Burr's fire. He composed a second letter that noted he had found nothing in Hamilton's missive that reflected "sincerity and delicacy which you profess to value." Burr accused Hamilton of hiding behind words, writing "Political opposition can never absolve gentlemen from the necessity of a rigid adherence to the laws of honor and the rules of decorum." Burr added that the issue between them had nothing at all to do with "grammatical accuracy", rather the issue remained "whether you have authorized this application either directly or by uttering expressions or opinions derogatory to my honor." After reading the letter, Hamilton informed Van Ness that he stood by his original response. Van Ness, who was acting as Burr's second, still hoping to avoid a duel, asked Hamilton if he could recollect the conversation in question. Some who have studied the exchange between the two parties have concluded that Van Ness was trying to give Hamilton some flexibility in disavowing the insults in order to avoid the duel. Hamilton, however, refused to change his position.

Later on the same day, Hamilton asked Nathaniel Pendleton to serve as his second. He sent Pendleton to Van Ness with another letter requesting that the matter be delayed. Van Ness met with Pendleton who conveyed a summary of the conversation which, as Hamilton remembered: "turned wholly on political topics and did not attribute to Colonel Burr, any instance of dishonorable conduct, nor relate to his private character." Hamilton's second letter did little to satisfy Burr. As far as Burr was concerned, Hamilton seemed to be complaining that Burr was asking for too much as Hamilton requested "greater latitude" in any disavowal he would issue. Refusing to budge, Burr demanded a general disavowal and as to this demand, Hamilton refused. On June 27, 1804, Burr's formal challenge was delivered to Hamilton.

Thus it was that Burr and Hamilton met on the Weehawken dueling ground. Their seconds were also present as was Hamilton's physician, Dr. David Hosack. Hamilton had written a document that was to be made public should he not survive the duel. In it he wrote that he intended to throw away his first fire. He also noted his moral objections to dueling and of Burr said, "I am conscious of no ill-will to Col. Burr, distinct from political opposition, which, I trust, has proceeded from pure and upright motives." As Burr's biographer Nancy Isenberg pointed out in her book

The final resting place of Vice President Aaron Burr who some refer to as a "Fallen Founder."

Fallen Founder, had Hamilton placed "all of his vicious letters about Burr before him, he might have had to alter his plea to posterity." Despite his pledge to throw away his first and possibly second fire, Hamilton delayed the start of the duel to test his vision. He then leveled his gun from various positions and put on his spectacles.

The two men stood with about thirty feet of ground between them. At Pendleton's command of "Present," they would be permitted to discharge their weapons. After the command was given, both of the seconds agreed that Hamilton and Burr fired within seconds of each other. They disagreed on who fired first. The bullet from Hamilton's pistol struck a tree branch that hung several feet above Burr's head. Burr's shot entered Hamilton's right hip, continued through the liver, and came to rest in the doomed man's spine. Hamilton fell to the ground and, according to Van Ness, Burr started toward the man he had just shot with "a manner and gesture of regret." Van Ness stopped Burr and hurried him to his boat waiting on shore. Hamilton's doctor raced to his side where Hamilton proclaimed that his wound was mortal. His prognosis was correct and he passed away the following day.

The duel that literally killed Hamilton also wounded Burr's already sagging political career. Though his adventures in the country were not yet over, he would never hold another political office. Hamilton may have lost the duel but, in the days and years to follow, he would be lionized as an American hero and Burr would, unfairly, be painted as a villain by numerous historians.

Hamilton was laid to rest in Manhattan in the Trinity Churchyard Cemetery. Burr died at the age of eighty in a Staten Island hotel. He was laid to rest in the Princeton Cemetery. There is a story that in his later years Burr read a comic English novel by Laurence Sterne titled *Tristam Shandy*. The story goes that Burr referenced a passage in the book where the main character, Uncle Toby, chases a fly out of a window rather than killing it. Referring to that story Burr is said to have remarked, "Had I read Sterne more and Voltaire less, I should have known that the world was wide enough for Hamilton and me."

If You Go:

There are a number of other luminaries buried in the Trinity Churchyard Cemetery. John Jacob Astor the businessman, merchant, and investor who became America's first multi-millionaire can be found at Trinity.

Also buried here is Robert Fulton who is often given credit for inventing the steamboat which is not the case. He did construct a steamboat called the *Clermont* and made it a commercial success by establishing the first permanent commercial route on the Hudson River.

Revolutionary War General Horatio Gates was laid to rest here. Gates claimed credit for the American victory in the Battle of Saratoga. He was blamed for the defeat at the Battle of Camden in 1780. He remains a controversial figure as a result of his participation in the Conway Cabal which sought to replace George Washington as commander of the American forces.

James Lawrence a United States Naval Officer, whose dying words "Don't give up the ship" made him famous, is buried here.

There are also three members of the Continental Congress, Francis Lewis, Walter Livingston, and Martin Luther, whose final resting place is at Trinity. Lewis signed the Declaration of Independence.

4

"40 Heroes"

FLIGHT 93 CRASH SITE

County: Somerset
Town: Shanksville
Address: 6424 Lincoln Highway

Just about every adult American remembers where he or she was on September 11, 2001. On that day, the deadliest terrorist attack in U.S. history took place when four commercial airliners were hijacked by members of the Islamic extremist group Al Queda. Two of those planes, American Airlines Flight 11 and United Airlines Flight 175, were crashed into the North and South towers, respectively, of the World Trade Center Complex in New York City. A third plane, American Airlines Flight 77, hit the western side of the Pentagon just outside Washington, D.C.

The nation's capital was also the target of the fourth plane, United Airlines Flight 93. Instead, it crashed into a field in Stonycreek Township, Pennsylvania, near Shanksville, after its passengers tried to overcome the hijackers. Nearly 3,000 people were killed during the attacks on September 11, a number that almost certainly would have been higher if not for the heroic actions of those aboard Flight 93.

Flight 93 was a regularly-scheduled nonstop flight from Newark, New Jersey, to San Francisco, California, set to depart at 8:00 A.M. The flight was delayed due to heavy air traffic and took off at 8:42 A.M. with 37 passengers and seven crew members. Four of the passengers were terrorists with plans to hijack the plane and fly it into the U.S. Capitol building. They had successfully boarded the plane with knives and boxcutters.

The hijacking began at 9:28 A.M., when the terrorists infiltrated the plane's cockpit. Air traffic controllers heard what they believed to be mayday calls and sounds of a struggle. At 9:32 A.M., a hijacker (later identified as Ziad Jarrah) was heard over the flight data recorder directing

This monument marks the opening of the Flight 93 memorial.

the passengers to sit down and stating that there was a bomb on board. The flight data recorder also shows that Jarrah reset the autopilot, turning the plane around and heading it towards Washington. By this time, the first two planes had already hit the World Trade Center in New York.

At 9:39 A.M., Jarrah once again announced that there was a bomb on board, that the plane was returning to the airport, and that the passengers should remain quiet. Air traffic controllers did not hear from the flight again.

The passengers began making calls using airphones and cell phones. A total of ten passengers and two crew members were able to complete phone calls. By now, the third plane had hit the Pentagon. Huddled in the back of the plane making calls and exchanging information, the passengers learned the fate of the three other hijacked flights, realized what was going on, and began to plan an insurrection.

One of the passengers, Tom Burnett, made several phone calls to his wife, Deena. He pumped her for information and interrupted her several times to tell the others what she was saying. During one of the calls, he told her:

"I know we're all going to die. There's three of us who are going to do something about it. I love you, honey."

This is a view of the actual crash site. The remains of the victims are buried here.

Another passenger, Todd Beamer, was heard by a GTE phone operator over an open line saying to his fellow passengers:

"Are you guys ready? Okay. Let's roll."

Flight attendant Sandra Bradshaw called her husband and told him she was preparing scalding water to throw on the hijackers. She ended by saying:

"Everyone is running up to first class. I've got to go. Bye."

At 9:57 A.M., the passengers and crew began their assault on the cockpit. Jarrah began to roll the aircraft left and right to knock the passengers off balance. The cockpit voice recorder captured sounds of crashing, screaming and the shattering of glass.

According to the *9/11 Commission Report*, Jarrah and another hijacker discussed intentionally crashing the plane into the ground before the passengers could break through to the cockpit—even though such a move would obviously prevent the hijackers from destroying their intended target in Washington (which was still more than 150 miles away

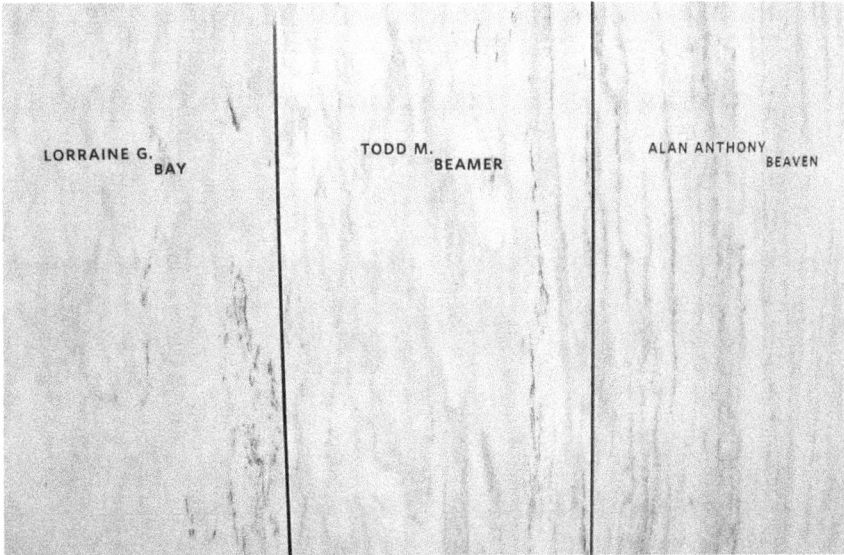

This is a wall constructed to the memory of the passengers and crew on the flight.

at that point). There were indications that the passengers were using a food cart to ram the cockpit door. The plane headed down and rolled onto its back, at which point one of the hijackers can be heard on the voice recorder shouting "Allah is great! Allah is the greatest!" The Report concludes that the hijackers remained at the controls but must have judged that the passengers were only seconds from overcoming them. With the sounds of the counter-attack continuing, the aircraft plowed into an empty field in Shanksville . . . about 20 minutes flying time from the U.S. Capitol.

Flight 93 fragmented violently upon impact. All human remains were found within a 70-acre area surrounding the impact point. By December 21, 2001, all of the people on board the flight had been identified. Investigators were not able to determine if any of the victims were dead before the plane crashed. It was later revealed that on the day of the crash, two F-16 fighter jets from the 121st Fighter Squadron of the D.C. Air National Guard had been scrambled and ordered to intercept Flight 93. Since time constraints at take-off had prevented the pilots from being able to arm their jets with missiles, their plan—had they reached Flight 93—was to ram the Boeing 757's cockpit and tail areas (hopefully ejecting from their respective jets just prior to impact).

THE 40 HEROES OF FLIGHT 93
THE CREW & PASSENGERS

CREW MEMBERS	AGE	HOMETOWN
Captain		
Jason M. Dahl	43	Littleton, Colorado
First Officer		
LeRoy Homer	36	Marlton, New Jersey
Flight Attendants		
Lorraine G. Bay	37	East Windsor, New Jersey
Sandy Waugh Bradshaw	38	Greensboro, North Carolina
Wanda Anita Green	49	Oakland, CA & Linden, N.J.
CeeCee Ross Lyles	33	Fort Pierce, Florida
Deborah Jacobs Welsh	49	New York City, New York

PASSENGERS	AGE	HOMETOWN
Christian Adams	37	Biebelsheim, Rheinland-Pfalz, Germany
Todd M. Beamer	32	Cranbury, New Jersey
Alan Anthony Beaven	48	Oakland, California
Mark Bingham	31	San Francisco, California
Deora Frances Bodley	20	San Diego, California
Marion R. Britton	53	Brooklyn, New York
Thomas E. Burnett, Jr.	38	Bloomington, Minnesota
William Joseph Cashman	60	West New York, New Jersey
Georgine Rose Corrigan	55	Honolulu, Hawaii
Patricia Cushing	69	Bayonne, New Jersey
Joseph DeLuca	52	Succasunna, New Jersey
Patrick Joseph Driscoll	70	Manalapan, New Jersey
Edward Porter Felt	41	Matawan, New Jersey
Jane C. Folger	73	Bayonne, New Jersey
Colleen L. Fraser	51	Elizabeth, New Jersey
Andrew (Sonny) Garcia	62	Portola Valley, California
Jeremy Logan Glick	31	Hewitt, New Jersey
Kristin White Gould	65	New York City, New York
Lauren Catuzzi Grandcolas and Unborn Child	38	San Rafael, California
Donald Freeman Greene	52	Greenwich, Connecticut
Linda Gronlund	46	Greenwood Lake, New York
Richard Guadagno	38	Eureka, CA & Trenton, N.J.
Toshiya Kuge	20	Osaka, Japan
Hilda Marcin	79	Mount Olive, New Jersey
Waleska Martinez	37	Jersey City, New Jersey
Nicole Carol Miller	21	San Jose, California
Louis J. Nacke, II	42	New Hope, Pennsylvania
Donald Arthur Peterson	66	Spring Lake, New Jersey
Jean Hoadley Peterson	55	Spring Lake, New Jersey
Mark David Rothenberg	52	Scotch Plains, New Jersey
Christine Ann Snyder	32	Kailua, Hawaii
John Talignani	74	Staten Island, New York
Honor Elizabeth Wainio	27	Baltimore, Maryland

Although the details of what happened on board Flight 93 will never be fully known, all 40 passengers (not counting the hijackers) and crew are recognized as heroes.

Two years after the attacks, federal officials formed the Flight 93 National Memorial Advisory Commission responsible for making design recommendations for a permanent memorial. A temporary memorial had been formed from spontaneous tributes left at the crash site by visitors in the days and weeks after the attacks. The first phase of the permanent memorial was dedicated on September 10, 2011, the day before the 10th anniversary of the crash. On September 11, 2012, the remains of those killed were buried in a private ceremony for family members and police, fire and emergency workers who had responded to the scene exactly 11 years earlier. The remains, which had been kept in three caskets in a crypt for 10 years, were placed to rest after being looked after by Somerset County Coroner Wallace Miller.

The National Park Foundation has received over $40 million for the memorial from more than 110,000 individuals, foundations and corporations. The funds have already been used to build the new park's Memorial Plaza, Wall of Names, 40 Memorial Groves and the Field of Honor. A visitors' center is opened in 2015, containing a permanent collection of artifacts and a learning center.

At the National September 11 Memorial in New York, the names of the 40 victims of Flight 93 are inscribed on Panels S-67 and S-68 at the South Pool.

In April 2012, the United States Navy launched a newly-constructed warship which it dubbed the USS *Somerset*. The name honors the passengers of Flight 93. Flight 93 has also been the subject of various films and documentaries, including the 2006 Hollywood feature film *United 93*.

If You Go:
The Flight 93 crash site is in a very remote location. However, if you do decide to make that trek then we recommend you also pay a visit to the Quecreek Mine Rescue site, located in Lincoln Township not far from the crash site. It was there in 2002 that nine miners were trapped underground for over 78 hours. In an amazing rescue that unfolded before a live national television audience over the course of several

days (July 24–28), all nine miners were saved and eventually made full recoveries.

A memorial park is located at the farm field just west of Route 985 where the drilling operations to rescue the miners took place. Driving directions and other helpful information may be found at http://www. quecreekrescue.org. There is a bronze statue of a miner at the park's entrance, and at the rescue site itself you will find the "Monument for Life"—a plaque mounted to a large boulder which sits in front of a red oak tree surrounded by nine pine trees. This dramatic rescue operation has inspired books and movies and is a testament to the human spirit.

5

General Slocum Fire

1021 VICTIMS

County: Queens
City: New York
Cemetery: Lutheran All Faiths Cemetery
Address: 67-29 Metropolitan Avenue, Middle Village

School had recently let out for the summer and hundreds of German-American children and their mothers headed for their annual retreat—a picnic across the Long Island Sound to Locust Grove, a picnic site in Eatons Neck, Long Island. On the morning of Wednesday, June 15, 1904, the enthusiastic passengers with their picnic baskets and blankets boarded the ship PS *General Slocum* which had been chartered for $350 by St. Mark's Evangelical Lutheran Church of the Little Germany district of the Lower East Side of Manhattan. The paddle-wheeler was known as the largest passenger ship serving the New York Harbor area and its experienced captain, William H. Van Schaick, had an impeccable safety record. But, within a half-hour of leaving the dock, the ship was engulfed in flames and over a thousand souls were lost, the greatest loss of life in the New York metropolitan area prior to September 11, 2001.

The morning of Wednesday, June 15, 1904, was a typical late-spring day with bright sun and a light breeze. The men of Little Germany headed out their doors to work, wishing their loved ones a fun day on Long Island, never imagining it would be the last time they would see most of them. The mothers, attired in their typical ankle-length dresses and large hats arrived at the dock with their grade-school-aged children, who were excited to ride on the big ship. Each mother handed a crewman a ticket for herself and every child 10 and older. In all, Captain Schaick was informed that nearly 1000 tickets had been collected. While the passengers boarded, a German band played on deck, accompanied by

Illustration of the General Slocum *afire in the East River.*

the adults, who sang along. Joining them on deck in song was Reverend George Haas, the pastor of St. Mark's and other leaders of the church. Haas brought his entire household including his wife Anna, 12-year-old Gertrude, Emma Haas, and Elizabeth Hanson. Only 16-year-old George stayed behind.

Around 9:30 A.M., Captain Schaick gave the order to head out. A bell rang and the steam engine came to life. The lines were cast off, and the great ship was turned into the East River for its two-hour journey. Aboard were about 1350 souls, including hundreds of unticketed children, crew, catering staff, and the 1000 ticketed passengers. Per the *New York Times*, "As she cast off and stood out into the stream her flags were flying, the band was playing a lively air, and her three decks were crowded to their capacity with a happy throng that looked for a pleasant day's outing at Locust Point, on the Sound."

Built in Brooklyn in 1891, the *General Slocum* was 235 feet long and 37.5 feet wide made of oak and yellow pine. The ship was powered by a steam engine which drove a sidewheel. There was a crew of 22, including the captain and two pilots. The *Slocum* could handle up to 2,500 passengers and had at the ready ample life preservers. The prior

Old postcard of the General Slocum *before the tragedy.*

month, a fire inspector had found the ship's fire equipment to be in "fine working order."

The ship first steamed north in the East River at 15 knots, passing Blackwell's Island (now Roosevelt Island). Around 10 A.M., a small fire started aboard the ship. There were conflicting accounts of exactly where, but the captain wasn't notified until ten minutes had passed. Some of the crew, seeing puffs of smoke rising through the deck, rushed to the fire hoses, but they were rotten and burst as soon as the water pressure filled them. The crew informed the captain there was a "blaze that could not be conquered—like trying to put out hell itself."

Van Schaick realized he was passing 97th Street, with Randalls Island ahead to port and Long Island to starboard (this is very close to the current Robert F. Kennedy Bridge). Around him were opportunities to dock or ground the ship, but he feared the flames would spread due to the flammable buildings and materials laying on the docks. Said the Captain, "I started to head for One Hundred and Thirty-fourth Street, but was warned off by the captain of a tugboat, who shouted to me that the boat would set fire to the lumber yards and oil tanks there. Besides I knew that the shore was lined with rocks and the boat would founder if I put in there. I then fixed upon North Brother Island." His plan was to beach

The burnt and twisted hulk of the ship.

the *Slocum* sideways so that the passengers could more easily escape. But North Brother Island was another mile away, and the winds in the Long Island Sound were fanning the flames as he turned into them.

"It was only a matter of seconds until the entire forward part of the boat was a mass of flames," continued the *New York Times*. Passengers began to panic on all three decks. "All this time full speed ahead was maintained, and the flames, fanned fiercely by the wind, ate their way swiftly toward the hapless women and babies that were crowded on all the decks astern."

Van Schaick said he looked out from his pilothouse and saw "a fierce blaze—the wildest I have ever seen." He kept the ship pointed into the wind, headed for North Brother Island, just minutes away.

As the mass of panicked passengers pressed to the stern, trying to escape the flames, young children were trampled. The crew handed out life vests, but many of them burst, the canvas covers rotted, cork falling on the deck. They had been hanging on the deck, unused, for thirteen years. Mothers wrapped their young ones in life vests and tossed them into the river only to see them sink and drown. Many of the vests had been weighted down with iron to trick the inspectors into believing they were full of material. The crowd watched in horror as a man, engulfed in flames, leaped over the side of the ship only to meet his end as the giant paddle wheel crushed him. A boy was seen to climb the ship's flagstaff and hang until he was overcome by the heat and plummeted into the flames. When the middle deck gave way from the heat and the added weight, it crushed those beneath and knocked many overboard. Women and children began jumping into the water, but many did not know how to swim and their clothing quickly weighed them down. Amid the chaos,

Captain William H. Van Schaick

a woman gave birth and hurled herself and newborn overboard, only to drown. The *New York Times* described the scene as "a spectacle of horror beyond words to express—a great vessel all in flames, sweeping forward in the sunlight, within sight of the crowded city, while her helpless, screaming hundreds were roasted alive or swallowed up in waves."

Reverend Haas later recounted "At that time most of the women and children were jammed in the rear of the boat, where the band was playing. Why the captain did not point the boat for the meadows I do not understand. He kept on, and the fresh wind from the Sound drove the fire back through the different decks with lightning rapidity.

"In three minutes from the time the fire started all the decks were ablaze . . . I was in the rear of the boat with my wife and daughter. Women were shrieking and grasping their children in their arms. Some mothers had as many as three or four with them. Our case seemed hopeless. Death from fire was to be escaped only to die in the water.

"With my wife and daughter, I had been swept over the rail. The fire then looked as if it would devour us the next instant. I got my wife and daughter out on the rail, and then we went overboard. I was in such an excited state that I don't remember whether we were pushed over or jumped.

"When I struck the water I sank, and when I rose there were scores about me fighting to keep afloat. One by one I saw them sink around me. But I was powerless to do anything. I was holding my wife and

Some of the hundreds of bodies that washed up on North Brother Island.

daughter up in the water as best I could, almost under the side of the boat, when someone, jumping from the rail directly above me, landed on top of us. My hold was broken, and we all went under together. When I came up my wife and child were gone."

Along the East River and Long Island Sound, boats sped to the scene and began pulling a few people out of the water, but mostly encountered the corpses of young children. A large white yacht flying the insignia from the New York Yacht Club was seen to arrive as the burning *Slocum* passed 139th Street. The captain of the yacht only observed the situation but offered no assistance.

Captain Van Schaick kept the *Slocum* on course. "I stuck to my post in the pilothouse until my cap caught fire. We were then about twenty-five feet off North Brother Island. She went on the beach, bow on, in about twenty-five feet of water . . . Most of the people aft, where the fire raged fiercest, jumped in when we were in deep water and were carried away. We had no chance to lower the lifeboats. They were burned before the crew could get at them."

City Health Commissioner Darlington was at Riverside Hosptial on North Brother Island when the *General Slocum* was beached. "I will never be able to forget the scene, the utter horror of it," he said. "The patients

Outdoor morgue by the hospital on North Brother Island in the East RIver.

in the contagious wards, especially in the scarlet fever ward, went wild at things they saw from their windows and went screaming and beating at the doors until it took fifty nurses and doctors to quiet them. They were all locked up. Along the beach, the boats were carrying in the living and dying and towing in the dead." North Brother Island became a scene of courage and panic.

At the hospital, the staff quickly prepared their fire hoses to battle the blaze. The fire whistle was blown and dozens of rescuers headed to the shore. Some swam out to the ship to rescue people while nurses threw debris into the water for drowning passengers to hold onto. But, it was impossible to get too close to the hot burning wreck.

Edward McCarroll, one of the firefighters, dove off of his boat, the *Wade*, to rescue an 11-year-old girl to safety. He jumped in and was about to rescue another when a woman grabbed him by the throat and nearly pulled him under. She shouted, "You must save my boy!" McCarroll rescued both mother and son and hoisted them onto his boat. Meanwhile, tugboat crews were moving about pulling living and dead from the water. Soon, the sands of North Brother Island was covered by the bodies of 150 deceased, mostly women, one still clutching her lifeless baby. Pre-school-aged orphans walked about the beach, dazed, unable to find their mothers. Many would be unclaimed by relatives for many hours or days.

Captain Van Schaick, his feet blistered from the blaze beneath, his mission accomplished, jumped into the water and swam ashore. It was believed to be the last person off the boat. Now partially blinded and crippled, he was hospitalized at Lebanon Hospital.

Of 1,358 who boarded the ship that morning, 1,021 perished. Fortunately, there were miracles. A little boy who fell into the river clutching his stuffed toy dog was fished out, unharmed, still holding his prize. One tugboat crew, in particular, pulled alongside the *General Slocum* and risked catching fire in order to rescue over 100. A nurse, who did not know she could swim, dove into the water and rescued children, again and again, discovering she was quite capable in the water. One of the quarantined measles patients at the hos-

Large monument to the unknown victims at Lutheran All Faiths Cemetery in Queens, N.Y..

pital ran into the water, despite her fever, and rescued several children. One 10-month-old boy floated to shore, uninjured but orphaned, and lay unclaimed at a hospital until his grandmother identified him days later. Willie Keppler, 11 years-old, had joined the excursion without permission from his parents. He managed to survive but was afraid of returning home to be punished. Upon seeing his name among the dead in the newspapers, he said, "I thought I'd come home and get the licking instead of breaking my mother's heart. So I'm home, and my mother only kissed me and my father gave me half a dollar for being a good swimmer."

There were also antiheroes and opportunists. Souvenir hunters walked the beaches and made the search for bodies difficult. Some stripped the bodies of their jewelry.

Detail of the monument.

Meanwhile, the *General Slocum* drifted, burning above the water line, until it struck Hunts Point in the Bronx, a thousand yards away, where it remained for weeks. Divers searched for bodies in its sunken remains. Police and rescue parties combed the riverbanks for miles in search of bodies.

As word spread throughout Little Germany, thousands gathered at St. Marks Church to await word about survivors. Others rushed to the East 23rd Street pier which had been designated as a temporary morgue where the corpses were laid out as they arrived. Policemen were sent into the city to find available coffins. Wagons, loaded with ice were sent to preserve the bodies. As the crowds of curiosity seekers, opportunistic undertakers, and news reporters swelled, the police tried to allow the friends and relatives through. By the afternoon, many of the families began to lose hope, and many discovered they had lost wives and or children. Some lost their entire families. Around 5 P.M. that evening, young George Haas and his sister Emma returned home without their family members.

The *New York Tribune* reported that on the night of June 15, 1904, "grief-crazed crowds" lined the shore where the bodies were being brought in by the boatload: "Scores were prevented from throwing themselves into the river."

The following morning the New-York Tribune said "The pastor was prostrated last night. Much of the time he was unconscious . . . With the exception of Mr. Haas's son George, who did not

Fountain honoring the children at Tompkins Square Park on Manhattan.

go on the excursion, these two are apparently the only ones left of a large family."

Over the following days, thousands walked past the hundreds of unclaimed victims in their open coffins. The well-preserved drowning victims were quickly identified. Some of those who were burned and disfigured were identified by their jewelry or clothing. The sixty-one that were never identified, including many found days later, were buried in a common grave.

For days, funerals were held every hour in the churches of the Little Germany neighborhood. Unable to handle the grief, several men and women took their own lives.

Two weeks later, the funeral of George's wife Anna, aged 46, was held in their East 7th Street house. The *Evening World* said, "It was rendered

Detail from the fountain.

doubly pathetic because the bodies of the pastor's daughter, Gertrude, his mother-in-law, Mrs. Mary Hanson, his sister-in-law, Mrs. William Dietmore, and her son Herbert, have not been recovered."

"Because of the ghastly burns he received in the destruction of the *Slocum*, Dr. Haas sat behind a screen during the funeral services," said the newspaper.

During the service, word came that the body of Anna's sister, burned beyond recognition, had been identified by marks on the body. Her coffin was hurried to the Haas house and the service became a double funeral. Little Gertrude's body was among the last to be identified.

Among the telegrams and letters George Haas received were one from President Theodore Roosevelt,

"Accept my profound sympathy for yourself, your church, and your congregation."

and from Kaiser Wilhelm of Germany,

"Being most profoundly affected by the news of the indescribably horrible catastrophe which has overtaken the Lutheran congregation, I command you to express to it my innermost feelings of sorrow."

Funeral procession for many victims of the General Slocum *disaster.*

Captain Van Schaick faced criminal charges and was sentenced to 10 years in Sing Song prison, though he only served four until he was pardoned by President William Howard Taft on Christmas Day, 1912.

The Knickerbocker Steamship Company paid a small fine despite evidence that its safety records had been falsified.

The Little Germany neighborhood, which had been in decline for decades as families moved to other parts of the city, quickly faded following the disaster. The church whose congregation chartered the ship was converted to a synagogue in 1940 as Jewish immigrants settled the neighborhood.

The last survivor, Adella Wotherspoon (nee Liebenow) lived to be 100 and passed in 2004. Victims were buried throughout New York City. Fifty-eight identified deceased were laid to rest in the Cemetery of the Evergreens in Brooklyn. Many, including the unidentified, were buried at the Lutheran Cemetery in Middle Village, Queens, now Lutheran All Faiths Cemetery where there is a historical marker and an annual ceremony.

In 1906, a memorial fountain was erected in Tompkins Square Park in Manhattan by the Sympathy Society of German Ladies. It is inscribed "They are Earth's purest children, young and fair."

The ship was salvaged and converted into a barge named *Maryland* which sank off of the New Jersey coast in December of 1911, laden with a cargo of coal. No one died in that incident.

The burning of the *General Slocum* was the worst maritime disaster in New York's history and the second worst on US waterways, It has been memorialized or referred to in numerous books, films, television programs, and plays.

If You Go

The best way to pay tribute to the *General Slocum* victims is to visit the Lutheran All Faiths Cemetery in Queens where many are buried, including the unknown in a mass grave which is marked by a large monument. Every year, around the anniversary of the disaster, a memorial service is held.

The former German Evangelical Lutheran Church of St. Mark building still stands at 325 West 6th Street near Tompkins Square Park in Manhattan where you can find the fountain dedicated to the lost children. There are numerous restaurants in the Tompkins Square area.

The grave of Captain William Van Schaick was unmarked for many years but now contains a granite stone. It is located at Oakwood Cemetery in Utica, New York.

6

"An Act of God?"

JOHNSTOWN FLOOD VICTIMS

County: Cambria
Town: Johnstown
Cemetery: Grandview
Address: 801 Millcreek Road

Heavy rainfall caused water to rise in the streets of Johnstown, Pennsylvania in late May 1889. That seemed normal and didn't raise any alarms. Being built on the fork of Little Conemaugh and Stony Creek rivers, flooding had been a problem since its founding. On June 1, 1889, Americans woke to the news that Johnstown had been devastated by the worst flood in the nation's history. A neglected dam and phenomenal storm led to a catastrophe in which 2209 people died. It's a story of great tragedy and when the full story came to light, many believed that if it was a "natural" disaster, then surely man was an accomplice.

The Little Conemaugh and the Stony Creek rivers meet in Johnstown and form the Conemaugh River. In 1889, Johnstown was a town of Welsh and German immigrants with a population of about 30,000 including surrounding towns. High above the city, the South Fork Dam was built by the Commonwealth of Pennsylvania between 1838 and 1853 as part of a cross-state canal system. The reservoir behind the dam, Lake Conemaugh, supplied water to the city.

As railroads replaced canal barge transportation, the canal was abandoned by the Commonwealth and sold to the Pennsylvania Railroad. The dam and the lake were subsequently sold to private interests. One of the private interests was a group led by Henry Clay Frick, chairman of Carnegie Brothers Company, who had made a fortune selling coke. Their intent was to modify the lake and convert it into a private resort for the wealthy of Pittsburgh. They formed the South Fork Fishing and

Detail of "The Great Conemaugh Valley Disaster—Flood & Fire at Johnstown, Pa.,"
subtitled "Hundreds Roasted Alive at the Railroad Bridge." Reproduced from a
lithograph print published by Kurz & Allison Art Publishers, 76 & 78 Wabash Avenue,
Chicago, Illinois.

Hunting Club and bought it in 1879. The purpose of the club was
to provide the members and their families an opportunity to escape
the noise, heat, and dirt of Pittsburgh. There were sixty-one members
at that time including Andrew Carnegie, Henry Clay Frick, Andrew
Mellon, Philander Chase Knox (who served as US Attorney General,
US Senator, and Secretary of State), and Benjamin Thaw, the uncle of
Harry Thaw. They built a 47-room clubhouse with a huge dining room
and 16 houses along the lake's shores. The club's boat fleet included a
pair of steam yachts, many sailboats, and canoes and the boathouses to
house them. The club did engage in some periodic maintenance of the
dam, but also made some harmful modifications to it. They lowered
the dam to make its top wide enough to hold a road, and they installed
fish screens across the spillway to keep expensive game fish from escap-
ing, which had the unfortunate effect of capturing debris keeping the
spillway from draining the lake's overflow.

On May 30th, 1889, unusually heavy rains hit the area. The U.S.
Army Signal Corps estimated 6 to 10 inches of rain fell in 24 hours. At
around 3:10 PM, the South Fork Dam burst. The collapse sent twenty
million tons of water roaring downstream toward Johnstown. On its way
it picked up debris, such as trees, rocks, houses, and animals. When it hit

Debris being removed from the railroad bridge.

Johnstown, it was about 40 feet high and a half-mile wide and traveling about 40 miles an hour. Just outside of East Conemaugh, a locomotive engineer, John Hess, was sitting in his locomotive. He heard the rumbling of the approaching flood and, correctly assuming what it was, tried to warn people by blowing the train whistle and racing toward the town riding backwards. His warning saved many people who were able to get to high ground. Hess himself miraculously survived despite the locomotive being picked up and tossed aside by the wall of water and debris. At 4:07 PM, the wall of water hit Johnstown. At first, it sounded like a low rumble that grew to a roar like thunder.

It was over in ten minutes, but for some, the worst was still yet to come. Darkness fell, thousands were huddled in attics, others floating on the debris, while many more had been swept downstream to the old Stone Bridge at the junction of the rivers. There, much of the debris piled up against the arches and caught fire, killing eighty people who had survived the initial flood wave. The fire burned for three days. The pile of debris reached seventy feet in height and took three months to remove because of the masses of steel wire from an ironworks factory binding it. Dynamite was eventually used to clean it.

Debris on Main Street.

Many bodies were never identified, hundreds of the missing never found. The official death toll registered 2209 people killed or presumed lost. Among the dead were 99 entire families, 396 children under the age of ten, and 777 unidentified victims.

Emergency morgues and hospitals were set up, and commissaries distributed food and clothing. Across the country and around the world, people responded with a spontaneous outpouring of time, money, food, clothing, and medical assistance. A total of $3.7 million was collected from the U.S. and eighteen foreign countries.

The American Red Cross, which was formed in 1881 by Clara Barton, arrived in Johnstown on June 5, five days after the disaster. This was the group's first major disaster relief effort, and Clara Barton herself was to lead the relief efforts. She and many other volunteers worked tirelessly and didn't leave for more than five months.

The media response to the disaster was immediate. Over 100 newspapers and magazines sent writers and illustrators to Johnstown. The Johnstown Flood was the biggest news story since the Civil War. The dead were lined up in morgues throughout the city and in communities further down the river until some survivor in search of a loved one came to identify them. The living set up tents, often near the place their homes had been located, and began the task of cleaning up and starting life again. Although not noted for their accuracy, the reports touched the hearts of readers. Residents of Johnstown and Americans in general began to turn their wrath on the members of the South Fork Fishing and Hunting Club. Newspapers all across the country denounced the sportsmen's lake. *The Chicago Herald*'s editorial on the disaster was entitled "Manslaughter or Murder?" On June 9, the *Herald* carried a cartoon that showed the members of the club drinking champagne

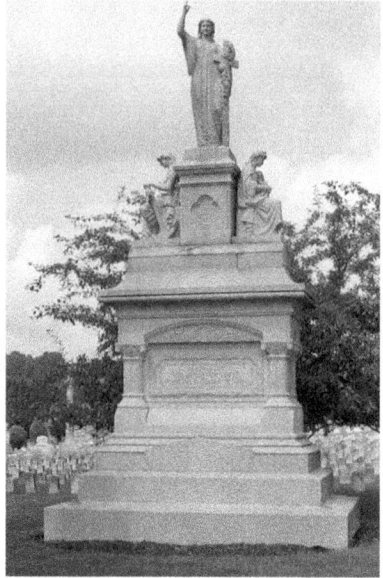

Memorial to 777 unidentified victims of the Johnstown flood.

on the porch of the clubhouse while, in the valley beneath them, the Flood is destroying Johnstown. A *New York World* headline on June 7 declared, "The Club is Guilty."

In the immediate aftermath of the tragedy, the club contributed 1000 blankets to the relief effort. A few of the club members served on relief committees. Only about half the club members contributed to the disaster relief effort, including Andrew Carnegie whose company gave $10,000 and who later rebuilt Johnstown's library. However, no club member ever expressed a sense of personal responsibility for the disaster.

The club had very few assets aside from the clubhouse, but a few lawsuits were brought against the club anyway. Legal action against individual club members was difficult as it would have been necessary to prove personal negligence—and the power and influence of the club members is hard to overestimate. Despite the accusations and the evidence, they were successfully defended by the firm of Knox and Reed, both partners of which were club members (Philander Knox and James Reed). The Club was never held legally responsible for the disaster. The court held the dam break to have been an Act of God and granted the survivors no legal compensation.

Memorial to those who had their graves destroyed by the Johnstown flood.

Many bodies were never identified and hundreds of the missing never found. The cleanup operation took years with bodies being found months later and, in a few cases, years after the flood. In 1989, on the 100th Anniversary of the flood, 106 year-old survivor Elsie Frum was interviewed by news organizations. Her father was alerted by John Hess's train whistle and had gotten his family to safety, thus saving young Elsie's life. Frank Shomo, reportedly the last survivor of the Johnstown Flood, died in 1997 at the age of 108.

There is a large, beautiful memorial marking the resting place of 777 flood victims who could not be identified in Grandview Cemetery in Johnstown. The State Flood Commission purchased the plot, called "The Unknown Plot," for burying the unidentified and bought markers for each grave. It was dedicated on May 31, 1892, exactly three years after the flood.

The Johnstown Flood Museum is located on Washington Street in Johnstown in a large beautiful brick building that was built for the city, as the new library, by Andrew Carnegie. The museum provides exhibits and artifacts that tell the story of the flood and the film *The Johnstown Flood*, winner of the 1989 Academy Award for Best Documentary Short Subject, is shown each hour at the museum's theater. The Johnstown Flood National Memorial is located about ten miles northeast of Johnstown. The park preserves the remains of the South Fork Dam. The visitor center features multi-media exhibits including a fiber optic map, which describes the path of the flood.

If You Go:

Grandview Cemetery is the final resting place of Congressional Medal of Honor recipient George W. Reed. Reed was awarded his medal for his bravery in action at the Second Battle of Weldon Railroad, Virginia during the siege of Petersburg in the Civil War in 1864.

There is also an impressive grave marking the remains of Boyd "Buzz" Wagner, the World War II fighter ace. Wagner rose to Lieutenant Colonel in the Army Air Corps during World War II. He shot down eight Japanese planes and earned the title as America's first fighter ace. He was a recipient of the Purple Heart and the Distinguished Flying Cross.

John McCrory, the founder of the McCrory Five and Ten Cent, store chain is also buried there in the family mausoleum above whose entrance is inscribed "McCrorey" the original spelling of the family name. His hundreds of stores would come to be known as the second of the great five-and-dime chain stores following Woolworth's and preceding Kresge.

Pete Duranko, the Notre Dame All-American from the 1966 national championship team and eight year NFL veteran, is also buried in Grandview Cemetery, as is Congressman John Murtha. Murtha represented Pennsylvania in Congress for 36 years and was the first Vietnam Veteran elected to the U.S. House of Representatives.

7

"The Kelayres Massacre"

JOSEPH BRUNO

County: Schuylkill
Town: McAdoo
Cemetery: Saint Patrick's
Address: Lincoln Street

It was election eve in Schuylkill County Pennsylvania in the year 1934. Kline Township Democrats, expecting a big day at the polls in the morning, organized a parade. A local barber named Carl Vacante carried an American flag in front of the marchers who carried red torches. In addition vehicles carrying children were part of the parade. The marchers approached the home of Joseph Bruno a prominent Republican in the area. As they did some of the marchers began to chant "down with the Brunos." Suddenly shots rang out and five of the marchers were killed and many others were wounded. The incident became known as the Kelayres Massacre.

The Joseph Bruno family was active in real estate, bottling beer and politics dating back to the early 1890s. The family had members who held positions such as president of the school board, county detective, justice of the peace and inspector of weights and measures. Joseph Bruno's brother Philip was a tax collector, a Coal and Iron Policeman who also supplied various establishments with slot machines. By 1930 the Bruno family established political control over Kelayres.

Bruno used his position on the school board to enrich himself and his family. The schoolhouse in Kelayres burned to the ground under mysterious circumstances in 1932. The school board that Bruno controlled turned down an offer by a local coal company to rebuild the school. When construction on the new school began the trucks that were used were supplied by Bruno's brothers and Bruno himself acted as the

A parade turned into a bloodbath and became the Kelayres Massacre.

purchasing agent. In that same year Bruno purchased the Lofty School for one dollar. He converted the building into a school bus garage, and the board agreed to rent the building for $30.00 a month.

Bruno was defeated in the school board election in 1933. However as justice of the peace he impounded the ballots and demanded a recount. Ballots were altered, and they favored Bruno. The controversy over the election led to Bruno's resignation but not before he arranged for his son Alfred to replace him.

Bruno's tenure on the school board was marked by corruption. Teachers were expected to give money to Bruno to keep their positions. By 1934 the teachers had formed a union to oppose the Brunos.

On election eve in 1934 the Brunos remained confident that they would prevail. The local democrats, equally as confident that the tide was turning in their favor, organized the fateful march. The purpose of the march was to signal the end of the 27 year long Republican rule that was

The home of Joseph Bruno after the massacre.

headed by Bruno. Bruno family members occupied homes on two of the three corners at Center and Fourth streets and the democrats decided to March past those homes.

As the marchers approached the homes gunfire rang out. The gunfire came from both sides of the street causing the marchers to scatter in all directions. It was over in about a minute. Three people, William Forke, 37, Frank Fiorella, 65, and Joseph Galosky, 30, died at the scene. Two others Dominic Perna, 37, and Andrew Kostician were rushed to a local hospital. Kostician died the following day, and he was wounded because upon hearing the shots he ran to the scene to search for his daughter. Perna died two days after being wounded. At a minimum 13 other march-ers had been hit and required medical attention.

The initial calls to local police were ignored and believed to be prank calls because Bruno was well known and respected by the local authori-ties. When the police did make their way to Kelayres, they witnessed the carnage. They also found an angry mob planning to dynamite the Bruno household. When the police questioned Bruno and the other people in the house Bruno claimed to have heard shots and that they were aimed at his house. However when the police searched the house they found a shotgun, a pump gun, three doubled-barreled shotguns, three repeat-ing rifles, automatic pistols and revolvers. In addition they discovered a dresser filled with ammunition. Bruno and six other members of his family were arrested.

In the election held the following day the Democrats swept the state. In Keylares out of 682 votes cast only 24 went to Republican candidates. Democrat George Earle was the first of his party to be elected Governor in decades. He along with a future Governor by the name of David Lawrence

Joseph James Bruno

would attend the funeral for the five victims of the massacre. The funeral itself drew approximately 20,000 mourners. Many local businesses closed on the day of the funeral including banks, the post office, stores, schools and some of the local collieries. Five hearses took the bodies through the town of McAdoo to their final resting place. As the hearses passed them a number of women screamed in Italian "If you do not send those murderers to the electric chair, we will kill them ourselves."

At the trials the prosecutors produced witnesses who testified that the shots had come from the homes occupied by the Brunos. Witnesses for the defense claimed that the shots came from the home of Dan McAloose who was a local Democratic leader. At his initial trial Bruno was convicted of manslaughter. He appealed the verdict and received a second trial. At that trial Bruno was convicted and sentenced to life while his son Philip was sentenced to ten to twenty years. The other family members were acquitted. However at a third trial both Joseph and Philip

Here are the graves of Philip (left) and Joseph Bruno (right). Two men who were considered civic leaders yet opened fire on unarmed marchers killing five and wounding countless others.

were convicted of first degree murder while James, Arthur and Alfred Bruno were convicted of manslaughter.

Joseph Bruno had been convicted and sentenced to three life sentences. He was jailed in the Schuylkill County Prison in Pottsville. Two years later Bruno complained about a sore tooth. A prison guard was assigned to take Bruno to a doctor. Believe it or not when the guard couldn't find a parking place he told Bruno to get out of the car in front of the doctor's office and to wait for him there while he found a place to park. When he returned to the office Bruno was nowhere to be found.

About eight months later Bruno was found and apprehended lving under an assumed name in New York City. He was returned to the Schuylkill County Prison where he served time for the next ten years until his sentence was commuted. All the others involved in the massacre had had their sentences commuted earlier in the 1940s. Bruno died in Kelayres of natural causes in 1951.

If You Go:

You are very near the center of Hazleton where you can visit a number of sites connected to the Lattimer Massacre (p. 55) including a very sad scene of 14 of the victims of that massacre with their tombstones standing side by side at the Saint Stanislaus's Polish Catholic Cemetery located at 652 Carson Street. We also recommend a visit to the Battered Mug located on the corner of Beech and Pine Streets. We enjoyed the best pierogies we had ever tasted on our visit there. In addition you are close to a number of people we covered within this volume including Jack Kehoe of the Molly Maguires (p. 105) and the man many consider to be the greatest athlete of all time, Jim Thorpe. If you visit Jim Thorpe we suggest a visit to the old jail which is now a museum where a number of the alleged Mollies were hanged. In addition you can't go wrong by visiting the Molly Maguire Pub where you will find good food and drink at reasonable prices. Finally the town of Jim Thorpe is very near the Poconos, so depending on the season you can enjoy white water rafting or skiing.

8

"The Lattimer Massacre"

MICHAEL CHESLOCK

County: Luzerne
Town: Hazleton
Cemetery: Hazleton
Address: 120 North Vine Street

On September 17, 1897, the *Hazleton Daily Standard* published the following verse:

> If the courts of justice shield you
> And your freedom you should gain,
> Remember that your brows are marked
> With the burning brand of Cain.
> Oh, noble, noble, deputies
> We always will remember
> Your bloody work at Lattimer
> On the 10th day of November.

The verse was a testament to yet another act of violence involving labor and management in the anthracite coal region of Pennsylvania. This incident became known as the Lattimer Massacre.

The coal region is located in northeastern Pennsylvania. It is largely made up six counties: Lackawanna, Luzerne, Columbia, Carbon, Schuylkill, and Northumberland. Coal was discovered in the area in 1762. This discovery would have a profound influence on those who chose to settle in the coal region in the 1800s. The coal industry went through a tremendous growth spurt after the civil war. This growth provided tremendous wealth for the few who had the capital to obtain mining rights and the land beneath where the vast deposits of coal could be

Mine workers marching to their slaughter outside of Lattimer, Pa., September 10, 1897.

found. For a minority of people who worked for the mining companies it provided a good job and a decent income. These people were mine bosses, superintendents, and supervisors. The majority of the employees were the actual miners who were faced with extremely dangerous work, harsh conditions and low pay coupled with the fact that they were forced to live in company supplied housing and purchase their goods at company owned stores. Often a miner's wages failed to cover his and his family's expenses, and he went into debt to the company. These conditions led to conflict, sometimes violent, between labor and management (see Chapter 14 titled "The Molly Maguires," p. 127).

The jobs in the mines were generally filled by the latest groups of immigrants to enter the region. This meant that in the 1890s most of the miners were of Italian or Slavic decent. At this time the company owned town of Lattimer housed an Italian population. Similar company owned towns in the area were largely occupied by Slavic miners and their families. In either case they were renting their homes from mine owner Ariovistus Pardee, who was one of the wealthiest men in America at the time.

As newcomers, these miners were often assigned the most difficult and dangerous jobs available. In addition, they were often subjected to

ANOTHER TRIAL CERTAIN

FOR SHERIFF MARTIN AND THE OTHER

LATTIMER MURDERERS.

Prosecutors Say the County's Honor Demands It.

Jury Feared Coal Barons and Wouldn't Punish "Best Families."

VERDICT IN ADVANCE.

So Also Was Judge's Charge. Sheriff Tells What He'll Do in Next Trouble.

WHAT *IS* CRIME IN PENNSYLVANIA ANYHOW?

It seems to be settled that in the mining regions deputy sheriffs have the right to kill unarmed strikers on sight. They may pursue them and shoot them down as they would mad dogs. And in the end the deputy sheriffs are glorified as martyrs—not hanged as murderers.

From the New York Evening Journal, 10 March 1898, p. 5.

prejudice. For example the Slavic miners were often called "hunkies." They were also angry about the "alien tax" that had been passed by the Pennsylvania General Assembly. This tax required a three-cent levy per day on all immigrant employees. When one considers that the immigrants' earnings were already set lower than their more established counterparts doing the same work, it becomes easy to see the anger that resulted from these conditions. Thus the stage had been set for the latest clash between labor and management in Pennsylvania's Anthracite Coal region.

A number of incidents occurred in the late summer of 1897 that led to the trouble that would eventually take place in Lattimer. In August, Gomer James, who worked for the mine owners in a management position, decided to make a central stable for all of the mules who worked in the mines to save money. Mine owners at this time valued a trained mule more than a miner since it cost about $200 to buy and train the animal. One of the savings was that a single crew could now be given the job of feeding and watering the mules. Another consequence of the decision was that the mules were no longer kept at the mines where they worked and the mule drivers had to travel to the central stable to pick them up. In many cases this added two hours to the workers day as they had to wake an hour early to get to the stable to pick up the mule and then spend an hour after work returning the animal. The workers were angry because they received no compensation for this extra time.

On August 13, 1897, a majority of the mule drivers who worked at the Honeybrook mine went on strike. In addition they formed a human fence and refused to allow anyone to enter the mine to get to work. When word of this reached Jones, he grabbed a crowbar, rushed to the scene and attacked the nearest striker, hitting him across the shoulders. The other strikers rushed to intervene and soon had Jones on the ground where they began to beat him. The local supervisor, Oliver Welsh, then intervened stopping the beating and promptly firing all the strikers. In breaking up the fight, Welsh suffered a blow to the head from a stone; it took eight stitches to close the wound.

News of what happened at Honeybrook quickly spread across the coal fields. The result was that more miners joined the strike. Within three days more than 800 miners had joined the effort to better their treatment. They demanded a wage hike, the right to shop at stores other than those owned by the company, the freedom to choose their own doctor and an end to the alien tax. The strikers appointed a team of leaders to negotiate with management on their behalf.

The strike ended on a temporary basis when the strikers' leaders negotiated a ten cent pay increase. While the miners were happy with the increase, they remained disturbed that their other issues had not been addressed, and as a result on August 25, 1897, the strike was renewed with a march. Local newspapers reported that anywhere from 300 to 500 miners had taken to the streets to march in protest of their working conditions.

On September 4, 1879, the miners issued a list of demands. These demands included a fifteen cents per day raise for every employee, the right

FIRING ON THE MINERS. AN ACCURATE VIEW OF THE FIELD WHERE THE TRAGEDY TOOK PLACE
Drawn by an Inquirer Staff Artist.

By a Philadelphia Inquirer staff person, 12 September 1897, front page.

to seek out and pay for the doctor of their choice, they would be paid if they reported to work even if work wasn't possible because machinery was out of order and they would not be compelled to shop in company stores or use the company butcher. The coal companies divided in their response to these demands. By September 6th the men at Coleraine and Milnesville were back at work. The mine owners here agreed that the miners could shop where they wished though the company stores would remain open. That same day, Sheriff Martin of Luzerne County met with supervisors of the Cross Creek Coal Company, and it was decided that none of the strikers' demands would be met. The coal company agreed that it would furnish funds to pay for an armed force of deputies to aid the Coal and Iron Police. Sheriff Martin was dispatched to Hazleton with instructions to raise such a force. Martin had no trouble finding men, and within a day, he deputized approximately eighty volunteers who he armed with new Winchester rifles. Martin also issued a proclamation that he sent to the *Wilkes-Barre Times*. The proclamation put the striking miners on notice in that it warned against any unlawful assembly or any acts of violence.

On September 9th a group of miners from Lattimer met with their counterparts from Harwood. The Harwood miners were already on strike, and the delegation from Lattimer expressed their desire to join in and close both of Pardee's mines in the area. The largely Slavic miners from Harwood agreed that Pardee would give no concessions unless he was faced with a show of unity from the miners. Therefore, it was decided that the Harwood miners would march to Lattimer the next day where the Lattimer miners would join them in the strike.

September 10, 1897, was a warm and sunny day. Approximately three hundred men appeared at Harwood to join in the march to Lattimer. A few of the men carried American flags to display during the march. The vast majority of the marchers did not speak English nor were they American citizens. Michael Cheslock, who did speak English and had applied for American citizenship, was selected to be one of the leaders of the march. The large group set off for Lattimer; they were unarmed and marched peacefully.

As soon as Sheriff Martin received word of the procession, he mobilized his forces. As the marchers neared Hazleton, they were met by Martin and his posse. Martin pulled his gun pointed it at a marcher and ordered the group to disperse. The miners, who felt they were doing nothing wrong, refused. Around this time a fight broke out, and one deputy grabbed a flag from a marcher and tore it to bits. At this point the chief of the Hazleton police intervened. The fighting stopped when the chief said the march could continue but could not go through Hazleton. The marchers agreed and proceeded on around the city.

Martin ordered his men to trolleys bound for Lattimer. Later some of the trolley passengers would report that tensions were high, and there was talk of a shooting. One deputy was overheard saying "I bet I drop six of them." A reporter notified the *Wilkes-Barre Times* that serious trouble was coming. Word of what was happening spread through the area. Mothers, in Lattimer, went to the local schoolhouse to remove their children, a wise move in light of what was about to unfold. The Lattimer

This monument sits at the site of the massacre.

mine shut down. Martin and his men arrived and were joined by coal and iron police. Now in command of an armed force of about 150, Martin assembled his men at the forked entrance to the town of Lattimer.

It was 3:45 that afternoon when the marchers approached Lattimer led by a man carrying the American flag. The miners' ranks had by now swelled to over 400 men. Martin approached the marchers and told them they were participating in an unlawful assembly. He ordered them to disperse. Many of the marchers couldn't understand what the sheriff said and just as many could not hear him. Michael Cheslock and other leaders of the march attempted to talk with Martin, but the sheriff was having none of that. He attempted to grab the American flag from the marcher in front. Failing there, he grabbed a marcher from the second row, and when other marchers came to his defense, a scuffle ensued. Martin pulled his pistol, but it misfired, and at this point someone yelled "fire." Eyewitnesses would claim it was the sheriff, but he would deny the charge. Whoever gave the order, the deputies opened up. Michael Cheslock was shot between the eyes and killed immediately. The marchers, seeing what was happening, turned to run, but the deputies continued to fire. Some ran toward the schoolhouse where the teachers inside soon saw shots piercing the walls and sending wood splinters flying. The shooting went on for at least a minute and a half, and when it was over 19 of the marchers lay dead and another thirty-six were wounded. Some of the deputies walked through the dead and wounded kicking them. Some of the marchers begged for help, and one eyewitness heard a deputy respond to these pleas by saying, "we'll give you hell, not water, hunkies!" Sheriff Martin surveyed the area around him, and in a classic understatement muttered, "I am not well."

Wagons were called in to move the dead and wounded to local hospitals and undertakers. Many of the dead were taken to Boyle's and Bonin's who, as undertakers, were assigned the responsibility of preparing the bodies for burial. Undertaker Boyle would later testify that the bodies left in his care had been shot in the back. Boyle's decedents run a funeral home in Hazleton to this day. The funeral director at present is named Thomas Boyle. Tom and the author went to high school together.

The next few days were bedlam in the coal country. Many of the deputies headed to the Jersey Shore to wait out the events. The Governor of Pennsylvania sent the state militia to Hazleton to preserve order since

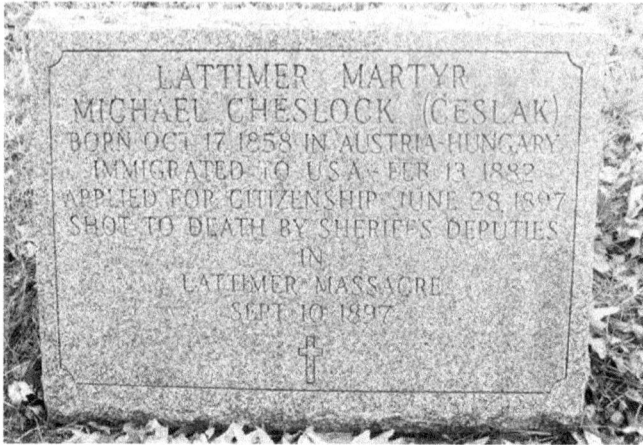

The grave site of Michael Cheslock who was the first miner killed during the Lattimer Massacre.

most expected there would be reprisals. To the surprise of many, the immigrants remained peaceful. Large funerals continued in the days to follow, some drawing crowds of as many as eight thousand people.

The story of the massacre was covered in the press throughout the country. Generally the sheriff and his deputies were found to be at fault. *The Philadelphia Inquirer* said that the massacre was,

> "a human slaughter in which men were mowed down like grain stalks before a scythe, by the deadly bullets which stormed for fully two minutes. An exact list of the dead and wounded is impossible to be obtained tonight, but the Inquirer counted twelve dead men in the field. Two others died at the hospital and a number of others are expected to die at any moment."

Sheriff Martin was being hounded by the press, so he finally told his side of the story. He said he received word of the march from one of his deputies who told him that the miners were heavily armed. In response he gathered his deputies together and told them to remain calm no matter what happened. He said when the marchers arrived in Lattimer, he read them the proclamation but that they paid no attention to him and continued to march. Martin said he told the leader to stop, but that order was also ignored. He said he tried to arrest the leader, but when he did, he was surrounded by the strikers who began kicking him. He then told the reporters,

"I realized something needed to be done at once or I would be killed. I called to the deputies to discharge their firearms into the air over the heads of the strikers, as it might probably frighten them. It was done at once but it had no effect whatever on the infuriated foreigners, who used me so much the rougher and became fiercer and fiercer, more like wild beasts than human beings."

Martin went on to say that the miners were desperate and did not value human life. He claimed that his deputies were ordered to shoot only to protect their own lives and the property they were there to defend. He said that he felt bad about giving the order to fire but insisted that it was his duty in light of the situation.

Soon after this interview, Martin changed his story. He said the marchers were not on company property; that they were on a public road. When asked if the marchers had done anything that was not peaceful, he said no. He denied giving the order to fire saying; that had been done by someone else. Soon after Martin and his deputies were arrested and charged with murder.

On February 1, 1898, the trial of Martin and his deputies began in Wilkes-Barre. It took over a month to complete and testimony was received from about 200 witnesses. On March 9, 1898 the jury returned with a verdict of "not guilty." News of the verdict sparked outrage not only in the United States but throughout Eastern Europe as well. A Slovak cartoon shows a dead miner laying at the feet of justice. Justice is not depicted as being blind but is seen looking at a bag of money.

In many ways, the martyred miners of Lattimer inspired the working people of America to do something about their working conditions. After

Here lies 4 of 14 victims of the Massacre who are buried side by side.

These 14 tombstones lined up side by side mark the graves of miners shot to death during the massacre.

the massacre, more than 15,000 workers joined the United Mine Workers of America. In time that union became the most powerful representative of the anthracite workers. At the peak of its power, it represented 150,000 workers in the region.

In 1972 a monument was erected in Lattimer at the site of the massacre. An inscription on the monument reads,

> "It was not a battle because they were not aggressive, nor were they defensive because they had no weapons of any kind and were simply shot down like so many worthless objects, each of the licensed life-takers trying to outdo the others in butchery."

Michael Cheslock is buried in the Hazleton Cemetery. His grave is easy to find if you use the Diamond Avenue entrance to the cemetery. As you enter, Cheslock's grave is to your right just a few yards away from your entry point. Cheslock was 39 years old when he was killed.

If You Go:

Also buried in the Hazleton Cemetery is Sergeant Robert H. Sinex who fought with the Union during the Civil War. According to one of his death notices, he was a secret service agent who saw Lincoln's assassination and participated in the capture of John Wilkes Booth. If you wish to visit his grave, we suggest a stop at the cemetery office. The Hazleton Cemetery is located on the same side of Hazleton as the Saint Stanislaus's Polish Catholic Cemetery, and a visit to this site is a must. Fourteen of the miners shot at Lattimer are buried here in a manner to get your attention. The fourteen are lined up side by side against the cemetery wall. Their tombstones are identical and all contain the same information. At the top of the stone is the miners name and inscribed underneath the name on each marker it reads, "Shot September 10, 1897."

This cemetery is located at 652 Carson Street in Hazleton, and the wall you are looking for is the one with the school building right across the street. If you visit Saint Stanislaus's you are right next to the Most Precious Blood Cemetery. You may want to stop in here to visit the grave of Jack "the Dandy" Parisi. Parisi was a member of the notorious group Murder Incorporated which accepted and carried out murder contracts from mob bosses throughout the country. A government agent once said of Parisi, "if you hung him up by his thumbs for eight hours he might tell you his name."

If you are in need of refreshments you have plenty of options in Hazleton. We had a pint and the best perogies we have ever tasted at a small pub called the Battered Mug located on the corner of South Pine and Beech streets. If you are in Hazleton you are close to many people that we covered within this volume including Jim Thorpe, Black Jack Kehoe of the Molly Maguires, Congressman Dan Flood and Mary Jo Kopechne. As it would be very difficult to visit all the sites in one day, we recommend spending the night at the Comfort Inn located in West Hazleton. The hotel is clean, reasonably priced and has a friendly staff. In addition it houses a nice lounge called "Timbers" that offers live entertainment on the weekends.

9

"Lincoln Assassination"

JOHN WILKES BOOTH

County: Baltimore City
Town: Baltimore
Cemetery: Green Mount
Address: 1501 Green Mount Avenue

On the morning of April 14, 1865, the owners of Ford's Theater in Washington, D. C., received word from the White House that President Lincoln and his wife Mary would be attending that evening's performance of the play *Our American Cousin.* An actor who had appeared on the Ford stage less than a month before stopped by the theater that afternoon and learned of the president's plans. The actor who had previously plotted to kidnap the president now saw another way to avenge the defeat of his beloved Confederate States of America. With that thought in mind, John Wilkes Booth set off on what would be a most busy day that would reach its climax with the first successful assassination of an American president.

It appears that one of the first things Booth did was sit down and write a letter. Later that afternoon, the assassin met up with another actor and friend, John Matthews, not far from Washington's Willard Hotel. After a brief discussion about Confederate prisoners that had just been brought to the city, Booth asked his friend if he could do him a favor. Booth indicated that he might have to leave Washington that night but he had a letter he wanted to be published in the *National Intelligencer* and he asked Matthews to deliver it for him the next day. Matthews agreed and took the letter and placed it in his coat pocket.

Shortly after the two exchanged the correspondence, Matthews called Booth's attention to a carriage that was carrying General Ulysses Grant and his wife. Booth then shook his friend's hand saying, "Perhaps I will see you again." Then, he hurried his horse after the carriage. Mrs. Grant

Ford's Theater in Washington, DC, where Lincoln was shot.

would later recall a man sweeping by them on horseback before turning and riding back toward their carriage where the rider "thrust his face quite near the General's and glared in a disagreeable manner."

Booth's next stop was at a local boarding house run by Mary Surratt, a widow and the mother of a friend of the actor's named John Surratt, Jr. who was a Confederate courier. Mrs. Surratt told Booth her son was out of town on rebel business and was not expected back that night. She also said that she was getting ready to leave and was heading to her country tavern located outside of Washington in Surrattsville, Maryland. Booth had a wrapped package with him. He asked her to deliver it to her tavern keeper, John Lloyd. The actor said he would stop by the tavern later that

The tavern owned by Mary Surratt located outside of Washington where Booth stopped to gather weapons and supplies after the assassination.

evening to pick up the package as well as guns, ammunition, and supplies that her son had previously left there for him. Booth told Mrs. Surratt that Lloyd should have these things ready for him. The woman agreed to do as Booth had asked.

As evening descended on Washington, Booth gathered his small group of conspirators that he had put together to carry out his plan to kidnap Lincoln. They met at the Herndon House just around the corner from Ford's Theater. Seated with Booth were Lewis Powell, David Herold, and George Atzerodt. This was only a portion of the gang Booth had assembled for his original kidnapping plan. As stated earlier, John Surratt was out of the city on a rebel mission and two of Booth's boyhood friends, Samuel Arnold and Michael O'Laughlen, who were part of the original plan, were also unavailable or couldn't be located on such short notice

Booth laid out his plans in hushed tones. With Lee having just surrendered, kidnapping the President would not be enough to save the Confederacy. Booth explained that Lincoln would not be the only target. They would also add Vice President Johnson and Secretary of State Seward to their list. With their reduced numbers, Booth explained that capturing the three men was not possible. Instead, they would murder them.

The home of Doctor Samuel Mudd who treated the ankle Booth broke after leaping to the stage in Ford's Theater after killing Lincoln.

Booth told Herold to guide Powell (who didn't know his way around Washington) to Seward's residence where Powell would carry out the assault and Herold would lead both on their escape out of the city. Atzerodt was given the assignment of killing Vice President Johnson while Booth would slip into Ford's Theater and kill Lincoln as he watched the play. Booth had eager accomplices in Powell and Herold but Atzerodt balked at the assignment. Booth then threatened to implicate him anyway and get him hanged as well as advising the reluctant Atzerodt he would blow his brains out. Indeed Booth had already implicated all at the table in the letter he had left with John Matthews which justified the murders and was signed with the names of all the conspirators. Booth's final words to his reluctant co-conspirator were, "You had better come along and get your horse."

Back at Ford's Theater, Lincoln had entered to an ovation from the crowd, many of which had purchased tickets after learning that the President would attend the show. He made himself comfortable in the presidential box where he seated himself in a walnut rocker. Mrs. Lincoln sat next to her husband. The Lincoln's were joined by Major Henry Rathbone and his fiancée Clara Harris, who were seated about seven feet away from the President. Actress May Hart remembered watching the

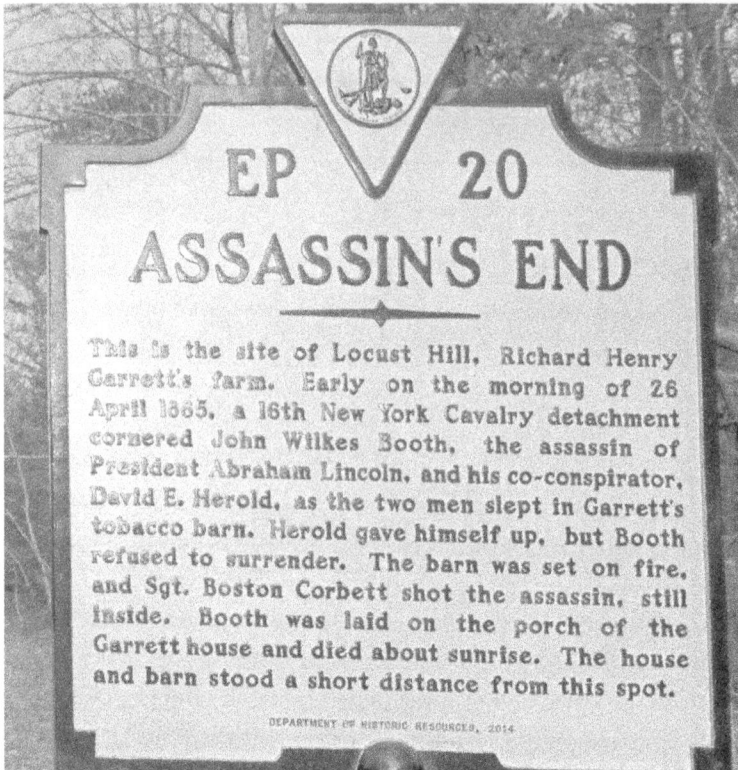

Sign erected to mark the spot where one Lincoln assassin conspirator was captured and where the famous actor who had taken the life of the president was shot and killed.

President as he sat twelve feet above the actors. His eyes were on the stage but, as she recalled, his mind seemed elsewhere.

Booth, of course, was well known to the employees at the theater. As the performance went on, he entered and left multiple times. When he entered for the final time, he was humming a tune. From the stage, Helen Truman, who had been studying Mrs. Lincoln, noticed John Wilkes Booth near the entrance to the Presidential box. When Booth saw her staring at him, he gave her a quick bow.

Booth quietly entered the box. He knew every line of the play and he awaited one he knew would bring laughter from those in the crowded theater. Harry Hawk was on stage alone when he said, "Don't know the manners of good society, eh? Well, I guess I know enough to turn you inside out, old gal. You sockdologizing old man-trap." Booth pulled his

The barn where John Wilkes Booth met his end was located in this area.

single shot .44-caliber derringer from his pocket. His left hand held a sharp Rio Grande camp knife. While the audience convulsed in laughter, Booth squeezed the trigger sending a metal ball into Lincoln's head where it traveled through his brain before coming to rest behind the President's right eye. Lincoln slumped forward in the rocker as though he had fallen asleep.

Based on his battlefield experience, Major Rathbone knew he had just heard a gunshot and, when he turned to look in the president's direction, he saw a cloud of smoke. The Major then rushed toward Lincoln. Booth had used his only shot so he went to his knife in the tussle with Rathbone. The assassin took aim at the Major's heart but Rathbone deflected the blow with his left arm which took the brunt of Booth's force and sliced flesh from the elbow to almost the shoulder. Booth then looked to leap to the stage with the knife still in hand. As he did, his right foot caught on the decorations covering the presidential box and he landed awkwardly. He felt a stab of pain in his left leg near the ankle. Booth then stood stage center holding the bloody knife above his head and with a wild look in his eyes shouted, "Sic semper tyrannis (Thus always to tyrants)." Then he shouted, "The South is avenged." Quickly he made his way off stage and headed for the theater's rear exit which led to Baptist Alley. When

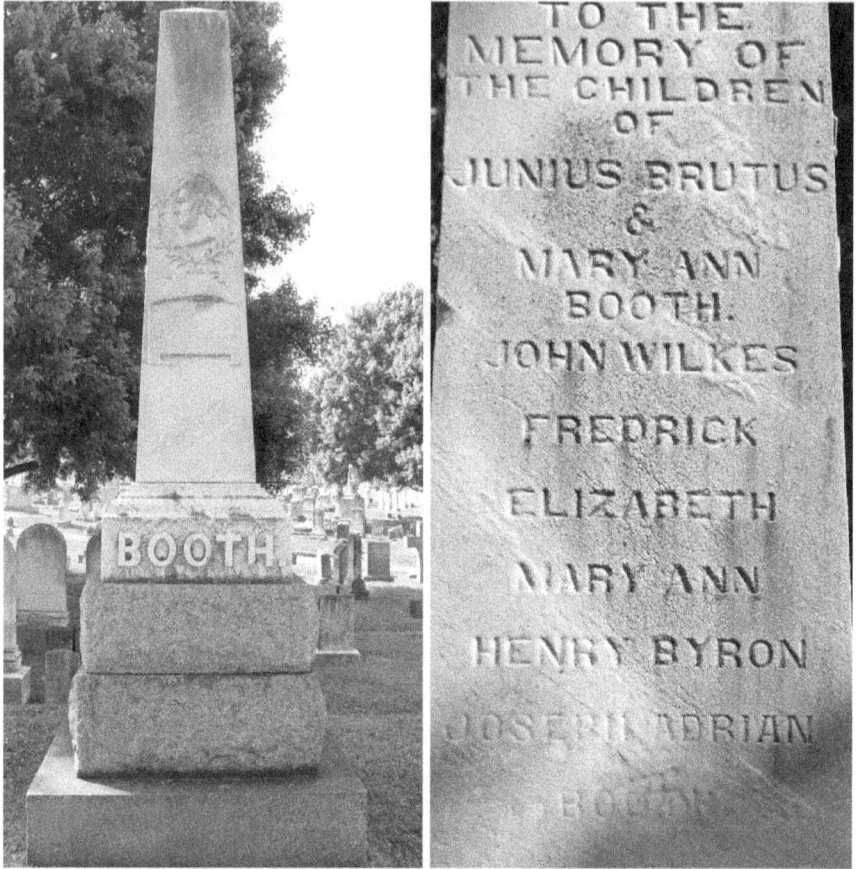

The Booth family plot located in Baltimore's Green Mount Cemetery.

he opened the door and reached the alley, he looked for his horse which he had left in the hands of a theater employee. Mounting his steed, he escaped the clutches of army Major Joseph Stewart, who had left the audience to chase Lincoln's killer. Stewart tried to grab the reins but Booth, who was an expert horseman, outmaneuvered him and, urging his horse, rode away at a gallop.

While Booth carried out his murderous deed at Ford's Theater, David Herold and Lewis Powell arrived at the Washington, D. C., Mansion that served as the home of Secretary of State Seward. Seward was confined to bed after having been involved in a serious carriage accident days earlier. Booth's instructions to the duo were straightforward: enter the house, locate Seward, and kill him with a pistol or, failing that, with a knife. Powell, a tall and strong ex-confederate soldier, would carry out the deed and Herold would lead their escape across the Potomac where they would meet Booth.

The two conspirators kept watch on the house observing two doctors come and go. Finally, the gaslights in the home began to go dim and Powell made his move. Carrying a wrapped package, he rang the bell at the front door. The door was opened by a black servant who saw a tall well-dressed man holding a small package. Powell claimed to be a messenger from one of Seward's doctors and said he had medicine that the doctor had ordered him to deliver. The servant allowed Powell to enter and reached out to take the package. Powell refused to turn the package over saying he had been instructed to deliver it to the secretary and explain how the medicine should be used. The servant insisted that he could deliver the medicine and any instructions to Seward and the two argued for up to five minutes with Powell repeating "I must go up."

Powell grew tired of arguing with the servant and began climbing the stairs. The servant stayed with him telling him he was going to get in trouble for not handing over the medicine. The pair were met at the top of the stairs by Seward's son Frederick. Powell explained to the young Seward why he was there. Frederick said his father was asleep but he would take the medicine and the instructions for its use. In a room just feet away lay the Secretary of State who was being looked after by his daughter Fanny. She had heard the discussion going on outside the room and opened the door slightly to see what was going on. She saw her brother talking to a stranger and said, "Fred, father is awake now." Powell, trying to get a look inside the room, asked, "Is the Secretary asleep?" Fanny made the mistake of replying, "Almost." Frederick interceded, shutting the door, but now Powell had the information he needed. Frederick Seward finally told Powell to give him the medicine or take it back to the doctor. Powell put the package in his pocket and began walking down the stairs behind the servant. When Frederick Seward turned and headed toward his father's bedroom door, Powell turned and ran up the stairs. When Seward again faced Powell, the assassin held a revolver inches from his face. The trigger was pulled but all that was heard was a click. The weapon had misfired.

Powell still had five more rounds in his gun but, rather than trying to shoot again, he used the revolver as a club and brought it down hard on

Lincoln pennies cover a stone in the Booth family plot.

The final resting place of Michael O'Laughlen who died in prison for his part in the assassination. He was also laid to rest in Green Mount.

The grave of Samuel Arnold who was also laid to rest In Green Mount. Arnold was originally sentence to life in prison but both he and Doctor Samuel Mudd were pardoned by President Johnson.

Frederick's head, breaking both Seward's skull and the weapon. The servant ran into the street yelling "Murder." Inside the room, unbeknownst to Powell, Fanny sat with Sergeant George Robinson, an army nurse, who was there to care for the Secretary's injuries. Fanny asked Robinson to check on what was going on outside the room. When Robinson opened the door, Powell struck Robinson in the head and, knife in hand, headed toward the bed. Fanny raced to the bed as well screaming, "Don't kill him." In the darkness of the room, Powell raised his knife three times and tried to plunge it into Seward. Two of the blows missed and the third cut opened the Secretary's cheek but did not mortally wound him. By now, Robinson had regained his senses and another Seward son, Augustus, summoned by his sister's screams, also entered the room and began fighting the would-be assassin. Fanny opened a window and screamed, which was enough for Herold. Figuring Powell had been thwarted, he rode away to meet Booth.

Meanwhile, Sergeant Robison and Augustus Seward had successfully maneuvered Powell back into the Hall, though Robinson was stabbed twice in the process. With his own face just inches from Seward's son, Powell said in a calm voice, "I'm mad. I'm mad." Powell landed another solid blow; a punch that felled Robinson. Then, he escaped down the stairs, out the door, and looked around frantically for David Herold. Finding only his own horse, he dropped his knife, jumped in the saddle, and trotted away. He would be arrested a few days later at Mary Surratt's tavern in Surrattsville.

The final assassin in the plot, George Atzerodt, sat at a bar at the Kirkwood House perhaps trying to drink up the courage to carry out his assignment and murder the Vice-President. Evidently, there wasn't enough whiskey available and Atzerodt got on his horse and headed out of Washington. The decision not to murder Johnson would not save him. Of the three assassination attempts, only Booth was successful. President Lincoln was carried from Ford's Theater to a house across the street (the Peterson House) where he died the following day.

While Lincoln lay dying, Booth waited on the Maryland side of the Potomac for his fellow conspirators. Only Herold joined him and the two set off on a twelve-day flight from justice. Their first stop was at the Surratt Tavern to pick up the package Mary had delivered and the weapons and supplies that waited for them there. Upon leaving the tavern, they set out to get Booth the medical help he needed for the broken leg he had suffered when he jumped to the stage after the assassination. It was about a four-hour ride to the farm of someone Booth felt he could count on; Doctor Samuel A. Mudd. Mudd knew Booth, though he would claim that the actor never informed him of the murderous deed he had just carried out. He treated Booth's wounds and made an improvised splint for Booth's broken leg; a fracture that the doctor described as being about two inches above the ankle. Mudd then invited Booth and Herold to spend the night in his house and the tired co-conspirators eagerly accepted.

Booth became the focus of a massive manhunt that eventually cornered both him and Herold inside a barn on a farm owned by a man named Richard Garrett located in Virginia. Herold was captured and Booth killed by the troops who surrounded the barn. The search for the assassins is covered in depth in the book *Manhunt* written by James L. Swanson.

The capture of Herold did not save his life. On July 7, 1865, he was hanged along with Powell, Atzerodt, and Mary Surratt. Doctor Mudd and others received prison sentences as a result of their involvement in the assassination. The bodies of the condemned conspirators and Booth

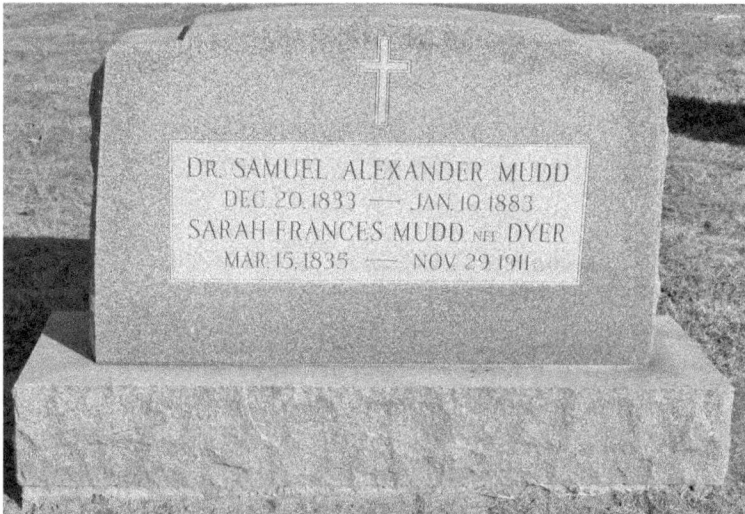

Dr. Mudd was laid to rest in the Saint Mary's Catholic Cemetery in Bryantown, Maryland.

were buried at the Old Arsenal Penitentiary, now Fort Leslie McNair, where the executions took place. In 1869, President Johnson allowed Mary Surratt's daughter Anna to have her mother's remains removed to their final resting place in Washington's Mount Olivet Cemetery. The President also responded to a request from Edwin Booth and released the remains of Lincoln's assassin to the Booth family. Booth was quietly laid to rest in the Booth family plot in Baltimore's Green Mount Cemetery. Another of Booth's conspirators, Samuel Arnold, is also buried at Green Mount. Arnold was involved in Booth's plan to kidnap Lincoln. As a result, he was sentenced to life in prison. Before leaving office, President Johnson pardoned Arnold and Doctor Mudd. Arnold died in Baltimore in 1906. Mudd passed away in 1883 and was laid to rest in Saint Mary's Catholic Cemetery in Bryantown, Maryland.

If You Go:
Should you decide to visit Booth in Baltimore's Green Mount Cemetery there are other graves you might want to check out. Allen Welsh Dulles can be found there. He served as the Director of the CIA from 1953 until 1961. He was also a key member of the Warren Commission which investigated the assassination of John F. Kennedy. Confederate General Joseph Eggleston Johnston was also laid to rest here. Johnston died of pneumonia after catching a cold while serving as a pallbearer at the funeral of Union General William T. Sherman. The author Walter Lord, whose most famous work *A Night to Remember* told the story of the sinking of the *Titanic*, can be found here as well. While you are in Baltimore you might want to check out the Inner Harbor where you can find numerous eating and drinking establishments.

A visit to Washington can include a tour of Ford's Theater, the scene of the Lincoln assassination. There are numerous attractions in the nation's capital to fill your day and many excellent restaurants as well. Should you

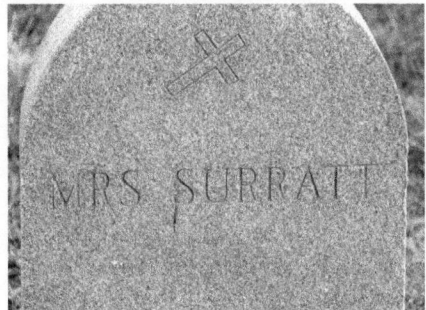

Mary Surratt is buried in Washington's Mount Olivet Cemetery. Many believe her execution was unwarranted.

like, you can also trace Booth's escape from Washington with a visit to Mary Surratt's tavern, a stop at the home of Dr. Mudd, and a quick stop along the highway in the area where Booth met his end.

The grave of conspirator David Herold is at the foot of his parents' graves, unmarked, at Congressional Cemetery in Washington, DC.

10

"Malcolm X"

MALCOLM LITTLE

aka: el-Hajj Malik el-Shabazz

County: Westchester
Town: Hartsdale
Cemetery: Ferncliff Cemetery
Address: 200 Secor Road

Malcolm X was an African-American Muslim minister and human rights activist. He was the public voice of the Black Muslim faith, challenged the mainstream Civil Rights Movement, and articulated concepts of racial pride and black nationalism in the 1950s and 60s.

He was born Malcolm Little on May 19, 1925, in Omaha, Nebraska. He was the fourth of eight children born to Louise and Earl Little. Louise was a homemaker and Earl a preacher and active leader of the Universal Negro Improvement Association (UNIA), for which Louise served as secretary. Due to Earl's civil rights activism, the family faced frequent harassment and threats from white supremacist groups such as the Ku Klux Klan, and one of its splinter factions, the Black Legion. Because of this, the family relocated, in 1926, to Milwaukee, Wisconsin, and, shortly thereafter, to Lansing, Michigan.

The racism they encountered in Lansing proved even worse than in Omaha. Shortly after the Littles moved in, a racist mob set their house on fire and it burned to the ground. Two years later, in 1931, things got much worse. Earl Little's dead body was found laid out on the city's streetcar tracks. Although he was very likely murdered by white supremacists (from whom he had received frequent death threats), the police officially ruled his death a suicide, thereby voiding the large life insurance policy he had purchased for his family in the event of his death. In 1937, Louise had an emotional breakdown, and was committed to Kalamazoo State

A Young Malcolm addresses a crowd.

Hospital in 1938, while her children were split among various foster homes and orphanages in and around the Lansing area. Malcolm went to live with family friends.

Initially, Malcolm did quite well at Lansing's West Junior High School. He excelled academically, and was elected class president. However, in 1939, at the age of 13, he dropped out of school after a white teacher told him that becoming a lawyer—his aspiration at the time—was not a realistic goal for a black man, and suggested carpentry. In 1941, Malcolm and his long-time friend, "Shorty" Jarvis, moved to Boston, where Malcolm lived with his older half-sister, Ella, who got him a job shining shoes at the Roseland Ballroom. He soon became acquainted with the city's criminal underground, and got into selling drugs. He got a job as kitchen help on the *Yankee Clipper* train that ran between New York and Boston, and fell further into drug dealing, gambling, racketeering, robbery, and pimping. He began wearing flamboyant, pinstriped zoot suits, straightened his hair, frequented nightclubs and dance halls, and became known as "Detroit Red" because of his reddish hair.

Following a move to Harlem, New York, in 1943, Malcolm was declared "mentally disqualified for military service," when he told draft board officials that he wanted to be sent down south to "organize them nigger soldiers, steal us some guns, and kill us some crackers." In 1945, he and four accomplices committed a series of burglaries targeting wealthy

The black leader ponders his next move.

white families; in 1946, he was arrested, convicted, and sentenced to eight to ten years in prison.

In prison, Malcolm became a voracious reader, devouring books from the prison library. During this time, his brother Reginald would visit and discuss his recent conversion to the Muslim religion and his joining the Nation of Islam ("NOI"). At the time, the NOI was a small sect of black Muslims who embraced the ideology of Black Nationalism—the idea that, in order to secure freedom, justice, and equality, black Americans needed to establish their own state entirely separate from white Americans. Intrigued, Malcolm began to study the teachings of NOI leader Elijah Muhammad. Muhammad taught that white society actively worked to keep African-Americans from empowering themselves and achieving political, economic, and social success.

Malcolm soon became a member of the NOI, and maintained a regular correspondence with Muhammad. In 1950, he began signing his name "Malcolm X." He abandoned his surname "Little," which he considered a relic of slavery, in favor of the surname "X"—a tribute to the unknown name of his African ancestors.

After serving six years of his sentence, Malcolm X was released on parole in August, 1952, and went to visit Elijah Muhammad in Chicago. He was soon appointed as a minister and national spokesman for the NOI. He was also assigned to establish new mosques in Detroit and

Malcolm X with Muhammad Ali.

Harlem. He utilized newspapers, as well as radio and television, to communicate the NOI's message across the country. His charisma, drive, and conviction attracted an astounding number of new members. Malcolm was largely credited with increasing membership one hundred-fold, from 500 in 1953, to 50,000 in 1963. He was articulate, passionate, and a gifted orator, exhorting blacks to cast off the shackles of racism "by any means necessary," including violence. Such militant proposals won Malcolm X large numbers of followers as well as many fierce critics. The crowds and controversy surrounding Malcolm made him a media magnet. He was featured in a week-long television special with Mike Wallace in 1959 called "The Hate that Hate Produced." The program explored the fundamentals of the NOI, and tracked Malcolm's emergence as one of its important leaders.

In 1960, he established a national newspaper, *Muhammad Speaks*, in order to further promote the message. He also attracted the government's attention, and as membership in the NOI continued to grow, the FBI infiltrated the organization, and placed bugs, wiretaps, and other surveillance devices to monitor the group's activities.

In 1955, Betty Sanders met Malcolm X after one of his lectures. She joined the NOI in 1956, and the couple fell in love. They married in

Malcolm X always at ease in front of a microphone.

January, 1958, and their union produced six daughters, including twins, who were not born until after their father's death.

By the early 1960s, Malcolm X had emerged as a leading voice of a radicalized wing of the Civil Rights Movement, presenting an alternative to Dr. Martin Luther King Jr.'s vision of a racially-integrated society achieved by peaceful means. Dr. King was highly critical of what he viewed as Malcolm's destructive demagoguery. "I feel that Malcolm has done himself and our people a great disservice," King once said.

In 1963, Malcolm X became deeply disillusioned when he learned that his hero and mentor had violated many of his own teachings. He learned that Elijah Muhammad was secretly having relations with as many as six women within the NOI organization. As if that were not enough, Malcolm found out that some of these relationships had resulted in children.

Shortly after his shocking discovery, Malcolm was asked to comment on the assassination of John F. Kennedy. Malcolm X said that it was a case of "chickens coming home to roost." The NOI publicly censured their former shining star, and he was prohibited from public speaking for ninety days. Malcolm felt he was silenced for another reason: he had refused Muhammad's request to help cover-up the affairs and children.

Malcolm X with Fidel Castro.

Malcolm felt guilty about the masses he had led to join the NOI, which he now believed was a fraudulent organization built on too many lies to ignore.

On March 8, 1964, Malcolm X publicly announced his break from the Nation of Islam. He expressed a desire to work with other civil rights leaders, saying that Elijah Muhammad had prevented him from doing so in the past. On March 26 of that year, in Washington, D.C., Malcolm X and Martin Luther King Jr. met each other for the first and only time, as both men attended the Senate's debate on the Civil Rights bill. In the months that followed, Malcolm X founded the Muslim Mosque, Inc., a religious organization, and the Organization of Afro-American Unity, a secular group that advocated Pan-Africanism.

One of the men that Malcolm X inspired to join the NOI was boxer Cassius Clay (later known as Muhammad Ali). They had a very close relationship, and when Malcolm X left the NOI and converted to Sunni Islam, he tried to convince Ali to join him. Ali declined, and refused to speak to him again. A decade later, when Ali, himself, decided to leave the NOI and become a Sunni Muslim, after the death of Elijah Muhammad in 1975, he wrote, "turning my back on Malcolm was one of the mistakes that I regret most in my life."

Malcolm and Betty at rest.

In 1964, Malcolm X went on an extended trip through North Africa and the Middle East, including a pilgrimage to Mecca ("The Hajj") in Saudi Arabia. The journey proved to be both a political and spiritual turning point in his life. He discovered that orthodox Muslims preached equality of the races. When he returned, Malcolm said he had met "blonde-haired, blued-eyed men I could call my brothers." He converted to traditional Islam, and again changed his name, this time to el-Hajj Malik el-Shabazz. He was less angry and more optimistic about a peaceful resolution of America's race problems.

Meanwhile, the conflict between Malcolm and the NOI intensified, and he was repeatedly threatened. FBI informants, working undercover, warned officials that Malcolm had been marked for assassination. In June, 1964, an FBI informant received a tip that "Malcolm X is going to be bumped off." On February 14, 1965, the home in East Elmhurst, New York, where he lived with Betty (who at the time was several months pregnant with twins) and their four daughters, was firebombed. The family escaped without physical injury.

On the evening of February 21, 1965, at the Audubon Ballroom in Manhattan, where Malcolm X was about to speak, three gunmen rushed the stage and shot him fifteen times at point-blank range. The

39-year-old was pronounced dead on arrival at New York's Columbia Presbyterian Hospital.

Somewhere around 22,000 people attended the public viewing at Unity Funeral Home in Harlem, and 1,500 attended his funeral on February 27, at Harlem's Faith Temple of the Church of God in Christ. After the ceremony, friends took the shovels away from the waiting gravediggers at Ferncliff Cemetery and buried Malcolm themselves.

Later that year, Betty gave birth to their twin daughters.

Malcolm X's assassins were convicted of first degree murder in March 1966 and given sentences of twenty years to life in prison. The three men were all members of the NOI. Two of the men were released on parole in the 1980s, and have long denied involvement in the killing. The third man—the only one to confess and admit to his role in the assassination—was paroled in 2010.

Malcolm had begun a collaboration, in 1963, with Alex Haley on his life story, *The Autobiography of Malcolm X*. He told Haley, "If I'm alive when this book comes out, it will be a miracle." Haley completed and published it some months after the assassination. In 1998, *Time* named *The Autobiography of Malcolm X* one of the ten most influential nonfiction books of the 20th century.

Malcolm's legacy has moved through generations as the subject of numerous documentaries, books, and movies. A tremendous resurgence of interest occurred in 1992, when director Spike Lee released the acclaimed movie, *Malcolm X*. Denzel Washington played the title role and received an Academy Award nomination for Best Actor. Many cities have renamed streets after Malcolm X, most notably New York, where Lenox Avenue in Manhattan was renamed Malcolm X Boulevard. In 1999, the U.S. Postal Service issued a Malcolm X postage stamp. In 2005, Columbia University announced the opening of the Malcolm X and Betty Shabazz Memorial and Education Center. The memorial is located in the Audubon Ballroom, where Malcolm X was assassinated. Collections of his papers are held by the Schomburg Center for Research in Black Culture and The Robert W. Woodruff Library.

If You Go:

Betty Shabazz (1934–1997), Malcolm X's wife, is buried beside him at Ferncliff Cemetery. After witnessing Malcolm's murder, Betty struggled to raise six children on her own. She went back to school and received a master's in Health Administration, and, in 1975, earned her doctorate in Education from the University of Massachusetts. In 1976, she joined the faculty of Medgar Evers College in New York. She worked in various high-level positions there until her death. She died on June 23, 1997, from injuries she suffered in a fire intentionally set by her grandson, who had been living with her at the time, 12-year-old Malcolm Latif Shabazz (see below).

Malcolm Latif Shabazz (1984–2013), the son of Qubilah Shabazz, the second daughter of Malcolm and Betty, had been sent to live with Betty after his mother was arrested and subsequently indicted for conspiring to murder Louis Farrakhan (Qubilah eventually reached a plea agreement and managed to avoid a prison sentence). He explained years after his grandmother's death, that he set the fire in the hopes of being sent back to live with his mother. He expected Betty to use another exit—one led to the outside directly from her bedroom—to escape. Instead, rather than run *away* from the fire, Betty was badly burned when she ran down a hallway *towards*, and then *through*, the fire in an apparent attempt to get to Malcolm's room to rescue him.

Malcolm's own life would be cut short at the hands of another. He was found beaten to death in Mexico City on May 9, 2013. The beating allegedly resulted from a dispute over a $1,200 bar tab for drinks and female companionship. Malcolm Latiff Shabazz, the first male descendant of Malcolm X, is buried near the graves of his grandpa and grandma at Ferncliff.

Three very prominent African-American leaders are also interred at Ferncliff. Among them is the famous actor, singer, athlete, and social reformer Paul Robeson (1898–1976), who was considered one of the great American "Renaissance Men." He was the son of an escaped slave who went on to win fifteen varsity letters at Rutgers University, graduated from Columbia Law School, and had a successful career in the performing arts. His performance of "Ol' Man River" in the film *Show Boat* is legendary. He was a political and social activist often criticized for his socialistic political views. He was accused of communist activities by

Wisconsin Senator Joseph McCarthy, and had his passport revoked. He died in 1976 at the age of 77.

Also buried at Ferncliff, is social reformer Whitney Young (1921–1971), who was Director of the National Urban League from 1961 to 1971. He advised three Presidents on civil rights issues, and was awarded the Presidential Medal of Freedom in 1969.

Famous author James Baldwin (1924–1987) is also interred at Ferncliff. A close friend of Malcolm X, he became one of the most important and vocal advocates for equality. For many, Baldwin's call for human equality in the essays of *Notes of a Native Son* (1955), *Nobody Knows My Name* (1961), and *The Fire Next Time* (1963), became an early and essential voice in the civil rights movement. He died of stomach cancer on November 30, 1987.

In addition, Ferncliff Cemetery has the graves of many other famous people, including:

Cab Calloway (1907–1994), legendary jazz singer/bandleader.
Thomas Carvel (1906–1990), founder of Carvel Ice Cream.
Joan Crawford (1905–1977), actress.
Jackie "Moms" Mabley (1894–1975), a comedian and veteran of the African-American vaudeville circuit.
Jeffrey Miller (1950–1970), victim of the Kent State shootings and subject of John Filo's iconic photo of the event.
Basil Rathbone (1892–1967), an actor most widely recognized for his many portrayals of Sherlock Holmes in the mid-1940s.
Charles Revson (1906–1975), founder of Revlon Cosmetics.
Ed Sullivan (1901–1974), television icon (see *Gotham Graves Volume One*, Chapter 23).

Notable figures residing at Ferncliff whose lives were cut short more recently include:

Basketball star Malik Sealy, an NBA guard named after Malcolm X (el-Hajj *Malik* el-Shabazz), who tragically died in a 2000 car accident at the age of 30.
Singer Aaliyah who died in a 2001 plane crash, at the age of 22.

Jam Master Jay, DJ for the pioneer rap/hip-hop group Run-D.M.C., who, in 2002, was shot and killed at the age of 37, inside a Jamaica, Queens recording studio.

Ferncliff also has its share of "alleged" Mafia members and others with mob ties, including

Sherman Billingsley (1896–1966), restaurateur and owner of the famous Stork Club.

Michael "Trigger Mike" Coppola (1900–1966), a Genovese crime family caporegime.

Vincenzo Rao (1898–1988), a Lucchese crime family mobster.

Gerlando Sciascia (1934–1999), a Bonanno crime family/Rizzuto clan caporegime.

Ferncliff is notable for having the only crematory in Westchester County. Approximately 10% of the cremations in the state are performed there and, because of local ordinances, no additional crematories can be constructed in the county. Notable people whose remains were cremated at Ferncliff, and whose ashes were taken somewhere else include:

Alan Freed (1921–1965), a radio DJ known as "The Father of Rock & Roll," whose ashes were moved to the Rock and Roll Hall of Fame in 2002.

Jim Henson (1936–1990), the Muppets creator, whose ashes were scattered at his ranch in Santa Fe, New Mexico.

John Lennon (1940–1980), whose ashes were scattered by his wife Yoko Ono in New York's Central Park, where the Strawberry Fields memorial was later created.

Nelson Rockefeller (1908–1979), the former Governor of New York, whose ashes were scattered on his estate in Sleepy Hollow, New York. Rockefeller was selected to become Vice President of the United States by Gerald Ford when Ford ascended to the Presidency following Richard Nixon's resignation in 1973.

Nikola Tesla (1856–1943), scientist of electrotechnics, best known for his contributions to the design of the modern alternating current (AC) electricity supply system.

11

"There's Something about Mary"

MARY MALLON

County: Bronx
City: New York
Cemetery: Saint Raymond's Cemetery
Address: 2600 Lafayette Avenue

The name Mary Mallon probably doesn't ring a bell in most people's minds. An Irish immigrant who worked as a cook, she never wanted nor expected to be famous. Yet one unexpected ingredient in her recipes gave her a unique place in American history. She was hounded, deprived of liberty and livelihood, and treated like a criminal. The courts declared her a menace and sent her into exile for more than two decades. The press bestowed upon her a nickname that would live on long after her death: Typhoid Mary.

Mary Mallon was born on September 23, 1869, in Cookstown (County Tyrone), Ireland. At the tender age of fifteen, she emigrated to the United States in search of a better life. She arrived in New York, and like many other immigrants, she took a job in domestic service. She had a talent for cooking and soon found employment as a cook for the wealthy city dwellers. Being a cook was a very respectable job and paid better than other domestic service positions. She did very well as a cook and maintained regular employment.

In 1906, Mary was hired by banker Charles Warren, when the Warrens rented a house in Oyster Bay for the summer. In late August, one of Warren's daughters became ill with typhoid fever. Soon, Mrs. Warren fell ill, then two maids, the gardener, and finally another daughter. Six of the eleven household members fell ill with typhoid fever.

Since the common way typhoid fever spread was through water or food sources, the owners of the property feared they would not be able to rent it again without correcting the source of the problem. The owners hired investigators who were unable to find anything of note. Then they hired a civil engineer with experience in typhoid fever outbreaks. His name was George Soper, and he quickly came to believe that the cook was the cause. He began to research Mallon's employment history and was able to trace it back to 1900. He discovered that, in the seven jobs she had held since then, 22 people had become ill

Mary Mallon

with typhoid, and, indeed, one young girl had died from it. Soper realized that this was more than a coincidence and that he needed stool and blood samples to scientifically prove she was the carrier.

In March 1907, Soper found Mary working as a cook in the home of Walter Bowen and his family. You might say George Soper lacked a certain sensitivity or people skills, as his approach to Mary would indicate. He walked in on Mary while she was working in the Bowen's kitchen, stated his suspicion that she was the cause of the typhoid outbreaks, and asked if he could take samples of her urine, feces, and blood. Mary was shocked, stated that she had never been sick in her life, and went after George with a carving fork. George retreated down a hall and out of the home. He tried again after tracking her to her home. This time, he brought an assistant, Dr. Bert Raymond Hoobler, for support. Again, Mary became enraged, made it clear they were unwelcome in her house, and shouted expletives at them while screaming and spitting.

Soper then decided to involve health officials and contracted the New York City Health Department. He handed over his research to Herman Biggs, who agreed with Soper and sent Dr. Josephine Baker to attempt to negotiate with Mary Mallon. Mary was quite wary of authorities by now. She refused to listen to Dr. Baker, and chased her away with a carving fork as well. Baker returned with five police officers and an ambulance. Mary was ready and escaped the house. Five hours of searching, later, they spotted a fragment of Mary's dress sticking out from a closet in

The press dubbed her Typhoid Mary.

the neighboring house. Mary came out fighting and swearing. Dr. Baker tried to soothe and cajole her into parting with her samples peaceably, but Mary would not cooperate. The police then manhandled her into the ambulance, and Dr. Baker sat on her while they drove to the Willard Parker Hospital.

Once at the hospital, Mary provided the requested samples that returned the results: she was indeed carrying the typhoid bacteria. Doctors suggested the removal of her gallbladder, but Mary refused, as she did not believe she carried the disease. She admitted poor hygiene, saying she posed no risk, so saw no purpose in frequent hand washing. She also refused to agree not to work as a cook. The New York City Health Inspector determined her to be an asymptomatic carrier, and ordered her held in an isolated cottage on North Brother Island, in the East River near the Bronx. Mary Mallon was taken by force, against her will, and was held without a trial. She had committed no crime. The city based their power on two sections of the Greater New York Charter.

Mallon attracted a great deal of media attention, and the press dubbed her "Typhoid Mary," a name she hated. She was called "Typhoid Mary" in a 1908 issue of the *Journal of the American Medical Association*, and later in a textbook that defined typhoid fever.

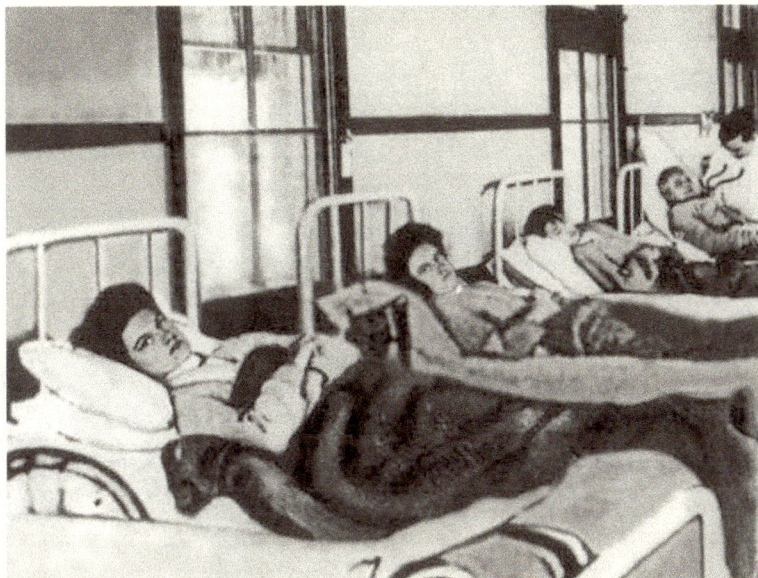

The after affects of the epidemic.

Mary believed that she was being unfairly persecuted and could not understand how she could spread such a deadly disease when she herself seemed healthy. In 1909, after having been isolated for two years, she began a campaign for her release, and sued the U.S. Government. "I never had typhoid in my life, and have always been healthy," Mallon wrote. "Why should I be banished like a leper and compelled to live in solitary confinement with only a dog for a companion?" She also submitted test results from a private laboratory that came up negative. There has been speculation that William Randolph Hearst helped fund Mallon's lawsuit, as newspapers followed this story. Locking up a healthy person seemed wrong to many people.

During her confinement, health officials had taken and analyzed stool samples approximately once a week, and those samples came back mostly positive (120 of 163 tested positive). Mary lost her case in the courts, and was returned to Brother Island where she languished for another year.

In 1910, a new Commissioner of Health took over. His name was Eugene Porter, and he decided that disease carriers should no longer be kept in isolation, and that Mallon could be freed under certain circumstances.

On February 19, 1910, Mary Mallon agreed that she was "prepared to change her occupation (that of a cook), and would give assurance by

House of Mary Mallon in Dorchester, Massachusetts.

affidavit that she would, upon her release, take such hygienic precautions as would protect those, with whom she came in contact, from infection." She was released from quarantine and returned to the mainland.

She found work in New York households as a laundress, but found this unsatisfying to her pocketbook and her ego. She had promised to report to the health authorities every 90 days, but, instead, she disappeared. She took work as a cook and used the name Mary Brown. For the next five years, she worked in a number of kitchens, and wherever she worked, there were outbreaks of typhoid. She changed jobs frequently, and authorities could not find her. In January, 1915, the Sloane Maternity Hospital in Manhattan suffered a typhoid outbreak. Twenty-five people became ill, and two of them died. Evidence pointed to a recently hired cook named Mary Brown, who had left just as people were getting sick. This time, police were able to find her and arrest her. She was returned to quarantine on North Brother Island on March 27, 1915. She was still unwilling to have her gallbladder removed.

Public sympathy for Typhoid Mary was quick to wane when it became apparent that she willfully ignored the health authorities and purposefully endangered life. It is unclear if Mary would have behaved differently if she understood the notion of a healthy carrier. She was an

Typhoid Mary's tombstone.

obstinate woman, and steadfastly denied ever having been sick, or that she made others sick.

Mallon remained confined on North Brother Island for the rest of her life, 23 more years. She helped around the tuberculosis hospital, and in 1922, gained the title of "nurse." Later, she was allowed to work as a technician in the island's laboratory, washing bottles.

In 1932, Mallon suffered a stroke that left her paralyzed. She was transferred from her cottage to the children's ward of the hospital on the island, where she stayed until her death from pneumonia on November 11, 1938, at the age of 69. An autopsy found evidence of typhoid bacteria in her gallbladder. She was buried at St. Raymond's Cemetery in the Bronx.

Since her death, the name "Typhoid Mary" has grown into a term for anyone who, knowingly or not, spreads disease or some other undesirable thing. A book titled *Typhoid Mary, Captive to the Public's Health* by Judith Walzer Leavitt was published in 1996. In it, the author tells the complete story of Mary Mallon and the problem of finding the balance between individual rights and protecting the community. Among the infections Mallon caused, at least three deaths were attributed to her. However, due to her use of aliases and refusal to cooperate, the exact number is not known. Some have estimated that she may have caused fifty fatalities. She may have suffered harsh treatment due to the fact that she was the first asymptomatic typhoid carrier to be identified by medical science, and there was no policy or guidelines for handling the situation.

If You Go:

St. Raymond's Cemetery also contains the graves of boxing champion Benny "Kid" Paret (1937-1962) and rock-n-roll singer/songwriter Frankie Lymon (1942-1968).

Paret was a welterweight champion in 1961, when he lost his crown to Emile Griffith. Six months later, he took back the championship from Griffith in a split decision. On March 24, 1962, they met for a third time, and the fight ended tragically. In the 12th round, Griffith launched a ferocious attack that had Paret hanging defenseless on the ropes. He slumped to the canvas, and never regained consciousness. He lapsed into a coma, and died ten days later, on April 3.

Lymon was considered one of the first African-American teenage pop stars. He formed the group Frankie Lymon and the Teenagers in 1956, at the age of 13, and their first single "Why Do Fools Fall in Love" was a huge top 40 hit. A year-and-a-half later, after many successful songs and appearances, Lymon broke from the group to become a solo act. Separated from one another, both Lymon and "the Teenageers" were unsuccessful and fell apart. On February 27, 1968, at the age of 26, Lymon died of an accidental heroin overdose. In 1993, Lymon and the Teenagers were inducted into the Rock and Roll Hall of Fame in Cleveland, and in 2000 they were inducted into the Vocal Group Hall of Fame in Sharon, Pennsylvania.

12

"The Mysterious Case of Mary Pinchot Meyer"

MARY PINCHOT MEYER

County: Pike
Town: Milford
Cemetery: Milford
Address: Route 209

She was born on October 14, 1920, in New York City, to a wealthy and politically connected family. Her father was a lawyer active in the Progressive party who contributed funding to the socialist magazine *The Masses*. Her mother was a journalist who wrote for magazines such as *The Nation* and *The New Republic*. Her uncle Gifford Pinchot was a two time Governor of Pennsylvania (see *Keystone Tombstones – Anthracite Region*, p. 80). She would eventually marry Cord Meyer who would go on to work for the Central Intelligence Agency. She would become a friend and lover of President John F. Kennedy. She was murdered in the fall of 1964, and many believe her death was related to her interest in the assassination of President Kennedy. Her name was Mary Pinchot Meyer.

Meyer grew up at the Pinchot family home named Grey Towers in Milford. As a child she met a number of left leaning intellectuals through her parents including Louis Brandeis and Harold Ickes. She was educated at Brearley School and Vassar College. It was during these years that she developed an interest in communism. This did not bother her father at all. He wrote a letter to his brother where he states, "Vassar seems to be very interested in communism. And a great deal of warm debating is going on among the students of Mary's class, which I think is an excellent thing. People of that age ought to be radical anyhow." It was during this period that she first met John F. Kennedy when she attended a dance at Choate Rosemary Hall.

Mary Pinchot Meyer was found shot and killed near her Georgetown home.

After she graduated from Vassar, Meyer began working as a journalist for United Press. By this time she had joined the American Labor Party. Joining that party resulted in the Federal Bureau of Investigation opening a file on her political activities. Like her parents, Meyer was a pacifist. In 1944 she met Cord Meyer. Meyer was a marine who had suffered serious combat injuries that resulted in him losing an eye. At the time the two had similar political views and on April 19, 1945, they were married. Shortly after their marriage the couple attended the conference held in San Francisco that resulted in the establishment of the United Nations. Cord Meyer went as an aide to Harold Stassen while his wife covered the conference for the North American Newspaper Alliance.

During this time period the Meyer's started a family. Their first son Quentin was born in 1945, followed by Michael in 1947. The couple had a third son named mark who was born in 1950. With three small children, Meyer settled into the role of being a housewife.

The couple at this time supported the idea of world government. However in 1950 after the family moved to Cambridge, Cord Meyer lost his enthusiasm for the idea. It was also around this time that he began working secretly for the Central Intelligence Agency (CIA). In 1951 he officially became an employee of the agency where he became a key player in "Operation Mockingbird" a covert operation designed to move the American media toward the positions supported by the CIA.

The Meyer family now moved to Washington, D.C. and settled in Georgetown. The couple was very visible in Georgetown social circles that included people like Katherine Graham, Clark Clifford and the high ranking CIA official by the name of Richard M. Bissell. In 1953 Senator Joe McCarthy accused Cord Meyer of being a communist. Allen Dulles was successful in defending Meyer, and he was able to keep his position with the CIA. In the summer of 1954 John F. Kennedy and his wife Jackie purchased Hickory Hill a house close to that of the Meyers. Mary Meyer and Jackie Kennedy became good friends and often went on walks together. As the Meyer's political views grew apart, it put a strain on their relationship. In 1956 their son Michael was killed after being hit by a car close to the family home. In 1958 Mary Meyer filed for a divorce. In the filing she alleged "extreme cruelty, mental in nature, which seriously injured her health, destroyed her happiness, rendered further cohabitation unendurable and compelled the parties to separate."

After the divorce Meyer and her two surviving sons remained in the family home. She began painting in a garage at the home of her sister who was married to the *Washington Post's* Ben Bradlee. In her book *A Very Private Woman* Nina Burleigh, who knew Meyer personally, wrote that during this period Meyer "was out looking for fun and getting in trouble along the way."

During this period Meyer began running into John Kennedy at social functions and parties. Many were aware that he was very much attracted to her, but Meyer knew about his womanizing and for a time that put her off. In addition Kennedy's plans to make a run for the presidency were, by this time well known, and she thought his woman-izing was reckless.

After Kennedy's election Meyer evidently changed her mind. Begin-ning in October 1961, she became a frequent visitor to the White House. The general consensus is that once their relationship became intimate Kennedy and Meyer got together at least 30 times. In addition it is gener-ally believed that on her visits to the White House Meyer brought with her marijuana and in some cases LSD. Meyer during this period told some friends she was keeping a diary.

How close was the relationship between Kennedy and Meyer? In an interview with Nina Burleigh, Kennedy aide Myer Feldman responded to a question with the following, "I think he might have thought more of her than some of the other women and discussed things that were on his mind not just social gossip." Burleigh wrote that "Mary might actually have been a force for peace during some of the most frightening years of the cold war."

In 1976 Ron Rosenbaum and Phillip Nobile wrote an article titled, "The Curious Aftermath of JFK's Best and Brightest Affair." They refer to Mary in the article as the "secret lady Ottoline of Camelot." They claimed to have been granted an interview with a source who did not wish to be identified but was in a unique position to comment on the couple's relationship. The interview went as follows:

"How could a woman so admired for her integrity as Mary Meyer traduce her friendship with Jackie Kennedy?"

"They weren't friends" was the curt response.

"Did JFK actually love Mary Meyer?"

"I think so."

"Then why would he carry on an affair simultaneously with Judith Exner?"

"My friend there's a difference between sex and love."

"But why Mary Meyer over all other women?"

"He was an unusual man. He wanted the best."

In 1983 former Harvard professor Timothy Leary claimed that Mey-er visited him and said that she was involved in a plan to avert nuclear war by convincing powerful men in Washington to take mind altering drugs with a goal of having them reach the conclusion that the Cold

War was meaningless. According to Leary the purpose of her visit was to find out how to conduct LSD sessions with these men. When Leary suggested that Mary bring the men here so he could conduct the session she responded by saying that was impossible since the man she was involved with was much too powerful.

In her book Burleigh confirms Meyer's own use of LSD and her involvement with Leary which occurred at the same time she was involved with Kennedy. While Burleigh draws no conclusions as to whether Kennedy participated in any LSD sessions she does note that the timing of her visits to Leary coincided with Meyer's known meetings with Kennedy. During a 1990 interview Leary was asked point blank whether he had any doubt that Kennedy was using LSD in the White House with Meyer. He responded by saying, "I can't say that." He pointed out that it was his assumption that Meyer had proposed to take LSD with Kennedy but that he had no proof it had actually happened. Pressed, Leary agreed, that it was possible, even likely, that Kennedy had taken LSD, but he would go no further than that.

On September 24, 1963, Kennedy went with both Meyer and her sister Tony for a visit to the family's Grey Tower estate in Milford, Pennsylvania. The purpose of the President's visit was to dedicate a gift from the Pinchot family to the United States Forest Service. The gift included

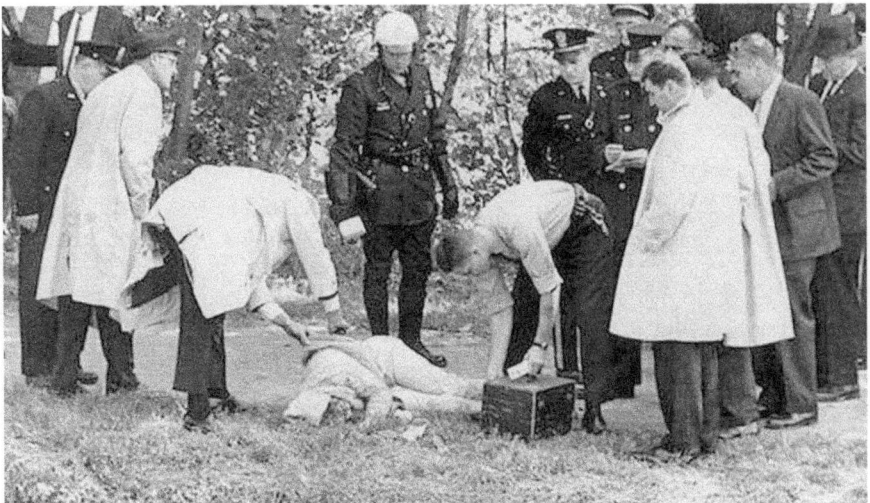

Mary Pinchot Meyer's murder scene.

a large piece of land and the Pinchot mansion which had served as the home of Meyer's uncle and former Pennsylvania Governor Gifford Pinchot. As documented by Peter Janney in his excellent book *Mary's Mosaic* Tony had no idea about the affair between her sister and the President. She said, "I always felt he liked me as much as Mary. You could say there was a little rivalry." Ironically on the same day as the dedication, the United States Senate ratified Kennedy's Limited Nuclear Test Ban Treaty with the Soviet Union and the United Kingdom.

Two months later, after Kennedy was assassinated, Leary said he received a phone call from Meyer who sobbed and said "They couldn't control him anymore. He was changing too fast . . . They've covered everything up. I gotta come see you. I'm afraid."

There is no way to document where Meyer was when she got word of the assassination. She spent the night at a friend's house in Georgetown. The friend recalled that Meyer was very sad and that they both cried but said very little.

As detailed in Janney's book Meyer spent the next year trying to solve the mystery surrounding Kennedy's death. From the first she was sure it had been a conspiracy, and one of the first people Meyer questioned was Kennedy aide Kenneth O'Donnell. O'Donnell respected Meyer largely because he was aware of the role she had played in the president's life. During one interview O'Donnell said he, "feared she had a hold on Jack." O'Donnell and another Kennedy aide by the name of Dave Powers were riding in the car directly behind Kennedy in the motorcade. Both were combat veterans of World War II. O'Donnell told Meyers about what he and Powers had witnessed that day, the smell of gunpowder and the fact that at least two shots were fired from behind the fence on what has become known as the grassy knoll. Twenty-five years later his account was confirmed by Speaker of the House Tip O'Neill. O'Neill recalled a conversation he had at a dinner with O'Donnell and Powers five years after the assassination. The two told O'Neill that two shots had come from behind the fence. When O'Neill responded, "That's not what you told the Warren Commission." O'Donnell readily agreed saying that the FBI told him it couldn't have happened that way so he testified the way "they wanted me to" because I didn't want to cause more pain or trouble for the family.

Dave Powers was interviewed on the radio in 1991 where he basically told the same story. It was around the time that Oliver Stone's film *JFK* had been released. After the broadcast Woody Woodland, who had done the interview, was walking Powers to his car when he asked Powers if he had seen the film. He replied that he had. Woodland then asked, "What did you think of it?" Powers responded, "I think they got it right." "Really?" was the reply from a surprised Woodland. "Yes," said Powers, "we were riding into an ambush. They were shooting from behind the fence." Woodland pointed out that was different from what Powers told the Warren Commission. Powers also admitted that that was true but added he had been told not to say that by the FBI.

Meyer began collecting information on the assassination. One of the people she sought out with regard to the assassination was William Walton, a gay man who had been her escort to many White House social affairs. Walton met Kennedy after World War II, and the two developed a close friendship. Kennedy's wife Jackie enjoyed Walton's company as well and when Kennedy was elected president, Walton enjoyed an almost unchecked access to the White House, and soon he became a close friend of Bobby Kennedy's as well. When Walton met Mary he found her to be distraught with grief. He told her that Bobby suspected something far deeper than Lee Harvey Oswald when it came to the death of his brother. He said Bobby had a plan to take back the presidency, but that it would be years before he could do anything about his brother's death. Despite this information Meyer continued her quest to learn more about Kennedy's death.

In the summer of 1964, Meyer began telling friends that she believed someone had been in her house while she was away. She told another friend that on one occasion she saw someone leaving the house as she was entering. Her friends confirmed that Meyer was frightened by these incidents. By this time Meyer had told a friend, Ann Truitt, that she had kept a diary that detailed her relationship with Kennedy. She asked Truitt to retrieve the diary should anything happen to her.

On October 12, 1964, Meyer was taking her daily walk on the Chesapeake and Ohio towpath in Georgetown. Henry Wiggins a car mechanic was working on a car on Canal Road when he heard a woman scream, "Someone help me, someone help me." Almost immediately he heard

This modest tombstone marks the final resting place of a woman who refused to believe the conclusions reached by the Warren Commission.

two gunshots. Wiggins ran to the edge of a wall overlooking the towpath where he saw a black man wearing a light jacket, dark pants and a dark cap standing over the body of a white woman. Wiggins would later tell police that the man was between 5 feet 8 inches to 5 feet 10 inches and weighed about 185 pounds. According to Wiggins the man turned and looked at him for a few seconds and after shoving something in his pocket turned and walked away disappearing down an embankment.

Meyer's body was taken to the Washington, D. C., morgue where an autopsy was performed by Deputy Coroner Doctor Linwood L. Rayford, a man who, by this time, performed more than 400 such procedures on gunshot victims. He found that Meyer had been shot twice: once in the head and once in the back. He concluded that both shots were fired at close range. According to the doctor Meyer probably survived the first shot to the head though it would have rendered her unconscious. He noted that the second shot was fired with remarkable precision. That bullet severed the aorta and death would have been instantaneous. That bothered Rayford because he felt that it indicated that whoever killed Meyer was a professional.

Meanwhile the police had arrested a black man, Ray Crump, who was found in the area of the shooting and who stood 5 foot 4 inches tall. They conducted tests to show that he had fired the gun that killed Meyer but found no nitrates on either his hands or his clothes. They conducted an extensive search for two days that included the use of scuba divers and actually draining the canal near the scene of the murder. No gun could be found. Crump was eventually acquitted (for a detailed account of that story the authors strongly recommend Janney's book *Mary's Mosaic*).

Ann Truitt was in Tokyo when Meyer was killed. She called Meyer's brother-in-law Ben Bradlee and told him about the diary. The next day Bradlee and his wife went to the Meyer home when they arrived it was locked and when they entered they found James Angleton, the CIA counterintelligence chief already searching for the diary. There are various reports of what happened to it. Some believe Angleton burned it while others believe it remains in someone's possession.

In February of 2001, a writer asked Cord Meyer about Mary Meyer. He responded by saying it had been a bad time because his father had died that same year. Getting back to Mary Meyer the writer asked who could have committed such a heinous crime. Cord Meyer responded, "The same sons of bitches that killed John F. Kennedy."

Mary Pinchot Meyer was laid to rest in the Pinchot family plot in the Milford, Pennsylvania cemetery. She lies next to her son Michael.

If You Go:
Meyer's uncle and former Governor of Pennsylvania Gifford Pinchot (see *Keystone Tombstones Volume 1*) is housed in a large mausoleum in the Milford Cemetery. Just across the road from his gravesite is the grave of Charles Henry Van Wyck. He was a New York Congressman, a Senator from Nebraska and a Brigadier general in the Civil War (See *Keystone Tombstones Civil War*, chapter 30).

On February 22, 1861, Van Wyck survived an assassination attempt in Washington. The attempt took place on the same night that an attempt was made to assassinate President-Elect Lincoln in Baltimore. The attack on Van Wyck was apparently motivated by a harsh anti-slavery speech he delivered on the floor of the house. In the speech he denounced the southern states for the "crime against the laws of God and nature." He fought off the attack and survived only because a book and papers that he carried in his breast pocket blocked the thrust of a Bowie knife.

General Daniel Brodhead

Also buried in the Milford Cemetery is General Daniel Brodhead. He fought with George Washington on Long Island and wintered with the Continental Army at Valley Forge in 1777-1778.

13

"Beverly Hills Nightmare"

JOSE (1944–1989) AND KITTY (1941–1989) MENENDEZ

County: Mercer
Town: Princeton
Cemetery: Princeton Cemetery
Address: 29 Greenview Avenue

The horrible, grisly murder of Jose and Kitty Menendez has fascinated the public for over two decades, inspiring movies, books, podcasts, miniseries, and television specials. Is it because it's set in glamorous, tony Beverly Hills? Or because they were killed by their children? Is it the gruesome, bloody crime scene? Perhaps it's because of their children's defense or because most of it played out live on television.

Jose Menendez was born in Havana, Cuba in 1944. He came to the United States when he was 16, following the Cuban Revolution. His father was a popular soccer player who owned his own accounting firm, while his mother was a Cuban Hall of Fame swimmer. When Castro took over in Cuba, Jose's family decided to leave Cuba for the United States and settled in Hazleton, Pennsylvania.

Jose had no financial resources and didn't speak or understand English, but was determined to succeed in American. He studied hard at Hazleton High, worked part-time to earn spending money and excelled in athletics. He had a dream of attending an Ivy League college but couldn't afford it. Instead, he accepted a scholarship to Southern Illinois University for swimming. It was at SIU that Jose met and fell in love with Mary Louise "Kitty" Andersen.

Kitty was three years older than Jose and was a senior communications major. She was a middle-class girl from the Chicago suburb of Oak Lawn. Her parents had a difficult marriage and divorce, and it left her emotionally scarred. She hated her abusive father and had no contact with

The Menendez family : things aren't always what they seem.

him for many years after her parents divorced. In 1962, her senior year at SIU, she competed in and won the Miss Oak Lawn beauty pageant.

Shortly after Jose and Kitty met they became inseparable. Both of their families had difficulty accepting their relationship, so in 1963, after Kitty graduated, they eloped. After their marriage, they moved to New York City where Jose enrolled at Queens College and Kitty got a job teaching grade school. Jose graduated in 1967 with a degree in accounting. Joseph Lyle Menendez, who went by his middle name, was born January 10, 1968. Kitty quit teaching and became a full-time mom. After a brief time living in Illinois, Jose went to work for Hertz and the family settled in New Jersey. Erik Menendez was born on November 27, 1970, in Gloucester Township, New Jersey.

In 1980, Jose's career at Hertz ended. He was reassigned to RCA's record division, the company that owned Hertz. By 1985, Jose had risen to become executive vice president for RCA Records worldwide operations. Jose was a hard-driving person and this trait carried over to raising his sons. He had rules for everything. As they grew older, the brothers were drawn to each other for companionship and solidarity to face their father's demands.

In 1986, Jose's career took the family to Calabasas, California. He took a position as the president of LIVE Entertainment, a video distribution and duplication company. Erik began attending high school in

The brothers on trial.

Calabasas and showed a talent for tennis, while Lyle applied to Princeton but was rejected. He enrolled at a local community college and reapplied to Princeton where this time he was accepted. During his first semester, Lyle was accused of plagiarism in a psychology class. He was found guilty and suspended for one year. Lyle wanted to transfer to UCLA but Jose would not have it.

Erik was the number one player on his high school's tennis team. He and the team's captain, Craig Cignarelli, spent a lot of time together. They wrote a screenplay entitled "Friends," in which a son from a wealthy family kills his parents to obtain his inheritance.

In July 1988, Lyle and Erik were arrested for a series of burglaries from homes of their friends. The amount of stolen money and jewelry was estimated at over $100,000, which made their actions a felony. Jose was furious but did not want them to go to jail. He hired a top criminal defense lawyer and they worked out a deal where Erik, still a juvenile, took all the blame and got sentenced to community service. After graduating from high school, Erik competed in many tennis tournaments, then returned to Beverly Hills to await enrollment at UCLA.

After the burglary episode, Jose moved the family to a mansion at 722 North Elm Drive in Beverly Hills that was once rented by Prince and by Elton John. It was there in the den that Erik and Lyle killed their parents on August 20, 1989, at around 10 P.M.

They attacked their parents while their mother rested her head on their father's lap. They were watching television when Jose was shot point-blank in the back of the head with a 12-gauge shotgun, killing him instantly. Kitty got up and started to run but was shot several times and fell. The brothers had to leave the den and retrieve more ammo from their car to reload. Erik then delivered the kill shot to his mother's face. Both Jose and Kitty were then shot in the kneecap, to make the murders appear related to organized crime.

The boys were surprised not to hear any sirens after all that noise. They got in the car and dumped the guns somewhere off Mulholland Drive, then threw the spent shotgun shells and their bloody clothes in a dumpster at a gas station. At 11:47 P.M., after the brothers returned home, Lyle called 9-1-1 and cried, "Somebody killed my parents!" The brothers told the police, who arrived in minutes, that they had gone to the movies and then drove to Santa Monica to have drinks with a friend but missed him and returned home.

Lyle and Erik performed so well for the police that they were not suspected and police did not administer gunshot-residue tests. Early reports described the crime scene as a "gangland-style killing." A lack of evidence prevented the police from considering the brothers more thoroughly and police didn't formally interview them until two months after the murders.

In the months that followed, the boys spent lavishly and brought suspicion on themselves. They reportedly spent over $700,000 on cars, jewelry, and travel. Erik hired a full-time tennis coach. Lyle bought a restaurant in Princeton, New Jersey.

Authorities initially pursued the notion that it was a mob hit. As a wealthy executive in the entertainment business who had been shot at close range multiple times by 12-gauge shotguns and shot in the kneecaps, it seemed likely that it was a message killing.

The brothers decided they could not stay in the Beverly Hills mansion and told their friends they moved from hotel to hotel because they feared the mobsters who murdered their parents would come after them. Lyle hired bodyguards to travel with him for several weeks.

The police eventually became suspicious of the boys not only for their spending sprees but also because they had called a computer expert to erase files on Kitty's computer. After an October 24, 1989, interview with Detective Les Zoeller, Erik was shaken. He tried to reach Lyle but failed and, needing someone to talk to, contacted his psychologist, Dr. Jerome Oziel. During a session with Oziel, Erik admitted to the murders and told him how they had been inspired by the Billionaire Boys Club miniseries as well as how they purchased the weapons, planned the murder, and hid the evidence.

Lyle was furious when he found out that Erik told Oziel and threatened to kill Oziel if he told anyone. On November 2, the brothers met with Oziel again. Lyle threatened him again. Oziel made tapes and notes of his sessions.

On March 5, 1990, the police got a call from Judalon Smyth. She was Oziel's ex-mistress. She told police she had eavesdropped on a therapy session with the brothers and heard Lyle threaten Oziel. She claimed that Oziel had confessions and details on tape.

The police obtained a warrant for Oziel's tapes and, after listening to them, arrested Lyle on March 8, 1990, near the mansion. Erik, who was in Israel playing tennis, turned himself in upon his return three days later. Both were held without bail and kept separate from each other.

The families hired very good and very expensive legal counsel for Lyle and Erik. Selected to represent Erik was Leslie Abramson, and Jill Lansing was hired to represent Lyle. Their first task was challenging the admissibility of the tapes from Dr. Oziel. On August 6, 1990, Superior Court Judge James Albrecht ruled that all the tapes could be used as evidence against the brothers because Lyle had voided the doctor-patient privilege by threatening physical harm against Oziel. That ruling was appealed, delaying the proceedings for two years.

After the evidentiary ruling was overturned on appeal, the Supreme Court of California declared in August 1992 that several of the tapes were admissible but not the tape of Erik discussing the murders.

The Menendez brothers spent three years in the Los Angeles County Men's Jail waiting for their trials to begin. When they finally did, the trials were broadcast by the fledgling Court TV network and became a national sensation. The brothers were tried together yet each had a separate jury.

Leslie Abramson became famous for her flamboyant defense alleging that the brothers were driven to murder by a lifetime of abuse from their parents, including sexual abuse. Jose was described as a cruel, callous perfectionist and a pedophile. Kitty was portrayed as a selfish, mentally unstable alcoholic and drug addict.

The defense presented had one big obstacle—the brothers had never complained to their psychologist or anyone else about abuse, there was no medical evidence of abuse, and no photographs of bruises or history of abuse whatsoever. If this defense were to succeed, specific incidents of abuse would have to be recounted, and they were. The prosecution had to prove to the jurors that the brothers were liars and their tales of abuse were not true.

The trial started on July 20, 1993, and went on for months. On January 13, 1994, Erik's jury announced that it was deadlocked after 16 days of deliberation. On January 25, Lyle's jury also announced that they were deadlocked after 24 days of deliberation. Judge Weisberg declared mistrials. The male members of both juries voted for conviction. Los Angeles County District Attorney Gil Garcetti announced immediately that the brothers would be retried.

In February 1995, Judge Weisberg set a date for a new trial but this time there would be some changes. He ruled that the brothers would be retried together in front of a single jury, limited the number of witnesses, and the trial would not be televised. The trial began in August 1995 and lasted 23 weeks. Sixty-four witnesses testified (as opposed to 101 in the first trial).

Kitty and Jose buried in Princeton.

The trial was never about guilt or innocence. The defendants admitted that they killed their parents in cold blood and showed neither mercy nor remorse. Instead, they blamed their parents for abuse that transformed the victims into the killers. The prosecutors attempted to prove the brothers were lying sociopaths who invented sensational allegations of abuse.

On March 20, 1996, a jury of eight men and four women found the Menendez brothers guilty of two counts of first-degree murder as well as conspiracy to commit murder.

The penalty phase began two days later and was completed in three weeks. Even this part of the trial had stunning drama. A psychiatrist who had treated Erik since the murders, Dr. William Vicary, admitted under cross-examination that he doctored his notes at the request of Leslie Abramson. The notes omitted contained incriminating evidence against Erik. The jury decided to spare their lives and voted for a sentence of life in prison without the possibility of parole. The jurors later said that the abuse defense was never a factor and it rejected the death penalty because neither brother had a history of violence.

On July 2, 1996, Judge Weisberg sentenced the two to life without parole. The California Department of Corrections separated the Menendez brothers and sent them to different prisons. In 1998, both the California Court of Appeal and the California Supreme Court upheld the convictions and sentences.

Since entering prison, both brothers have married even though California does not allow conjugal visits for those convicted of murder. Lyle has married *twice*. He married Anna Eriksson in a telephone ceremony in 1997. They divorced in 2001 and in 2003 he married Rebecca Sneed at Mule Creek State Prison. Erik married Tammi Ruth Saccoman in a waiting room at Folsom State Prison in 1999.

Jose and Kitty Menendez are buried beneath a large, impressive marker in Princeton Cemetery in Princeton, New Jersey.

If You Go:

Princeton Cemetery is a large, beautiful cemetery containing the graves of many famous people, including: John Witherspoon (1722–1794), a signer of the Declaration of Independence; Aaron Burr, Jr. (1756–1836)

who, as Vice-President of the United States, shot and killed Alexander
Hamilton; and Grover Cleveland (1837-1908), who was the 22nd and
24th President of the United States, making him the only President in
American history to serve two non-consecutive terms in office (1885-89
and 1893-97).

Writer John O'Hara (1905–1970) and pollster George Gallup
(1901–1984) are also among those buried there.

14

"The Molly Maguires"

BLACK JACK KEHOE AND FRANKLIN GOWEN

Counties: Schuylkill, Philadelphia
Towns: Tamaqua, Philadelphia
Cemeteries: Old Saint Jerome's, Ivy Hill
Addresses: Corner of High and Nescopeck Streets, 1201 Easton Road

In Pennsylvanian history, there are few groups as interesting or as controversial as the Molly Maguires. Some historians view them as an Irish Catholic terrorist organization, while to others, they are no more than an organized labor movement created as a response to the persecution of Irish coal miners. Still, there are some who argue that the organization never existed. Undeniable, however, is the fact is that between June 21, 1877, and October 9, 1879, twenty Irish catholic men were hanged for murder and accused of belonging to a secret society known as the Molly Maguires. Ten of these men were hanged on June 21, 1877, a day that would become known as "Black Thursday" or "The Day of the Rope."

The Molly Maguire story began in the early 1860s and ended in 1879 when the last hanging took place. The center of action was the anthracite coal region in northeastern Pennsylvania. The alleged Mollies were most active in two counties Carbon and Schuylkill.

As a result of the potato famine in the late 1840s, many Irish immigrates landed in America. Those who settled in the Pennsylvania coal region found that the only jobs available to them were in the mines. The work was difficult and dangerous. In addition, the miners were forced to live in coal company provided housing and could only shop at the company store where prices were so inflated that it was not unusual for a miner to find himself in debt to the company as his wages could not cover his rent and other expenses. These conditions led to the beatings and murder of mine owners, foreman and superintendents. The mine

John "Black Jack" Kehoe, "King of the Mollies," soon before his execution in 1878.

owners and newspapers believed these beatings and killings were part of an organized conspiracy headed by Irishmen who called themselves the Molly Maguires.

During the Molly era, the miners were forming a union under the leadership of John Siney. The union was known as the Workingmen's Benevolent Association and through Siney, and the leadership of the organization as a whole, they sought to seek concessions through negotiations. At times, they used strikes as a tool. In December of 1874, what was called the long strike began in the coalfields. The strike lasted for just under six months and when the miners broke they were forced to return for lower wages than they had previously earned. The person responsible for this settlement was Franklin B. Gowen, the President of the Philadelphia and Reading Coal and Iron Company.

Gowen was born in Mount Airy, Pennsylvania on February 9, 1836. He was the fifth child of an Irish Protestant immigrant who made his living as a grocer. Franklin attended a boarding school, John Beck's Boys Academy, starting at age 9 and ending when he was 13. After serving an apprenticeship to a Lancaster merchant, he decided to study law and worked under an attorney in Pottsville, Pennsylvania which happened to be the county seat of Schuylkill County. In 1860 he was admitted to the County Bar and in 1862 he was elected District Attorney of Schuylkill County. He held this position until 1864 when he resigned in order to pursue a private practice. Among his clients was the Philadelphia and Reading Railroad. He soon left private practice to head that company's legal department. It proved to be a wise move for in 1869, Gowen was appointed acting President of the company.

By this time, Gowen already had the Molly Maguires in his sights. In 1873, he hired the Pinkerton Detective Agency for the purpose of infiltrating the Mollies. Several Pinkerton operatives were sent into the coalfields, including James McParlan, who arrived in Schuylkill County on October 27,1873, using the alias of James McKenna. In April of 1874, McParlan was initiated into the Ancient Order of Hibernians (AOH), a legal Irish Catholic organization. It was Gowen's belief that the Molly Maguires operated within this organization. It is worth noting that violence on both management's and labor's side increased once the Pinkertons arrived in the area.

The Pinkertons were not the only weapon used by Gowen in his attacks on the Mollies. He had his own private police force known as the Coal and Iron police. An 1868 act of the legislature authorized the creation of this private army. A deputy commissioner for Pennsylvania's Bureau of Labor Statistics held the opinion that the coal operators were their own personal government in the middle of a republic. There was no limit to the number of Coal and Iron policemen that could be hired by the Reading Coal and Iron Company, nor were there any background checks on those who applied to join the force. This police force patrolled the coal region unmolested by local authorities. In May of 1875, Pinkerton sent Captain Robert Linden to the coal fields. He immediately received an appointment as a Coal and Iron policeman. The power of this police force was absolute. They were more powerful than the civil authorities. Linden was instrumental in investigating the crimes that led to the arrests of the alleged Molly Maguires.

One of the most important murders in the Molly Maguire story took place in Tamaqua during the evening hours on July 5, 1875. The Tamaqua police force consisted of two men: Barney McCarron and Benjamin Yost. Yost had a history of running into trouble with an Irish minor named James Kerrigan. Yost had arrested Kerrigan on several occasions for public drunkenness, and in at least one instance subdued Kerrigan with his billy club.

One of the duties of the Tamaqua police force was to extinguish the gas street lights. As Yost was climbing a ladder to shut off one of the light, shots rang out, and Yost fell to the ground. McCarron Turned towards the sound of the shots and saw two forms running away. McCarron gave chase but the assailants escaped. Yost died several hours later and word spread that the murder had been carried out by the Molly Maguires.

The first Mollies that ended up on the gallows were arrested in September of 1875 for the murder of mine superintendent John P. Jones. Jones was shot and killed at a railroad station in Lansford while on his way to work by two men who quickly left the scene. A witness to the murder quickly made the trip to Tamaqua and spread the news. In addition, this man claimed to have seen a man waving something white in the woods outside Tamaqua an apparent signal that brought two other men to him. A posse was formed to investigate. The three men arrested for the crime were found in those same woods having a meal. The men were identified as Edward Kelly, Michael Doyle, and Jimmy Kerrigan. Both Kelly and Doyle carried documents that identified them as members of the AOH. The three were taken to the Carbon County jail in Mauch Chunk, now known as Jim Thorpe.

These initial arrests provided the break the Pinkertons were waiting for, and they quickly took advantage of it. The accused men requested separate trials, and Michael Doyle was the first to be tried. Meanwhile Kerrigan and Kelly were kept in solitary confinement in the county jail.

This initial trial set the tone for the ones that would follow. The jury would have no Irish or catholic members and would be made up largely

The tombstones in this old cemetery have been destroyed due to vandalism. Two alleged Molly Maguires are buried here including Alec Campbell. Almost all historians agree that one of the two interned here, placed their handprint on his cell wall prior to his execution. The print remains to this day as a sign of his innocence.

of Germans, including some who spoke little or no English. The District Attorney, while present, did not try the case. This duty fell to attorneys who worked for the railroad and coal companies. In the Doyle trial the prosecution was headed by General Charles Albright who worked for the Lehigh and Wilkes-Barre Coal Company. The general wore his civil war uniform, including his sword, throughout the trial. One has to wonder how he would have gotten past security today.

The prosecution called more than 100 witnesses that established that Doyle was seen in Lansford on the day of the murder. While no one testified that they had seen Doyle murder Jones, he was described as walking quickly toward the murder site and observed running away with a pistol in hand. The defense did not call a single witness in the case. In their summation the defense conceded that Doyle was in Lansford that day, but he was simply looking for work.

The prosecution case was at its weakest when it came to providing a motive for the murder. Detective McParlan's reports to his superiors laid out a scenario that would have provided a motive. According to the detective, Kerrigan (the head of the Mollies in Tamaqua) had been beaten by the policeman Yost. Another Molly, Hugh McGehan, had been blacklisted by the mine foreman, Jones. Kerrigan initiated contact with James Roarity, the head of the Mollies in Coaldale, in order to exact revenge for these perceived wrong-doings. Kerrigan and Roarity decided that McGehan and a man by the name of James Boyle would murder Yost with the assistance of Kerrigan. Doyle and Kelly, again with Kerrigan's help, would take care of Jones.

The only way the prosecution could introduce this evidence would be to call McParlan as a witness. Because McParlan was still gathering information and the use of his testimony would have exposed his identity as a detective, the prosecution went on without him. It didn't matter. On February 1, 1876, the jury pronounced Doyle guilty and on the 23rd he was sentenced to be hanged.

At later trials, McParlan claimed that it was a common practice among the Mollies to trade jobs. This was done to make it difficult for the townspeople to recognize the out of town assailants.

Something of greater importance to the Molly Maguire story took place during the trial. Jimmy Kerrigan confessed. In fact, he produced a 210 page confession and agreed to testify against his fellow Irishmen in return for immunity. This action earned "Powder Keg" Kerrigan a new nickname, he would henceforth be known as "Squealer" Kerrigan.

Based on McParlan's reports and information supplied by Kerrigan, a unit of the Coal and Iron Police led by Captain Linden made a series

On June 21, 1877, within the walls of the Schuylkill County prison (pictured above) in Pottsville six alleged Molly Maguires were executed by hanging.

of arrests. On February 4th this group set out and arrested James Carroll, James Roarity, Thomas Duffy, Hugh McGehan, James Boyle and Alexander Campbell for the murders of Yost and Jones. Six days later the Coal and Iron Police arrested Thomas Munley as a suspect in the murders of Thomas Sanger and William Uren. Another alleged Molly, Dennis Donnelly, would be arrested later for his part in the murders.

Sanger and Uren were shot and killed on September 1, 1875. On that morning Sanger, who was a mine boss, left for work accompanied by Uren who worked for him. While on the road, the duo was attacked by five heavily armed men who shot and killed them both. Sanger had been targeted for evicting Irishmen. Uren was simply in the wrong place at the wrong time.

Following these murders, a one page handbill titled "Strictly Confidential" began circulating in the coalfields. The paper claimed to present facts to be considered by the Vigilance Committee of the Anthracite Coal Region. The document goes on to list a number of murders that had occurred in the region and named the murderers and their residences. In terms of the Sanger and Uren case the handbill states, "On September

1st, 1875 at about 7 A.M. Thomas Sanger, a mining boss, and William Uren, a miner of Raven Run, were shot and fatally wounded by James O'Donnell, alias "Friday," and Thomas Munley, as the unsuspecting victims were on their way to work. Charles O'Donnell, Charles McAllister, and Mike Doyle were present, and accessories to this murder." The information in the handbill was almost certainly based on reports from Detective McParlan, and it is just as probable that it was distributed by the Pinkerton's.

The handbill began circulating in the fall of 1875, on December 10th of that year it would bear fruit. At about 3 in the morning of the 10th Charles and Ellen McAllister were asleep in their home in Wiggans patch. A small child lay between them and Ellen was pregnant. Ellen's mother was also in the house along with her unmarried sons James "Friday" O'Donnell and Charles O'Donnell. Four borders were also asleep in the house including James McAllister who was the brother of Charles.

Charles McAllister was awakened by a crashing noise: the kitchen door being smashed in. He told his wife to stay in bed and ran to the cellar where he made his way to his neighbor's through a door that connected the residences. His wife did not obey; she got up and opened a door that led to the kitchen and was shot and killed. Now pairs of men began searching every bedroom in the house. They brought James McAllister down the stairs into the yard where he freed himself and ran. Shots were fired, and he was hit in the arm but escaped. James O' Donnell also managed to escape. Charles O'Donnell was not so lucky; he was taken outside, and when he struggled free, he was downed by gunshots. Men gathered around his fallen body and emptied their pistols. The shots were fired so close to the body that they burned the flesh. The next day a note was found on the property that stated "You are the killers of Sanger and Uren." Black Jack Kehoe, the man Gowen considered to be the King of the Mollies, was the brother-in-law of both Charles McAllister and Ellen McAllister.

To this day no one knows who the men were who participated in what became known as the Wiggans Patch massacre. What we do know is that Detective McParlan felt responsible. Upon hearing of the killings, he sent a letter of resignation to the Pinkerton office in New York City. In the letter he states, "Now I wake up this morning to find that I am the murderer of Mrs. McAllister." His resignation was not accepted.

Events moved quickly as a series of Molly Maguire trials commenced. The second trial, that of Edward Kelly, began on March 29th. Again, there were no Irish on the jury and the prosecution team was the same. The jury returned a guilty verdict on April 6th, and six days later Kelly was sentenced to be hanged.

After these first two convictions, the Pottsville Courthouse in Schuylkill County was the scene of the next trial. Leading the prosecution in this case would be Franklin Gowen, President of the Philadelphia and Reading Coal and Iron Company. Gowen was well acquainted with the Pottsville Courthouse. As stated previously, he had served as Schuylkill County's District Attorney. The trial started on May 4 and involved the killing of the Tamaqua police officer Benjamin Yost. James Boyle, James Roarity, Hugh McGehan, Thomas Duffy and James Carroll stood accused of the murder.

This trial marked the first appearance of the detective James McParlan as a witness for the prosecution. The informer, Jimmy Kerrigan, would also testify. Just as the trial was getting underway, news spread that the coal and iron police had arrested ten more Mollies in Schuylkill County. Among the ten was Black Jack Kehoe. Kehoe was a respected man active in community affairs who had written to local newspapers denying the existence of an organization known as the Molly Maguires. He was also active in the leadership of the Hibernians. In addition, he had worked his way out of the mines and had much to lose if his leadership of such a group as the Mollies could be proven.

Detective McParlan was the main witness at this trial, and through his testimony, the prosecution was able to leave the impression that the AOH and the Molly Maguires were one and the same. McParlan detailed secret signs and sayings that members used to identify each other. He stated that the chief purpose of the organization was to protect, and, when necessary, seek revenge for members who felt they had been wronged in some manner. In this way he tied the murders and beatings of the mine owners and bosses to the organization. Jimmy Kerrigan also testified and supported McParlan's account.

The defense did call several witnesses in this case including Mrs. Kerrigan who testified that her husband told her he had murdered Yost. She also condemned him for allowing innocent men to take the blame for his crime. While she was being cross examined, one of the jurors became ill. On May 18th the trial was suspended pending his recovery, however his condition did not improve and on May 25th he died of pneumonia. All the work that had gone into the case was lost. The jury was dismissed, and the prisoners returned to the county jail to await a new trial.

Before the second Yost trial began, Alexander Campbell was brought before the court in Mauch Chunk for the murder of John P. Jones. Campbell, like many of the accused Mollies, was born in Ireland. He arrived in Pennsylvania in 1868 where he opened a saloon in Tamaqua. He later moved to the Lansford area where he operated another saloon, the Columbia house. Campbell was viewed by many to be the leader of the Mollies in Carbon County. What made the Campbell trial important was that all agreed he was not present when Jones was killed. He was charged as an accessory before the fact, accused of being involved in the planning of the murder. The prosecution alleged that Kelly, Doyle and Kerrigan spent the night before the killing at Campbell's tavern. The defense countered with several witnesses who said they had been at Campbell's that night and had not seen the three men. After an eleven day trial the jury quickly returned with a guilty verdict and on August 28th Campbell was sentenced to be hanged. Clearly, an Irishman owning a public tavern was a dangerous business to be involved in at the time.

Before Campbell's trial was over, another had begun in Pottsville where Thomas Munley was tried for the murders of Thomas Sanger and William Uren. The prosecution case rested entirely on the testimony of McParlan. Several of Munley's family members testified that he was at home on the day of the murder. Despite this testimony, Munley was found guilty and sentenced to death.

By then, the second Yost trial was underway with the accused being Boyle, Carroll, McGehen and Roarity. Thomas Duffy had requested and was granted a separate trial. McParlan and Kerrigan repeated their testimony and all four men were found guilty. They too were sentenced to be hanged. In addition, the separate trial did not help Duffy as he was also found guilty and received the same sentence.

The Pinkertons continued to investigate past murders including that of mine boss Morgan Powell who had been killed in 1871. Three men, John Donahue, Thomas Fisher and Alec Campbell, were arrested and tried for this murder. All three were convicted and sentenced to death. This was Campbell's second conviction.

The first ten executions took place on June 21, 1877, Black Thursday, or the Day of the Rope as it was referred to by locals. Four of the convicted Irishmen would be hanged in the Mauch Chunk jail. The other six would face the hangman in Pottsville.

The Mauch Chunk hangings occurred first. The gallows had been constructed so that all four men could be hanged at the same time. At around 10:30 in the morning, Alexander Campbell took his place on the gallows. In his final statement, he forgave his executioners. Michael

Joe Farrell stands in front of Jack Kehoe's grave holding the key supplied by a local resident which allowed us entrance to the aged cemetery. Kehoe has been called the "King of the Mollies" but he was almost surely innocent of the crime that sent him to the gallows.

Here is Jack Kehoe's Hibernian House looking much as it did the day he was arrested. It is still in operation and run by Kehoe's great-grandson.

Doyle was next, and he took his spot on the gallows. He said that he had come to this point because of his failure to follow the advice of his church on secret societies. John Donahue took his place and declined comment. Edward Kelly was the last to take his place and, led by his priest, forgave everyone and added that if he had listened to his priests, he would not have found himself on the gallows. The men were then readied for execution and at approximately 10:45, the trap was sprung and the four hurtled to their death. After the bodies were cut down and their hoods removed, the sheriff invited the spectators present to inspect the bodies.

In Pottsville, the authorities had decided to hang the prisoners two at a time. Between 8 and 10 AM, those with official passes were allowed into the prison where they scurried to find the best spots to watch the executions. Meanwhile, the area around the prison, including the hills, were packed with people.

Around 11 AM, the first two prisoners, James Boyle and Hugh Mc-Gehan emerged from the jail and made their way to the gallows. Both asked for forgiveness, and Boyle pardoned those who were about to hang him. Ten minutes later, the two were dead. The pair to follow were James Carroll and James Roarity. The latter had been convicted primarily based on the testimony of Jimmy Kerrigan who claimed that Roarity had paid him to have Yost killed. On the gallows, Roarity insisted that this was not so, and he added that Thomas Duffy had nothing to do with the Yost murder. Carroll simply stated that he was an innocent man. Both men were hung at around 12:20. Thomas Duffy and Thomas Munley were the last to the gallows. Neither said much beyond that it was no use and at 1:20, both were sent falling to their death.

At this point the Mollies, if they ever existed, were finished as a power in the coal region. Ten more would be hanged, and others would serve long prison terms. This was not enough to satisfy Franklin Gowen. He wouldn't be happy until he saw Jack Kehoe, who was already serving a seven year prison term, at the end of a rope.

Kehoe was a man who worked his way out of the mines. By 1873, he opened a tavern and rooming house in Girardville called the Hibernian House. He ran this business for three years and during this time became active in local politics. He was elected to the post of Constable in Girardville and was also named Schuylkill County delegate in the AOH. When local newspapers, based on information supplied by the Pinkertons, began linking the Hibernians to the Molly Maguires Kehoe publicly denied such charges. It was Kehoe's view that the Mollies were the fictional invention of the mine owners. Based on information supplied by Detective McParlan, Kehoe was arrested in 1876 and charged with conspiracy to commit murder. This charge did not carry a death sentence, but Gowen resurrected a murder that occurred in 1862 and named Kehoe one of the killers.

Frank Langdon was a mining boss in Audenried where Kehoe lived and worked. On June 14, 1862, he was assaulted by at least three men. He was able to return home, but he died three days later as a result of the beating. In January of 1877, Kehoe was tried for his murder. The evidence presented at the trial was murky at best. Kehoe was said to have threatened Langdon weeks before he was beaten, but other witnesses claimed to have seen Kehoe on a hotel porch at the time Langdon was assaulted. In his summation, Gowen described Kehoe as a man who made money by his traffic in the souls of his fellow men. Despite the lack of evidence, Kehoe was found guilty and sentenced to death.

Kehoe's lawyers fought the conviction to the State Supreme Court which denied the appeal. Next they petitioned the Board of Pardons where they produced sworn statements from John Campbell and Neil Dougherty (both of whom had been convicted of second degree murder in the matter) admitting their participation in the beating and swearing that Kehoe was not present. In September 1878, the Board voted 2-2 on the petition. A tie vote meant the conviction was upheld.

On December 18, 1878, Kehoe waited in his cell with one of his lawyers, Martin L'Velle. He told L'Velle that he was prepared to die. Shortly thereafter, Kehoe took his place on the gallows in Pottsville. Given the opportunity to speak, he proclaimed his innocence, adding that he had not even seen the crime being committed. After making his statement, Kehoe nodded to the sheriff signifying that he was ready. He was quickly shackled and strapped, and at 10:27 A.M., the trap door was sprung. Four other men would be hanged as Mollies after Kehoe, but public interest in the story and in the hangings was never the same. In September of 1978, the Governor of Pennsylvania, Milton Shapp, released a statement that included the following; "It was Jack Kehoe's popularity among the workingmen that led Franklin Gowen to fear, despise, and ultimately destroy him." On January 12, 1979, Shapp signed a posthumous pardon for Jack Kehoe. This is the only posthumous pardon issued in the history of Pennsylvania.

Kehoe is buried in the old Saint Jerome's Catholic Cemetery in Tamaqua. The two victims of the Wiggans Patch massacre, Ellen McAllister

On the Day of the rope four alleged Mollies were hanged together at the same time in the old jail in Jim Thorpe. The gallows were built in the middle of the cell block so the condemned men were able to hear the construction prior to their execution.

and her brother, Charles O'Donnell, were also laid to rest here. The cemetery is located on the corner of High and Nescopeck streets, and it is fenced in and locked. A neighbor who lives on that corner has a key that he is happy to share with visitors. When we were looking for a way in, he appeared and asked "You here to see Kehoe?" That's how we found our way into the cemetery. Two other alleged Mollies, Thomas Duffy and Jack Donahue, are also buried there in unmarked graves. Another place worth visiting in relation to Kehoe is his Hibernian House in Girardville, which is now run by his great grandson. Among the artifacts that can be viewed at this location is Kehoe's cell door from the Pottsville prison.

Alec Campbell is buried in Saint Joseph's Catholic Cemetery on Ludlow Street in Summit Hill. There are no grave markers in this cemetery due to acts of vandalism. A mock trial of Campbell was held in Jim Thorpe recently using the transcripts from his trial. A relative portrayed Campbell, and he was found innocent. Another alleged Molly, Thomas Fisher, lies there as well.

The Schuylkill County jail in Pottsville where many of the hangings took place is still in operation, but aside from plaques noting what happened, there is little to see. There is one interesting plaque that is on the wall at the jail's main entrance. The plaque notes that the largest

Final resting place of Franklin Gowen who was the man most responsible for the hangings of 20 alleged Molly Maguires during the 1870s.

mass execution in Pennsylvania history took place inside this prison. It also references the four executions that took place in Mauch Chunk that same day. What is striking is it ends by stating that the pardon of Jack Kehoe reflects "the judgment of many historians that the trials and executions were part of a repression directed against the fledgling mine workers union of that historic period."

The Carbon County jail, however, is now a museum where regular tours are conducted. A replica of the gallows stands where the original one once stood. In addition, visitors can view the mysterious handprint in cell 17. According to legend, as one of the Mollies (either Alec Campbell or Thomas Fisher) was about to be taken to the gallows, he put his handprint on the wall of his cell saying that it would remain forever as a sign of his innocence. Despite efforts to remove the print, it remains to this day.

Things went well for one of the other main characters in the Molly story. James McParlan was named manager of the Pinkertons' office in Denver Colorado. He passed away in Denver in 1919.

Franklin Gowen eventually lost his leadership position in the Philadelphia and Reading Coal and Iron Company. He returned to private practice. On December 13, 1889, according to the coroner who investigated the death, Gowen shot himself while staying in a hotel in

Washington, D.C. Many of Gowen's family and friends believed he was murdered. In 2002, a book written by Patrick Campbell (a descendant of Alec Campbell) entitled *Who Killed Franklin Gowen*, concludes that Gowen was a homicide victim. Gowen is buried in the Ivy Hill Cemetery just outside Philadelphia.

In 1969, a highly fictionalized major motion picture called *The Molly Maguires* was released. It was filmed largely in Pennsylvania including several scenes that take place in Jim Thorpe. Much of the movie was filmed in Eckley, not far from Hazleton. Eckley in now a museum and visitors are most welcome. In the movie, Richard Harris plays Detective McParlan and Sean Connery stars as Black Jack Kehoe. It's worth a look.

If You Go:

In the center of downtown Jim Thorpe, you can always visit the Molly Maguire Pub where one can find good food and drink at reasonable prices. The pub has a large outdoor deck that is open weather permitting. That same section of Jim Thorpe is home to many antique and specialty shops that you might want to check out.

In addition, the town is quite close to the Poconos, so white water rafting is available as well as skiing depending on the season. Finally, you can visit the Jim Thorpe Memorial which is the final resting place for that great athlete (see *The Best of Keystone Tombstones*, chapter 28).

15

"The Mob"

23 ORGANIZED CRIME FIGURES

County: Queens
Town: Middle Village
Cemetery: Saint John Cemetery
Address: 80-01 Metropolitan Avenue

When we were doing research for *Keystone Tombstones Volume Two* in 2012, we were checking for the remains of Philip "Chicken Man" Testa, a famous mob figure in Philadelphia who was killed in March 1981 by a bomb exploding in his house. The bomb was allegedly planted by rival mobsters. The incident was made famous by lyrics about the incident in Bruce Springsteen's song "Atlantic City." Testa, we found, was buried in Holy Cross Cemetery just outside of Philadelphia. We were amazed at the time to discover four more famous organized crime figures buried nearby in Holy Cross Cemetery. (See chapter 18, titled "Philadelphia's Sinners").

While doing research for this volume we found a situation that dwarfed the Philadelphia experience. We found at least 23 organized crime figures buried in Saint John Cemetery in Middle Village, Queens. They began arriving at St. John in 1928 and the most recent one was in 2002. Eight were murdered by other organized crime figures, two were executed, four died of natural causes in prison and one was released from prison on humanitarian grounds because he was dying.

The first to arrive was Salvatore D'Aquila.

1. Salvatore D'Aquila
Born: Nov. 7, 1873 – Palermo, Sicily, Italy
Died: Oct. 10, 1928 (age 54) – Manhattan, N.Y.

Salvatore D'Aquila

D'Aquila formed his own crime family in 1910 and operated in East Harlem and the Bronx. He was one of what came to be known as a "Mustache Pete"—an old school mafioso steeped in Old World ways. When a rival boss Giuseppe Morello went to prison, D'Aquila seized the opportunity to expand his operations into Brooklyn and Southern Manhattan. Ten years later Morello was released from prison and the two gangs began a violent competition. After a number of top associates were killed, D'Aquila was forced to retreat from Manhattan back to the Bronx. He actually purchased a home directly across from the main entrance to the Bronx Zoo.

On October 10, 1928, D'Aquila was on his way to a doctor appointment. As he walked down the street several men approached him. One of the men pulled out a pistol and shot him two times in the chest. D'Aquila fell to the ground where the man fired another seven bullets into his body.

The next to arrive at St. John were Rosario Parrino and Salvatore Maranzano.

2. Rosario "Sasa" Parrino
Born: 1890, New York
Died: May 31, 1930 (age 40) – Detroit, MI

3. Salvatore Maranzano
Born: July 31, 1886 – Castellammarese del Golfo, Sicily
Died: Sept. 10, 1931 (age 45) – Manhattan, N.Y.

Salvatore Maranzano

Parrino was a casualty of what was called the "Castellammarese War." This was a bloody power struggle for control of the Italian-American Mafia between Joe Masseria and Salvatore Maranzano. It was so called because Maranzano was based in Castellammarese del Golfo, Sicily. Parrino had moved to Detroit and joined the Milazzo family where he was a soldier and bodyguard. Milazzo refused to help Masseria in his war with Maranzano and he and Parrino were murdered on May 31, 1930, in a Detroit fish market.

Maranzano was nicknamed "Little Caesar," and he and others like Masseria were called "Mustache Petes"—an old school mafioso steeped in their Old World ways. The "Young Turks" were more forward thinking and willing to work more with non-Italians, like Bugsy Siegel and Meyer Lansky. Maranzano had Masseria killed by some "Young Turks" on April 15, 1931, and thus won the war and be-

Little Caesar's grave.

came the "boss of bosses." His reign was short, however, as Lucky Luciano and other "Young Turks" shot and stabbed Maranzano to death on September 10, 1931, and he became the next to arrive at St. John Cemetery.

The next to arrive was Charles Higgins.

4. Charles "Vannie" Higgins
Born: 1897 – Bay Ridge, N.Y.
Died: June 19, 1932 (age 35) – Brooklyn, N.Y.

Higgins was one of the most prominent bootleggers during the Prohibition era. He was known as "Brooklyn's Last Irish Boss." In 1928, Higgins sought to expand his operation by aligning himself with Jack "Legs" Diamond. While trying to move into Manhattan, Higgins and his allies came into conflict with Dutch Schultz resulting in what be-

Charles Higgins

came known as "The Manhattan Beer War." On June 18, 1932, Higgins attended a tap dance recital at the Knights of Columbus in Prospect Park to see his seven-year old daughter perform. He was gunned down in the street while trying to protect his daughter from the gunfire. Police took him to Methodist Episcopal Hospital where he died the next afternoon. Police questioned him but he refused to answer their questions.

The next two arrivals were in 1942.

5. Harry "Happy" Maione

Born: Oct. 7, 1908
Died: Feb. 19, 1942 (age 33) –
Ossining, N.Y.

6. Frank "The Dasher" Abbundando

Born: July 11, 1910 –
Brooklyn, N.Y.
Died: Feb. 19, 1942 (age 31) –
Ossining, N.Y.

Harry Maione   *Frank Abbundando*

Harry Maione and Frank Abbundando were both executed on February 19, 1942, in the electric chair at Sing Sing Prison in Ossining, New York. Both were members of "Murder, Inc.," the official murder-for-hire squad of the Syndicate. Maione was called "Happy" because his face displayed a perpetual scowl. He reportedly killed

Grave of mob figure known as the dasher.

Harry "Happy" Maione and Frank "The Dasher" Abbundando.

at least 12 men himself. Abbundando was nicknamed "The Dasher" and was reputed to have killed 30 people.

"Happy" and "The Dasher" would be joined 20 years later by Giuseppe Profaci.

7. Giuseppe "Joe" Profaci
Born: Oct. 2, 1897 – Villabate, Sicily, Italy
Died: June 6, 1962 (age 64) – Bay Shore, N.Y.

Giuseppe "Joe" Profaci arrived at St. John in 1962. Profaci was made boss of one of five mob families by Charles Luciano in 1931. As his empire grew he kept legitimate businesses on the side to insulate himself from tax evasion charges which were

Joe Profaci

very popular with prosecutors at that time. His original olive oil business was successful and led to his nickname as the "Olive Oil King." He was a devout Catholic who made generous donations to Catholic charities and his New Jersey estate contained a private chapel where he would invite priests to celebrate mass. On one occasion, two thieves stole a relic from a New York Catholic Church. Profaci mobsters recovered the relic and reportedly strangled the thieves with rosaries. Profaci was one of the 61 mobsters arrested in 1957 at the national mob meeting known as the Apalachin Conference in upstate New York. Charges against him were later dropped. He died on June 6, 1962, in Bay Shore, New York of liver cancer at the age of 64.

Just a few months earlier that year, St. John's had become the final resting place of perhaps its most infamous inhabitant (and the person that had made Profaci boss in 1931)—a true crime legend who ironically was born just

Mausoleum of the olive oil king.

a month and half after Profaci in a Sicilian town located a mere 35 miles from Profaci's birthplace of Villabate, Italy.

His name was Lucky Luciano.

8. Charles "Lucky" Luciano

Born: Nov. 24, 1897 – Lercara Friddi, Sicily, Italy

Died: Jan. 6, 1962 (age 64) – Naples, Italy

Charles "Lucky" Luciano is considered the father of modern organized crime. He was born Salvatore Lucania in Sicily in 1897. He immigrated to the United States when he was nine. He quit school at 14 and started making money in the

Charles Luciano

street. During the 1920s, Prohibition created opportunities for criminals to make a lot of money. Luciano became one of the "Big Six" of bootlegging. By 1925 he was grossing over $12 million a year. In 1929, Luciano was forced into a limousine at gun point by three men who beat and stabbed him and left him on a beach in Staten Island to die. The identity of his abductors was never determined. He was discovered by a police officer and taken to a hospital where he recovered.

As one of the "Young Turks" he was involved in the killing of Joe Masseria in a Coney Island Restaurant. He took over Masseria's position under Maranzano but Maranzano soon viewed him as a threat and ordered a hit on him. Luciano was able to strike first as previously described in this chapter. With Maranzano's death, Lucky became the dominant organized crime boss in the United States.

Luciano focused on improving how criminal gangs did business. He sought to create a national organized crime network to quell any conflicts, manage disputes and establish guidelines for conducting business. This organization became known as the Commission. One of the Commission's first tests came in 1935 when it ordered Dutch Schultz to drop his plans to kill Special Prosecutor Thomas Dewey. Luciano argued that a Dewey assassination would bring a massive law enforcement crackdown. Schultz announced that he was going to kill Dewey regardless of the Commission's instructions. Schultz was murdered by Murder, Inc. in a

The authors visit the man known as Lucky.

tavern in Newark, New Jersey on October 24, 1935 before he could carry out his plan.

In 1936 Luciano's luck ran out and he was tried and convicted on 62 counts of extortion and prostitution and sentenced to 30 to 50 years in prison. He was first imprisoned at Sing Sing but later moved to the Clinton Correctional Facility in Dannemora, New York.

During World War II, the U.S. government struck a secret deal with the imprisoned Luciano. The Navy worried about security issues on the New York waterfront and concluded a deal with Luciano for his organization's cooperation in exchange for a commutation of his sentence. On January 3, 1946, as a reward for his wartime cooperation,

Governor Thomas E. Dewey reluctantly commuted Luciano's sentence on condition that he did not resist deportation. He was deported to Italy in February but in October secretly moved to Havana, Cuba. There he met up with some of his old cohorts including Meyer Lansky and Bugsy Siegel. Lansky called a meeting of the heads of the major crime families in Havana in December. The ostensible reason was to see Frank Sinatra perform but the real reason was to discuss mob business with Luciano able to attend. Soon after the U.S. government learned that Luciano was in Cuba. He was fraternizing with Sinatra visiting numerous nightclubs so his presence was no secret. Under pressure Cuba sent him back to Italy. In Italy he was kept under close supervision and had his passport revoked.

Lucky Luciano died on January 26, 1962 of a heart attack at Naples International Airport where he had gone to meet with a movie producer to discuss a film based on his life. His family had his body returned to the U.S. and buried in a vault at St. John Cemetery under his birth name Salvatore Lucania.

The next to arrive was Vito Genovese.

9. Vito Genovese

Born: Nov. 27, 1897 – Risigliano, Naples, Italy
Died: Feb. 14, 1969 (age 71) – Springfield, Missouri

Vito Genovese served Luciano as his under-boss after being one of the four hitmen to kill Joe Masseria. In 1936 when Luciano went to prison, Genovese became acting boss of the crime family. In 1934, however, Genovese allegedly killed

Vito Genovese

another mobster named Ferdinand Boccia and in 1937 he fled to Italy to avoid prosecution. Frank Costello took over. He thrived in Italy and developed ties to Mussolini through Mussolini's son-in-law. When the Allies invaded Italy in 1943 Genovese switched sides and worked for the Army in Naples. In 1945 he was returned to New York to face murder charges for the Boccia killing. In 1946 two key government witnesses were murdered and the government was forced to drop the charges.

Freed from custody, Genovese wanted power back but Costello wasn't anxious to give it back so Genovese ordered Costello's murder. On May 2, 1957, Costello was shot in the head by Vincent Gigante. Costello wasn't seriously hurt and survived but decided to retire. When Genovese heard that Costello was planning a comeback with Albert Anastasia he arranged for Anastasia's murder in a barber shop on October 25, 1957. The next month Genovese called for a meeting of national Cosa Nostra leaders. The meeting became known as the Apalachin Conference and was held at the farm of Joseph Barbara in Apalachin, New York. The conference turned into a fiasco as it was raided by state police who apprehended 58 of the attendees (charging 20 of them with crimes).

In 1959 Genovese was convicted of selling a large quantity of heroin and sentenced to 15 years. He died on Valentines Day 1969 of a heart attack at the Federal Medical Center in Springfield, Missouri.

Carlo Gambino was the next to arrive at St. John.

10. Carlo Gambino

Born: Aug. 24, 1902 – Palermo, Sicily, Italy

Died: Oct. 15, 1976 (age 74) – Massapequa, New York

Carl Gambino

Carlo Gambino was actually known for being low-key and secretive. He became a made man at the age of 19, in 1921 and joined the D'Aquila family. He was one of the Young Turks and rose to power and took over the Mangano family renamed the Gambino family shortly after Anastasia's murder. Gambino quickly expanded his rackets all over the country. He was boss of the largest, wealthiest and most powerful crime family in the country and was head of the Commission.

Gambino made his own family rule against dealing drugs. "Deal and Die" was his policy. He ran the family for two decades managing to keep a low profile from the police and the public. He was cunning however and capable of brutal force. When a member of the organization, Mimi Scialo, became drunk one night and insulted Gambino in front of many others, he was found later encased in the cement floor of Otto's Social

Club in South Brooklyn. Gambino died on October 15, 1976, at his home in Massapequa, New York of natural causes.

Joe Colombo was the next to arrive at St. John.

11. Joe Colombo

Born: June 16, 1924 – Brooklyn, New York

Died: May 22, 1978 (age 53) – Blooming Grove, New York

Joe Colombo

Colombo's father Anthony was a member of the Profaci crime family and was found strangled in a car with his mistress in 1938. Joe followed his father into the Profaci family and became one of their top enforcers and soon became a capo. In 1961 Colombo was kidnapped by Joey Gallo and his crew who were demanding a more equitable split of income from Profaci. They reached an agreement and Colombo was released.

A few years after Profaci died in 1962 Colombo took over as boss. At the age of 41, Colombo was one of the youngest crime bosses in the nation and the first American born boss of a New York crime family.

Grave of Joe Colombo.

Mob boss Joseph Colombo is placed in an ambulance after he was shot three times.

In the spring of 1970, he did something unheard of for a Mafia chief. He created the Italian-American Civil Rights League to push back against unfair treatment of Italians by the federal government and the entertainment industry. On June 29, 1970, 150,000 people showed up in Columbus Circle in New York for an "Italian-American Unity Day" rally. Rather than hiding from the public like other mobsters, Colombo appeared on TV interviews and at fundraisers and speaking engagements. On June 28, 1971 he was getting ready to address the crowd at the second "Italian Unity Day Rally" when he was shot and seriously wounded by a man named Jerome Johnson. Someone in the crowd shot and killed Johnson and was never identified. Colombo remained paralyzed for the next seven years. On May 22, 1978 Colombo died of cardiac arrest. The Colombo family leadership was convinced that Joey Gallo was behind Colombo's shooting and Joey Gallo was gunned down by some Colombo family members in a Manhattan restaurant on April 7, 1972.

Seven years later two more organized crime figures were buried at St. John.

12. John Dioguardi

Born: Apr. 29, 1914 –
Lower East Side, NYC
Died: Jan. 12, 1979 (age 64) –
Lewisburg, Pa.

13. Carmine Galante

Born: Feb. 21, 1910 –
East Harlem, NYC

Died: July 12, 1979 (age 69) – Bushwick, N.Y.

John Dioguardi   *Carmine Galante*

The first to arrive for eternal rest in 1979 was John Dioguardi, aka, Johnny Dio. He was a capo in the Lucchese crime family who helped tie organized labor to organized crime. In the 1950s, Dio was one of the country's more powerful labor racketeers, and he aided Jimmy Hoffa's climb to the Teamster presidency through strongarm tactics and the creation of fraudulent locals called "paper locals." The scandal of the paper locals or Dio locals became an object of the U.S. Senate Committee on Government operations in 1955. Senator John McClellan, chair of the committee hired Robert F. Kennedy as the subcommittee chief counsel and investigator.

In February 1957, the Committee released FBI wiretaps which showed the Hoffa and Dioguardi conspiracy. In the midst of the paper locals scandal Dio was indicted for planning the acid attack on crusading newspaper columnist Victor Riesel, an attack that left the journalist permanently blind. Abraham Telvi was identified as the assailant but he was murdered a few months after the attack. Charges against Dio were dropped when witnesses refused to testify at his trial.

Johnny Dio was convicted of numerous crimes such as tax evasion, extortion, bankruptcy fraud and stock fraud, which had him in and out of prison during the 1960s. His last years were spent at Lewisburg Federal Penitentiary on what became known as "Mafia row," a series of cells on the same level and wing of the prison where a number of organized crime figures were housed. Dioguardi died of natural causes in a Pennsylvania hospital while in federal custody on January 12, 1979.

The second to arrive at St. John in 1979 was Carmine Galante who was boss of the Bonanno family. He was nicknamed "The Cigar" since he was rarely seen without one. He quit school in seventh grade and in 1930 was a suspect in the murder of a police officer but was never prosecuted because the prosecutors couldn't find a witness that would testify. In 1939 after serving over eight years in prison for attempted robbery he went to work as an enforcer for Vito Genovese who at the time was the underboss of the Luciano Crime Family. He had a reputation for viciousness and was a suspect in over 80 murders. By 1953 Galante had risen to underboss of the Bonanno family and was a close confidant of Joe Bonanno. He was sent to Canada to lead the family heroin business. The Bonannos imported heroin from Italy through Canada and then into the United States. In 1957 Canada deported Galante after trying to charge him with several murders. Soon he was indicted on narcotics charges in the U.S. His first trial was declared a mistrial due to several juror "dropouts." At his second trial in 1962 he was convicted and sentenced to 20 years in prison.

In 1974 Galante was released from prison, and Joe Bonanno having been forced to retire, he considered himself the rightful successor and seized control of the family. While in prison the Gambino family had taken over much of the drug business and Galante began taking it back. By 1978 Galante allegedly organized the murders of at least eight high-ranking Gambino family members. This brazen attempt to take over the narcotics market upset all the families and in 1979 the Mafia Commission ordered Galante's execution. On July 12, 1979 Galante was murdered as he finished lunch on an open patio at Joe and Mary's Italian-American Restaurant in the Bushwick section of Brooklyn. Galante's death picture showed a cigar still in his mouth.

Two years later Frank "Funzi" Tieri would be laid to rest at St. John Cemetery.

14. Frank "Funzi" Tieri

Born: Feb. 22, 1904 – Campania, Naples, Italy
Died: Mar. 31, 1981 (age 77) – Manhattan, N.Y.

Frank Tieri

In 1972, after the murder of Genovese acting boss Thomas Eboli, Tieri became the boss of the Genovese family. He was twice denied U.S. citizenship living as a resident alien in Brooklyn. Tieri played a key role in the assassination of Philadelphia crime boss Angelo Bruno and the opening of Atlantic City to the New York crime families. He was the first mobster to be convicted under the RICO act in 1981. At the sentencing Tieri's lawyers argued for leniency, saying he was dying. Prosecutors told the judge it was an act and the judge sentenced him to 10 years. Apparently it was not an act as he died two months later on March 31, 1981, at Mount Sinai Hospital.

It would be 1983 before Roy DeMeo would arrive at St. John Cemetery.

15. Roy DeMeo
Born: Sept. 7, 1942 – Brooklyn, N.Y.
Died: Jan. 10, 1983 (age 40) – Brooklyn, N.Y.

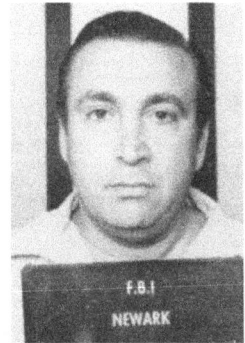

DeMeo was a member of the Gambino crime family infamous for heading the DeMeo crew, a gang suspected by the FBI of murdering as many as 100 people between 1973 and 1983. The vast majority of their victims' bodies were disposed of so thoroughly that they were never found. A set

Roy DeMeo

method of execution was established by the crew called the "Gemini Method." The name came from the Gemini Lounge (now a church) which was the primary hangout of the DeMeo crew as well as the site where most of the victims were killed.

The victim would be lured into the back of the building where he would be shot in the head with a silenced pistol and then the head wrapped in a towel to staunch the blood. Another member of the crew would stab the victim in the heart to prevent blood from pumping out of the gunshot wound. The body would then be stripped of clothing and dragged into a bathroom where the blood was drained out of the body. Then the body was laid on plastic sheets and dismembered. The body parts would then be put into bags, placed in cardboard boxes and sent to the Fountain Avenue Dump in Brooklyn.

By 1982, the FBI was investigating the enormous number of missing and murdered persons who were linked to DeMeo or who were last seen entering the Gemini Lounge. Paul Castellano was worried that DeMeo might cooperate with the government and ordered his murder. On January 10, 1983, he went to crew member Patty Testa's house for a meeting with his men. Ten days later DeMeo was found murdered in the trunk of his Cadillac. He was apparently killed by members of his own crew.

Aniello "Mr. Neil" Dellacroce was the next to arrive in 1985.

16. Aniello "Mr. Neil" Dellacroce
Born: Mar. 15, 1914 – New York
Died: Dec. 2, 1985 (age 71) – Queens, N.Y.

Aniello Dellacroce

Dellacroce was the underboss of the Gambino family during the reigns of Carlo Gambino (from 1957 to 1976) and Paul Castellano (1976 to 1985). He preferred to keep a low profile and was said to have a menacing stare. Once described as "the archangel of death," a famous New York City detective said "of all the gangsters

1985 murder of Paul Castellano and Thomas Bilotti outside of Sparks Steak House in Manhattan.

that I've met personally, and I've met dozens of them in all my years, there were only two who, when I looked them straight in the eye, I decided I wouldn't want them to be really personally mad at me. Aniello Dellacroce was one and Carmine Galante was the other."

In 1976 Gambino died and before he died he designated Castellano to become the boss. Dellacroce accepted this and served as Castellano's underboss and was a mentor to John Gotti. The Feds closed in on Dellacroce's operations and he was indicted for racketeering in 1985. He was very sick by that time and would not live to stand trial. He died of lung cancer on December 2, 1985 at the age of 71. Two weeks later Castellano, who had refused to visit Dellacroce as he was dying or attend his funeral, was gunned down with his new underboss Thomas Bilotti outside Sparks Steak House in Manhattan. Gotti than took over as boss of the Gambino family.

In May 1988 Paul "Paulie" Vario was buried at St. John.

17. Paul "Paulie" Vario
Born: July 9, 1914 – New York City
Died: May 3, 1988 (age 73) – Fort Worth, TX

Paul Vario

Vario was a capo in the Lucchese crime family. He allegedly had a very violent temper and his crew was one of the toughest and most violent crews in organized crime. His crew became famous for their hijacking at JFK International Airport. Vario's influence with the cargo haulers union made the airport particularly lucrative. He could threaten a labor strike in order to turn an investigation away if it got too close.

In the 1970s Vario started to attract the attention of the FBI. Vario was convicted of tax evasion in February 1973 and sentenced to six years in federal prison. While there he was part of the previously mentioned infamous Mafia Row. He was released from prison in 1975 and moved to Florida. In 1978 he approved of his crew's participation in the infamous Lufthansa Airlines robbery at JFK airport. That robbery netted the crew an estimated five million dollars in cash and $875,000 in jewelry. He died in Fort Worth Federal Prison while serving a ten year sentence for extorting payoffs from air freight companies at JFK. In the 1990s, Paul Vario was featured as a major character in the film *Goodfellas*. He is renamed "Paul Cicero" and portrayed by actor Paul Sorvino.

Later in 1988 Wilfred "Willie Boy" Johnson was buried at St. John.

18. Wilfred "Willie Boy" Johnson

Born: Sept. 29, 1935 – Canarsie, N.Y.
Died: Aug. 29, 1988 (age 52) – Brooklyn, N.Y.

Wilfred Johnson

Willie Boy had a very harsh and difficult child-hood and was in trouble at the age of nine and at twelve suffered serious head injuries in a fight. By 1949 he was running a gang of thugs who were used by the mafia to collect debts. He met John Gotti when he was 17 and they became friends. He followed Gotti into the Gambino crime family and became known as the "Terminator" because of his success in strong arm work.

Johnson turned on the mob in 1966 when he was imprisoned on an armed robbery charge. His capo Carmine Fatico promised to financially support Johnson's wife and two infant children but broke his promise and as a result Johnson's wife went on welfare. Willie Boy was grudgingly turned into an informant by the FBI and given the code name "Wahoo" because was part Native American. During the next 16 years he provided lots of useful information to law enforcement.

In 1985 his career as an informant came to an abrupt end. A Federal prosecutor trying to get Johnson to testify against Gotti revealed that he was an informant. Johnson's handlers in the FBI tried to convince him to enter the Witness Protection Program, but he refused. On August 29, 1988, Johnson was shot to death as he walked to his car in front of his house. He was shot once in each thigh, twice in the back, and at least six times in the head. The hit team then dropped jack-like spikes on the street to prevent pursuit as they drove away.

Two more organized crime figures were buried at St. John in 1991.

19. Philip "Rusty" Rastelli
Born: Jan. 31, 1918 –
Brooklyn, N.Y.
Died: June 24, 1991 (age 73) –
Queens, N.Y.

20. Carmine Fatico
Born: Jan. 19, 1910 –
New York
Died: Aug. 1, 1991 (age 81) –
Brooklyn

Philip Rastelli   *Carmine Fatico*

Rastelli was the boss of the Bonanno crime family from 1974 until his death although he spent all but two years of his reign in prison. He was the first member of the Queens faction to lead the family; all the previous bosses had come from Brooklyn. Rastelli allegedly ordered Galante's murder while in prison in 1979. In 1985 he was indicted and convicted the next year of racketeering and sentenced to 12 years in federal prison. He died of liver cancer in 1991 after being released on humanitarian grounds a few weeks before his death.

In August 1991, Carmine Fatico joined Rastelli at St. John. Fatico was nicknamed "Charlie Wagons" due to his penchant for hijacking transport trucks. He was an early mentor to John Gotti. He was placed in charge of family operations in East New York in 1951 by Albert Anastasia, and after Anastasia's murder, Carlo Gambino took over and kept Fatico as capo. His crew numbered about 120 men and grossed approximately $30 million a year.

In 1973 Fatico was indicted and as a condition of his bail he had to stay away from his crew. He designated Gotti as acting capo. In 1977 Fatico retired and Gotti officially succeeded him. He died of natural causes at the age of 81.

In 1992 two more organized crime figures would be buried at St. John.

21. Carmine Lombardozzi
Born: Feb. 8, 1913 –
Brooklyn, N.Y.
Died: Sept. 5, 1992 (age 79) –
Brooklyn, N.Y.

22. James Napoli
Born: Nov. 4, 1911 –
Hell's Kitchen, NYC

Carmine Lombardozzi   James Napoli

Died: Dec. 29, 1992 (age 81) – Manhattan, N.Y.

In September of that year, Carmine "The Doctor" Lombardozzi died of natural causes at the age of 79. Although only a capo for the Gambino family he was the biggest earner for the family. He ran the Gambino's loan-sharking operations and continued to practice his special brand of investment banking. He owned a large portfolio of prime real estate and ran an optical company which held the contract for eye glasses for the International Longshoremen's Association. He was one of those arrested at the infamous Commission meeting in Apalachia, New York in November 1957.

Lombardozzi was followed a few months later by James "Jimmy Nap" Napoli, who died of natural causes on December 29, 1992. He was a capo in the Genovese crime family. From the 1950s to the 1980s, he controlled one of the largest illegal gambling operations in the United States. He allegedly employed 2,000 people and grossed $150 million a year. He was intelligent and well respected and maintained relations to most of the major crime families. His wife Jeanne Napoli was a singer and theatrical producer of some note.

The last known organized crime figure as of this writing to be buried in St. John Cemetery was John Gotti.

23. John Gotti
Born: Oct. 27, 1940 – The Bronx, N.Y.
Died: June 10, 2002 (age 61) – Springfield, Missouri

John Gotti

Gotti grew up in poverty and turned to a life of crime at an early age. At 12 he was working as an errand boy for Carmine Fatico a capo in the Gambino family. At around this time he met Gambino underboss Neil Dellacroce who would become his mentor.

By the time Gotti was 21 he had been arrested five times but served little time in jail. In 1968 he served his first major sentence for hijacking. He served three years at Lewisburg. Paroled in 1972 he went back to work for Fatico who had moved operations to the Bergin Hunt and Fish Club in Queens. He was designated acting capo that year while Fatico was under indictment and as a condition of bail could not associate with known felons.

In 1974 he was arrested for murder and with the help of attorney Roy Cohn he was able to strike a deal and received a four-year sentence. He was released in 1977 and named official capo of the Bergin crew by Dellacroce who was kept as underboss by new boss Paul Castellano. Carlo Gambino died while Gotti was in prison and Castellano took his place.

In March of 1980 tragedy hit the Gotti family. John's youngest son, Frank (age 12), darted into the street on a motorized minibike from behind a dumpster. Almost immediately, he was struck and killed by the car of John Favara, Gotti's backyard neighbor. Favara was abducted in July and never heard from again.

Gotti rapidly became dissatisfied with Castellano's leadership and Castellano resented Gotti's outspoken personality and flamboyant style. Gotti became known as "The Dapper Don" for his expensive clothes and personality. In 1985 Dellacroce died and any goodwill between Castellano and Gotti dissolved when the boss didn't attend Dellacroce's funeral. Two weeks later on December 16, 1985 Castellano was gunned down at Spark's Steak House in Manhattan. Gotti, who watched the hit from his car, became boss soon after.

In 1985 Gotti was indicted by the Feds for racketeering and the trial began in August 1986. The trial was marked by witness intimidation, witness unreliability, perjury, and jury tampering. A juror named George Pape contacted Gotti's underboss Gravano and agreed to sell his vote for $60,000. A defense witness, bank robber Matthew Traynor, testified that U.S. Attorney and prosecutor Diane Giacolone offered him beer and drugs and a pair of her panties as a masturbation aid in exchange for his testimony for the prosecution. Pape was elected jury foreman and in March 1987 Gotti was acquitted. Five years later Pape was convicted of obstruction of justice and sentenced to prison. The verdict was a crushing defeat for law enforcement officials and Gotti became the mob's symbol of invincibility earning the name "Teflon Don" because charges against him just wouldn't stick.

The FBI then turned the conviction of Gotti into an organizational crusade. They pressured underboss Sammy Gravano into testifying against Gotti and finally got a conviction of murder and racketeering in April 1992. As a repeat offender he was sentenced to life in prison without parole and sent to federal prison in Marion, Illinois. In 1998 Gotti was diagnosed with throat cancer and died on June 10, 2002 in a federal prison hospital at the age of 61.

If You Go:

There are many other famous people buried at St. John Cemetery including Geraldine Ferraro (1935–2011). Ferraro represented New York's 9th District in Congress from 1979 to 1985. She is best known for being the first female Vice Presidential candidate from a major party when she was chosen as Walter Mondale's running mate in 1984.

Another political notable buried in St. John is former Governor of New York Mario Cuomo (1932–2015). Cuomo was raised in Queens and was appointed New York's Secretary of State in 1975. He won the Lieutenant Governorship in 1978 and the Governorship in 1982. He served three terms and became nationally known as the result of his 1984 Democratic National Convention keynote speech in support of the Mondale/Ferraro ticket. He was defeated for reelection in 1994, after which he practiced law and authored several books. He died of heart failure on January 1, 2015, just hours after his son Andrew was sworn in to a second term as Governor of New York.

Renowned photographer Robert Mapplethorpe (1946–1989) is also buried in St. John. He died of AIDS in 1989. His corpse was cremated and his ashes are interred at his mother's grave-site, etched with her maiden name "Maxey."

16

"America's Answer to the Ripper"

HERMAN WEBSTER MUDGETT
AKA DR. HENRY H. HOLMES

County: Delaware
Town: Yeadon
Cemetery: Holy Cross
Address: 626 Baily Road

One can reasonably argue that the most famous serial killer in history is Jack the Ripper. There have been numerous books written and films made about the Ripper. The actual Ripper was never found, and to this day there are numerous theories as to who he was and the suspects include members of the Royal Family. The Ripper murders began in the Whitechapel district of London in 1888, and some believe they continued until 1891. However most who have studied the case believe the Ripper was responsible for only five of the ten murders in that time frame and that his last victim was killed November 9, 1888. In contrast, America's answer to the Ripper may have tortured and killed as many as 200 people, mostly young women. He was born Herman Webster Mudgett on May 16, 1861, in New Hampshire. However, during his killing spree, he went by the name Doctor Henry H. Holmes, and that is how we shall refer to him in this chapter.

Holmes was known as a bright boy with strange tendencies. His father was a violent alcoholic, and his mother a Methodist who would read the bible to the young boy. Holmes was bullied at school, and he went through several traumatic experiences as a child. He and one of his few close friends explored a deserted house one day, and Holmes watched his friend fall to his death from a landing in the home. In addition bullies dragged him into a doctor's office and forced him into the arms of a

Herman Webster Mudgett

medical skeleton. The bullies' goal was to scare him. Instead he became obsessed with death.

As he hit his teens, his fascination with death manifested itself in the killing and dissection of animals. Holmes claimed his purpose in these mutilations was medical examination. Academically he continued to do well, and in 1884 he graduated with a medical degree from the University of Michigan in Ann Arbor. While at the university, he began an unusual business pursuit that would provide funds for him throughout his life. He began taking life insurance policies out on corpses in the medical school. He would steal the corpses and mutilate them in a manner to

The infamous Murder Castle: Holmes Motel at 63rd & Wallace on Chicago's south side.

show they had died in an accident. Then he would make his claim to the insurance company.

Holmes married his first wife in 1878. She bore him a son named Robert Lovering Mudgett who would go on to serve as city manager in Orlando, Florida. Holmes would marry two more times during his life without ever getting divorced. In addition he used his charm to prey on countless young women who fell for him and later died at his hands.

In 1886 Holmes moved to Chicago where he found work as a drugstore assistant. E. S. Holton, the owner of the store, was dying of cancer and his wife spent most of her time caring for her ailing husband. Holmes saw his opportunity, and he took it. When Holton died, Holmes persuaded Mrs. Horton to sell him the store. When the deal was complete, he murdered her and told those who asked about her that she had moved to California. In 1888 Holmes travelled to London where he sold skeletons to medical schools. He returned to the states in December of that same year, a time frame that becomes important later in his story.

Now that he owned a drug store that was making a good profit, Holmes began putting his plan into place. He purchased a vacant lot across the street from his store where he intended to build his "Castle."

It was a three story hotel that Holmes personally designed. The ground floor featured Holmes's drugstore. The second and third floors made up the hotel and featured secret passages, concealed chambers, staircases that led to brick walls, and soundproofed rooms with peepholes in the doors. In addition several of the rooms had been fitted with gas pipes that would allow Holmes to inject lethal gases into the area at the moment of his choosing. The basement was an addition to this house of horrors. It contained a dissection chamber and pits of lime and acid as well as cremation furnaces. Holmes constructed the "Castle" by using multiple contractors. Once part of the building was complete he would either fire or refuse payment to a contractor and hire another. As a result no one could piece together what Holmes planned to do in what would become known later as "the killing house."

The building was completed in time to take advantage of the many visitors to the 1893 Chicago's World Fair. The fair itself was a tremendous success and attracted visitors from all over the country. The fair marked the appearance of the first Ferris wheel which was a gigantic machine compared to what we have today. For example, each of the 36 cars on the wheel could hold as many as sixty people. The cars were 24 feet long and 13 feet wide and weighed 26,000 pounds. The fair itself, whose buildings reflected the big dreams of the era, was known as the "White City" and even received praise from that great critic of the "Gilded Age" Mark Twain. The owner of the new hotel, which he called the World's Fair Hotel, was eager to offer housing, and in many cases more, to those who chose to visit the fair.

Holmes didn't wait for the fair to open to begin more killings. In 1890 a man named Ned Connor went to work for Holmes as a watch-maker and jeweler. He and his very attractive wife named Julia and their daughter Pearl moved into an apartment above the drugstore. Holmes gave Julia a job as a bookkeeper and then seduced her. Ned Connor found out about the affair and left his wife and daughter. By this time in 1891 Holmes was living in the "Castle." He took out life insurance policies on Julia and Pearl that named him as the beneficiary. Around this time, Holmes began a relationship with a woman named Minnie Williams. Julia became angered by this turn of events especially in light of the fact that she was carrying Holmes's child. Holmes convinced Julia

The HOLMES CASTLE 2nd FLOOR

BACK ROOM

HALLWAY

LABORATORIES

THE MAZE

TRAP DOOR FROM 3RD FL.

ASPHYXIATION CHAMBER

HALLWAY

THE HANGING SECRET CHAMBER

BATHROOM WITH HIDDEN STAIRS TO BASEMENT

TRAP DOOR FROM 3RD FL.

SEALED ROOM

BLIND ROOM

CHUTE FROM ROOF TO BASEMENT

SECRET HIDING PLACE

BATHROOM

FIVE-DOOR ROOM

MYSTERIOUS CLOSED ROOM

HALLWAY

SECRET CHAMBER

DARK ROOM

RECEPTION ROOM

WAITING ROOM

WALLACE St.

63RD. Street

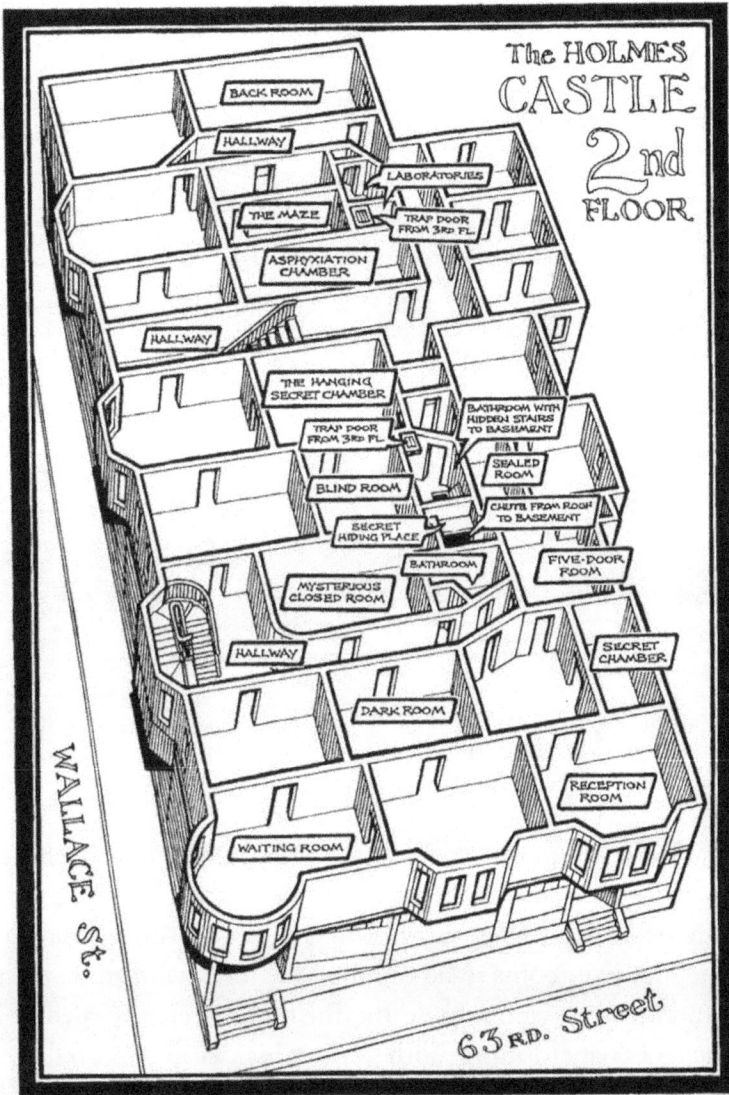

to have an abortion that he would perform. He led her to the basement where he aborted the child and killed Julia. He then killed Pearl using chloroform.

With his hotel now open, Holmes put his killing machine to work. Not only hotel staff but guests turned up missing. Holmes particularly enjoyed killing young women that he found attractive. Hotel staff were required to take out life insurance policies naming Holmes as the

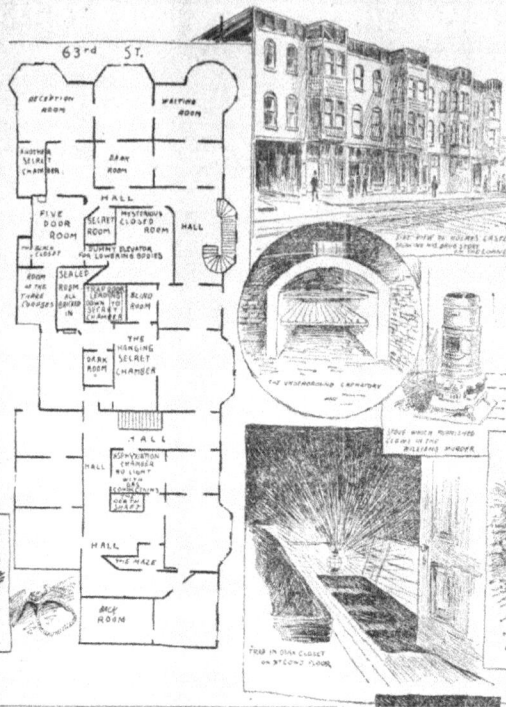

The Chicago Tribune of Sunday, August 18, 1895.

beneficiary. Holmes murdered his victims in a number of ways. He gassed some in their rooms, he tortured some on a stretching rack he kept in the basement, he dissected a few victims while they were still alive and he also had some fireproof rooms so he could fill the room with gases, ignite the vapors and burn the victim to death. The bodies were disposed of in his vats of acid or crematoriums. With some of his victims, he would remove the flesh and sell the skeletons to medical institutions. It is impossible to tell how many people he killed, but estimates range from 50 to 200.

When the World's Fair ended, the depression of 1893 was in full swing. With business way down at the hotel and his creditors on his back, Holmes left Chicago. He headed for Texas where he had inherited property from two sisters one of which he promised to marry. He never married her, but he did kill both sisters. He had hoped to build another Castle here, but he found that law enforcement officers were more aggressive in Texas than in Chicago so he headed back east.

In 1894, he and an associate named Benjamin Pitezel made a deal. Pitezel would take out a $10,000 life insurance policy, Holmes would find and disfigure a dead body claim that it was Pitezel and the two would split the money. Instead Holmes murdered Pitezel in Philadelphia by burning him alive to support the story of a laboratory accident. He then collected the money himself.

Pitezel had three of his five children with him at the time and Holmes took the three, a boy and two girls, through the northern United States into Canada. On the way in Indianapolis he killed the boy, cut up the body and burned it. In Toronto he put the girls into a trunk and gassed them to death. He then buried their bodies in the cellar of the house where he was staying.

Holmes had been jailed for a brief time for his involvement in a horseracing scam prior to his trip to Canada. While in jail, he told a cellmate about the plan he and Pitezel put together and he offered the cellmate $500 if he could find a lawyer that would assist Holmes with any legal questions should they arise. The cellmate found the attorney, but Holmes never paid him the $500 and as a result the cellmate told the police about the Pitezel scam. Holmes was arrested in Boston on November 17, 1894.

Following his arrest, the Chicago police searched the "Castle." In the basement they found the remains of some of Holmes's victims. They also found evidence that murders had been committed in other rooms in the hotel. Meanwhile a detective by the name of Frank Geyer was investigating the Pitezel case. He would eventually find the remains of the three children Holmes had killed during his trip to Canada. The public was satisfied that Holmes was a monster.

Holmes was put on trial in Philadelphia for the murder of Pitezel. He was convicted and sentenced to death. After his conviction he confessed to 30 murders. The Hearst newspapers paid him $7,500 (over $200,000 in today's dollars) for his confession. Holmes went to the gallows on May 7, 1896. The assistant superintendent, a man named Richardson appeared, more nervous than Holmes as he prepared the noose. Holmes turned to him and said, "Take your time, old man." Holmes neck did not snap, and as a result he died slowly. He was pronounced dead twenty minutes after the trap had been sprung.

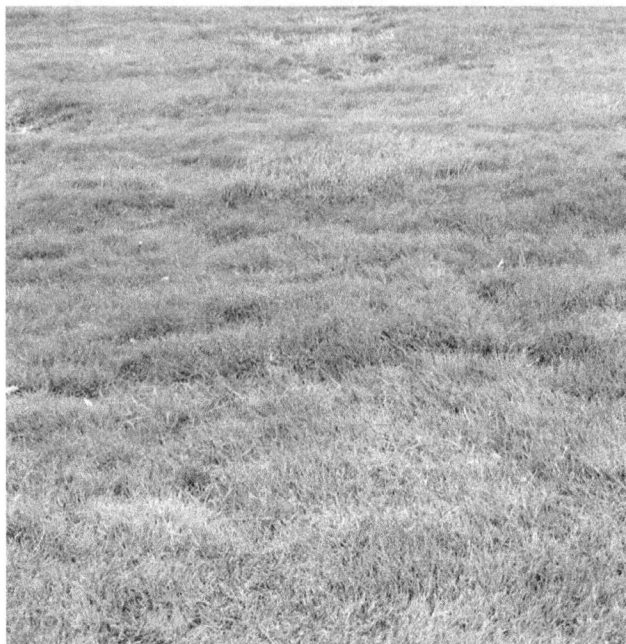

Here is the final resting place of America's first serial killer.

Holmes was buried based on instructions he left behind. First cement was poured into the coffin and then Holmes's body was put in which was then covered with more cement. His body was then taken to Holy Cross Cemetery just outside of Philadelphia. The grave was dug and the coffin placed inside. Workers then filled the grave with cement. The grave was left unmarked. Holmes wanted to make sure that neither medical researchers nor relatives of his victims could get to his body.

During his stay in prison, Holmes claimed that he was possessed by the devil. Events that occurred after his execution caused some to believe it. Detective Geyer became seriously ill. The warden at the Philadelphia prison where Holmes was held and executed committed suicide. An accidental electrocution took the life of the foreman of the jury that convicted Holmes. The priest who delivered the last rites to Holmes was found dead on church grounds. Finally a fire destroyed the office of the Chicago district attorney leaving only a picture of Holmes untouched.

Recently Jeff Mudgett, Holmes's great-great grandson, has written a book about his ancestor titled *Bloodstains*. The book provides evidence that Holmes may have been Jack the Ripper. Mudgett notes that there exist records documenting Holmes travelling to London in 1888 to sell skeletons to medical schools. He was not in Chicago when the five murders credited to the Ripper took place. When Holmes returned to Chicago in December of 1888, the Ripper murders stopped. Many believe that the Ripper possessed surgical skills which Holmes certainly had. Finally Mudgett had scientists at the University of Buffalo analyze letters written by Jack the Ripper and those written by Holmes while he was in prison. They reached the conclusion that the classifier performance number (97.95%) indicate that the writings of both men are similar in style. Was America's answer to the Ripper actually the Ripper himself?

When we visited Holy Cross Cemetery to photograph Holmes final resting place we had the section, range and lot number of the location of the grave. To be sure that our information was accurate we went to the cemetery office to verify it. The cemetery employee we spoke to told us, "We are not allowed to talk about that grave."

If you go:
See the "If You Go" section of the "Philadelphia Sinners" on page 190.

17

"New York's Finest"

JOSEPH PETROSINO

County: Queens
Town: New York
Cemetery: Calvary Cemetery
Address: 49-02 Laurel Hills Boulevard

Joseph Petrosino was one of New York's finest. He was a pioneer in the fight against organized crime, a protector of his community and had unique experiences as a New York City police detective.

He was born Giuseppe Petrosino in Padula, a village in southern Italy, on August 30, 1860. In 1873, at the age of 13, he was sent, along with a young cousin (Antonio Puppolo) to New York City to live with his grandfather who, shortly after Giuseppe's arrival, was killed in a streetcar accident. In 1874, Giuseppe's father, Prospero, a tailor, along with his mother, two sisters and three brothers, joined him in New York. At that time, many middle class Italians came to America hoping for a better life for their children. Such was the case for the Petrosinos. Prospero opened a shop in Manhattan that became successful enough to support his family.

Giuseppe or "Joe," being the eldest son, would take any job in order not to be a burden to the family. He was a newsboy in Little Italy and then a shoe-shine boy in front of the police headquarters on Mulberry Street. He developed friendships with many of the policemen who were customers. Being a police officer was his dream. He studied the English language and attended evening classes. In 1878, he obtained American citizenship and submitted an application for the police department. He was rejected. He applied over and over but at 5'3" tall did not meet the minimum height requirement of 5'7". His friendship with the police, especially with a captain, led to him getting a job as a "white winger" or

Joseph Petrosino

street cleaner. White wingers were named for the white uniforms they wore as they made their way through the streets picking up litter with small brooms and dustpans and depositing the trash in barrels on wheels that they pulled along. At that time, these jobs were controlled by the police department.

In the late 1800s, New York was hit with a great wave of poor southern Italian immigrants. Crime in the Italian ghetto was out of control. Knowing Italian, Petrosino soon became helpful to the police, who used him as an informant to catch Italian criminals. Finally the police commissioner bent the height requirement, and on October 19, 1883, he joined the NYPD and was issued badge number 285. He was the first

Italian-speaking officer to join the police department. Being fluent in several Italian dialects, he was able to investigate and solve cases that other officers couldn't. His ability to solve crimes in the Italian community was such that whenever a serious crime took place in that area, his supervisors would call out "send for the Dago." By all accounts, he was a tough cop. During this time, he befriended future President Theodore Roosevelt who was a police commissioner (at this time the NYPD was governed by a council of police commissioners) and loved Petrosino's toughness and courage.

On July 20, 1895, Roosevelt promoted him to detective sergeant and placed him in charge of the Homicide Division. During one months-long undercover investigation while on loan to the U.S. Secret Service, Petrosino worked as a tunnel digger and lived in a rooming house with suspected anarchists in New Jersey. This group had previously been involved with the assassination of King Umberto I of Italy. During this mission, he discovered evidence that this group would seek to assassinate President McKinley during a visit to Buffalo. He reported this to the Secret Service, and McKinley's reception was initially canceled. But even after Petrosino's competence and reliability were vouched for by then Vice-President Roosevelt, McKinley had the event placed back on his schedule. It was at this public reception on September 6, 1901, that McKinley was assassinated by Leon Czolgosz, an anarchist.

Petrosino was tough on Italian criminals who he saw as a shame upon decent Italians and Italian-Americans. He was particularly upset by the Black Hand, a criminal organization formed by some Italian immigrants near the turn of the 19th century. Typical Black Hand tactics involved sending a letter threatening bodily harm, kidnapping, arson, and murder. The letters would demand a specific amount of money delivered to a specific place. It usually contained threatening symbols and was signed with a hand drawn in black ink. One of the men considered the leader of the Black Hand Gang was Ignazio Lupo, also known as "Lupo the Wolf." Lupo got involved with the Unione Siciliana, a charitable organization that helped Sicilians living in America. The Black Hand infiltrated the Unione for its own purposes, and Lupo was elected chairman.

In 1901, Petrosino obtained a search warrant for the offices of the Unione Siciliana where he suspected there would be bodies of murder

One of New York's finest.

victims. He was correct, but no one in the NYPD expected the extent of what they uncovered. The building, which became known as the "Murder Stable," concealed approximately 60 bodies. An exact count was impossible because most of the corpses had been cut up. Some body parts were missing, and it was difficult to piece them together. Lupo was arrested but later released because of a lack of evidence tying the bodies to him. Petrosino was frustrated but determined to bring the Black Hand to justice.

On April 14, 1903, the body of a man was found in a barrel in Manhattan. He had been stabbed to death, his body chopped to pieces and his penis and testicles stuffed in his mouth. It was unknown who the victim was until Petrosino received an anonymous letter claiming the dead man was related to Giuseppe De Primo, who had recently been

sent to prison for counterfeiting. Petrosino went to Sing Sing Prison to interview
De Primo, who identified the victim as
his brother-in-law, Benedetto Madonia, a
member of the Black Hand from Buffalo.
De Primo claimed his brother-in-law was
murdered over a dispute about money in a
counterfeiting deal. Petrosino and his men
arrested Lupo, his underboss Joe Morello,
Vito Cascioferro, and other members of
the gang, but eventually they were released
for lack of evidence. During this investigation, however, Petrosino discovered that
Cascioferro was wanted for murder in
Italy and had fled to New York to avoid
a murder charge. Petrosino tried to have
Cascioferro deported, but he discovered
what Petrosino's plans were and fled to
New Orleans and later to Sicily.

In 1905, Petrosino was promoted
to the rank of lieutenant and placed in
charge of the Italian Squad, an elite corps
of Italian-American detectives assembled
specifically to deal with criminal activities
of organizations like the Mafia. They were
responsible for the deportation of over
500 Italian criminals.

This tombstone keeps watch over Petrosino's grave.

One of the Italians being extorted by the Black Hand was the famous
opera singer Enrico Caruso. Caruso was at first given an ultimatum to
pay $2,000 or be killed. Fearing for his life, he agreed to pay it. However,
before he could pay it, he received another demand for $15,000. He
turned to Petrosino for help. Petrosino supplied bodyguards for Caruso,
and when two men showed up to collect, he arrested them and had them
deported.

Among his high-profile exploits was the case of Angelo Carbone,
who was convicted of murder and sentenced to death in the electric

chair. Petrosino believed in Carbone's innocence and discovered who the real killer was, Allessandro Ciaramello, and began tracking him down. He tracked him through Delaware, Pennsylvania and New Jersey before finally catching him in Baltimore. Petrosino delivered Ciaramello to authorities a week before Carbone's scheduled execution. Ciaramello admitted his guilt, provided the murder weapon and agreed to return to New York. Carbone was released from Sing Sing prison.

Petrosino had neglected his personal life in order to focus on his job. That changed after the Italian Squad was formed. On April 7, 1907, he married Adelina Vinti in old St. Patrick's Cathedral. She was a 37-year-old childless widow who worked in her family's restaurant. On November 20, 1908, the couple had a baby girl, and he was delighted. He cut back on his work hours to spend more time at home.

In February 1909, the *New York Times* announced that "Police Commissioner Theodore Bingham has a secret service of his own at last." The newspaper report explained that Bingham had acquired private funding for the police organization and speculated that wealthy Italian businessmen or prominent industrialists like Andrew Carnegie and John D. Rockefeller might be footing the bill. "I have money and plenty of it," the commissioner boasted, "and it didn't come from the city." The paper noted that Petrosino was placed in charge of the new service and that he had not been seen in police headquarters for some weeks. When Bingham was questioned about this, he answered, "Why, he may be on the ocean, bound for Europe, for all I know."

Petrosino was in fact on his way to Sicily on a top secret mission. A recently passed federal law allowed the government to deport any alien who had lived in the country for less than three years if that alien had been convicted of a crime in another country. Petrosino had a long list of known Italian criminals who had taken up residence in the States. He intended to collect their penal certificates and other evidence of their criminal pasts in Italy to aid their extradition from the United States. Bingham's announcement to the press was a mistake, and articles about the secret mission appeared in the press all over the U.S. and Europe.

On March 12, 1909, after arriving in Palermo, Petrosino received a message from someone claiming to be an informant. The sender requested that Petrosino meet him in the city's Piazza Marina where he would

Inscription of Petrosino's tombstone.

give him information that he wanted. While waiting for the informant, Petrosino was shot to death. He was hit three times by bullets: once in the back, once in the throat and once to the side of the head. The gunmen fled, and one dropped a handgun on his way from the piazza. Petrosino was unarmed. The next day the Italian Squad received an anonymous letter stating that the New York Black Hand had arranged the murder. Legend has it that Don Vito Cascioferro, who had become the most powerful Mafioso in Sicily after being run out of the United States by Petrosino's pursuit, had been told of Petrosino's location and dispatched someone to lure him into a trap. Cascioferro left a dinner party with top Palermo politicians, went to the piazza, murdered Petrosino himself and returned to the dinner. He was arrested for Petrosino's murder but was released after an associate provided an alibi. Years later, he bragged about killing the police lieutenant, claiming it was the only time he killed someone with his own hands.

Petrosino's body was sent to New York aboard the steamship Slavonia arriving on April 9. On April 12, funeral rites were conducted at St. Patrick's Cathedral with over 200,000 people taking part in the funeral procession. The only New York police officer to ever be killed in the exercise of his duties overseas was laid to rest at Calvary Cemetery in Queens.

In 1987, the name of a small park in lower Manhattan was changed from Kenmare Square to Lieutenant Joseph Petrosino Square in his honor. Three biographical films have been made of Petrosino's Life: *The Adventures of Lieutenant Petrosino* (1912); *Pay or Die* (1960), starring Ernest Borgnine; and *The Black Hand* (1973), starring Lionel Stander. He has also been the subject of two Italian TV movies.

If You Go:

Ironically, Calvary Cemetery contains the graves of many organized crime notables. Very near the Petrosino grave are the graves of the Morello crime family and the Terranova brothers who he investigated in the famous Barrel Murder case.

Also buried near Petrosino in Calvary is Ignatius "Lupo the Wolf" Lupo. Lupo has been described as the most vicious of the Black Hand leaders. He was suspected of at least 60 murders and was never convicted until 1910 when he was sentenced to 30 years for counterfeiting. He was granted parole in 1920. In 1921, President Warren Harding freed Lupo from the constraints of his parole by granting him a commutation

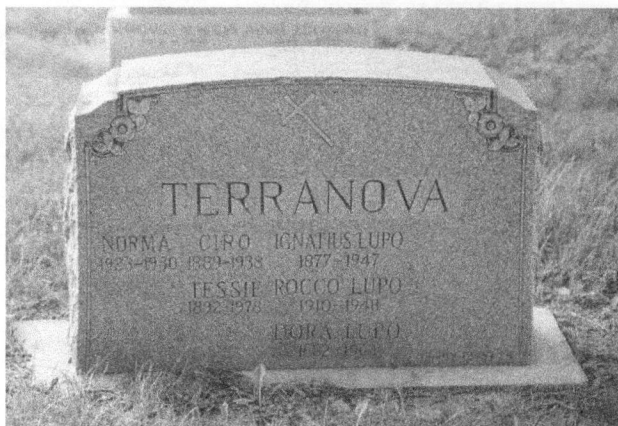

Terranova's brothers grave.

of sentence. In 1936, President Franklin Roosevelt—acting on a petition of New York Governor Herbert Lehman that showed Lupo was shaking down the New York City Bakers Union—signed an arrest warrant for Lupo, and he was sent back to prison. He was released in a few years in bad health and died in Brooklyn in 1947 at the age of 69.

Also buried in Calvary Cemetery is a victim of the Black Hand gang. In 1921, Joseph Varotta was kidnapped from in front of his home in Manhattan. The Gang demanded $2,500 for his return but the money could not be raised. A few weeks later, Varotta's body was found in the Hudson River near Piermont. His headstone reads: "Here rests the remains of Joesph Varotta, age 5 years, who was kidnapped by the Blackhands at 354 East 13th St., New York, May 24, 1921, was found June 11, 1921 at Piermont New York." Three members of the Black Hand Gang were tried and convicted of the murder and sentenced to death. New York Governor Alfred E. Smith commuted their death sentences to life in prison.

Tombstone of five-year-old Joseph Varotta who was a victim of the gang known as the Black Hand.

18

"Philadelphia's Sinners"

MICHAEL MAGGIO
ANTONIO POLLINA
ANGELO BRUNO
PHILIP TESTA
SALVATORE TESTA

County: Delaware
Town: Yeadon
Cemetery: Holy Cross
Address: Bailey Road and Leadon Avenue

"Well they blew up the Chicken Man in Philly last night/now they blew up his house too." These are the lyrics that open the classic Bruce Springsteen song "Atlantic City." The song was released in 1982, a year after the violent death of Philip "Chicken Man" Testa. Testa was killed in his home by a bomb. He and at least four other reputed Philadelphia Mafia figures are buried in Holy Cross Cemetery in Yeadon.

Michael Maggio was reputedly an old time Mafia Don from the 1920s until 1959. In 1934, Maggio, who was known as the "Cheese King" because of his successful cheese business, was arrested for the murder of his second wife (Anna, 32) and son (Joseph, 21) from a prior marriage. As the story goes, Maggio suspected them of having an affair and after catching them in bed he shot and killed them both. He pleaded guilty, and was sentenced to five years, but served less than two.

Maggio is credited with sponsoring a future mob boss, Angelo Bruno, for membership in the organization. At that time, the active boss of the Philadelphia mafia family was Salvatore Sabella. Bruno was a salesman for Maggio's cheese company and put in a good word to Sabella regarding Bruno's hard work ethic. Shortly thereafter, Bruno was running several small operations for Sabella. Michael Maggio died of natural causes at

Ruins of the Testa house.

the age of 69 in 1959. He is buried in a large beautiful Mausoleum with a large stained glass window.

Antonio Pollina accomplished what most people would never expect of the head of a crime family. He lived to be 100 years old. Known as "Mr. Migs," Pollina was named "don" by Guiseppe "Joe Ida" Idda shortly before Idda fled to Italy to avoided being indicted by federal authorities. Despite being named the boss, Pollina considered Angelo Bruno a rival and ordered his underboss to kill him. The underboss, Ignazio Denaro, informed Bruno and Bruno told "the Commission," a national Mafia board formed to resolve disputes among organized crime families and members. The Commission decided to remove Pollina and make Bruno the new boss of Philadelphia and advised him he could have Pollina killed for plotting against him. Bruno decided to let Pollina live, figuring the repercussion would be bad for the family. Pollina remained inactive in the mob for the rest of his life. He was a suspect in a number of murders over the years but was never convicted. He died in 1993 at the age of 100.

Angelo Bruno was born Angelo Annaloro in Sicily and emigrated to the United States in his early teens, settling in Philadelphia. After being

This man was known as the Cheese King he killed his wife and son (by a previous marriage) for sleeping with each other.

Known as Mister Migs this crime family head lived to the ripe old age of 100.

named the new boss of the Philadelphia family in 1959, he assumed the surname of his paternal grandmother and became Angelo Bruno.

Over the next twenty years, Bruno successfully avoided the intense media and law enforcement scrutiny and outbursts that plagued other crime families. He was known for instituting order and increasing the power of the Philadelphia mob family and connections to larger more established families in New York and New Jersey. He was given the nickname "The Gentle Don" as he preferred to settle disputes in a professional, non-violent manner. He also avoided lengthy prison terms despite several arrests. His longest term was two years for refusing to testify to a grand jury. Under Bruno, the Philadelphia crime family enjoyed the most peaceful and prosperous reign. Bruno did not allow his family to deal in narcotics, preferring more traditional operations like labor racketeering, illegal gambling, extortion, bookmaking, and loansharking. His philosophy was "make money don't make headlines." His position on narcotics, however, eroded some of his support since many factions below him felt they should have a piece of the action. Then in 1976, Atlantic City, New Jersey opened for gambling, and soon it became so lucrative that he agreed to let the New York and New Jersey families share in the profits. Bruno knew better than to try to challenge the New York families who were a lot stronger than his. This decision did not go over well with many of his underlings and further eroded his support. Several factions within the Pennsylvania family began conspiring to betray the aging Bruno.

On March 21, 1980, the sixty-nine year-old Bruno was killed by a shotgun blast in the back of the head as he sat in his car in front of his South Philadelphia home. It is believed that the killing was ordered by Antonio Caponigro (AKA Tony Bananas), Bruno's consigliere. A few weeks later, Caponigro's body was found stuffed in a body bag in the trunk of a car in New York City with about $300 jammed into his mouth and anus. The Commission reportedly ordered his murder because he assassinated Bruno without full permission. Other Philadelphia family members involved in Bruno's murder were tortured and killed.

Philip "The Chicken Man" Testa took over as mob boss in Philadelphia after the death of Angelo Bruno. He was born in Sicily and emigrated to the U.S. and settled in South Philadelphia in his teenage years. He was a dour-looking man with a pockmarked face. He stood about five feet

Angelo Bruno (right)

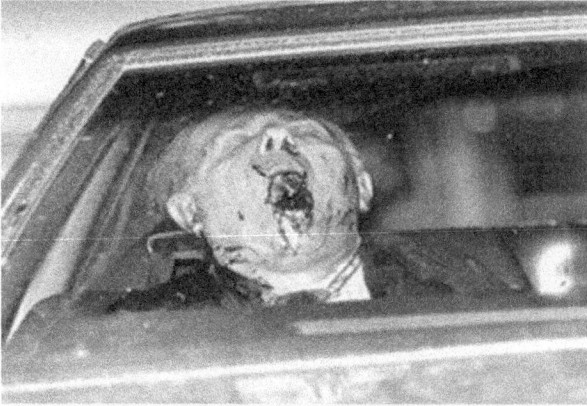

Crime scene photo of Angelo Bruno.

Known as the Gentle Don Bruno was killed by a shotgun blast to the back of the head. It appears that he had friends who were not so gentle.

eight inches and weighed 183 pounds. He reportedly had dark emotionless eyes and a pockmarked face, which is thought to be one of the reasons for his nickname. The pockmarks are believed to have been caused by a horrible case of chicken pox with the scars never fully healing. He had a thick mustache and preferred blue-collar clothing to the fancy clothing worn by most mafia dons. He became a father to his only son, Salvatore, in 1956 and they were very close. He was a staunch Roman Catholic and raised his son in the same fashion. He reportedly did not drink heavily and remained loyal to his wife. Testa

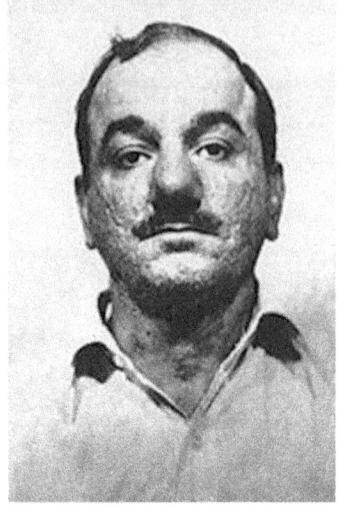

Philip "Chicken Man" Testa

conducted his business, legitimate and otherwise, out of a restaurant in Old City Philadelphia, which he owned, and his daughter Maria managed.

In February 1981, Testa was indicted by Federal authorizes for racketeering. The case was based on an investigation called Operation Gangplank and was one of the first built on the RICO Act by the U.S. Attorney's office in Philadelphia. On March 15, 1981, less than a year after the murder of Angelo Bruno, Philip Testa was killed by a bomb exploding in his home across the street from Stephen Girard Park. There were roofing nails in the bomb that apparently were to make it look like retaliation by allies of John McCullough, the roofing union leader who was killed mob style in December 1980. Testa's killing touched off a string of intra-family wars that lasted until 1995.

Salvatore "Salvie" Testa became a rising star in the mob after his father's murder. A 1974 graduate of Saint John Neumann High School, Salvie was a ruggedly handsome man who was six feet tall and 210 pounds. His parents had chosen Nicky Scarfo and his wife Domencia as his godparents. After the murder of his father, Salvie became a protegé of Nick Scarfo and was thought of as a son to Scarfo. Scarfo made him a captain (caporegime) a few months after his father's death. Newspaper accounts say that Scarfo used Salvie for over fifteen hits. He had "inherited" most of his father's business and an estate worth $800,000 that

Salvatore Testa with a couple escorts.

included a rundown bar in Atlantic City on a site where casino developer Donald Trump decided to build the Trump Plaza in 1984. Trump paid the young Testa $1.1 million for the right to tear it down.

Two of the hits were the men responsible for killing his father. On January 7, 1982, Chickie Narducci, the man who reportedly orchestrated the killing of Philip Testa, was shot ten times in the face, neck, and chest outside his home in south Philadelphia. On March 15, 1982, exactly one year after the bombing, Rocco Marinucci, the man who reportedly detonated the bomb, was found dead in a parking lot on Federal Street in Philadelphia. He had bullet wounds to the neck, chest, and head and his mouth was stuffed with three large, unexploded cherry bombs.

In April 1984, Salvie Testa was described as the "fastest rising star" in the Philadelphia mob in a front-page article of the *Wall Street Journal*. This made Nicky Scarfo jealous and worried that Testa was becoming too powerful, especially with his own group of young turks. According to newspaper accounts, on September 14, 1984, Scarfo ordered Testa's best friend, Joey Pungitore, to lure Testa into an ambush in the back room of the "Too Sweet" candy store on East Passyunk Avenue in Philadelphia.

Here lies "Chicken Man" Testa and his son Salvie.
Notice the grave goods left on the tomb.

Scarfo had requested that his godson be strangled to death, but his killers considered this too risky given Salvie's size and strength. His hog-tied body was found at the side of a dirt road in Glouster Township, New Jersey. He was wrapped in a carpet with a rope around his neck. He had been shot twice in the back of the head. He was 28 years old.

In May of 1988, Scarfo and eight associates were acquitted on all charges in the murder of Testa. A book about the Philadelphia mob was published in 2003. It's titled *Blood and Honor: Inside the Scarfo Mob – The Mafia's Most Violent Family* by George Anastasia.

If You Go:

Holy Cross Cemetery is a large and well maintained cemetery with many interesting graves. One such grave is that of Louis Van Zelst who was the bat boy and mascot for the Philadelphia Athletics from 1910 to 1914. Due to a childhood accident, his growth was stunted, and he had a hunchback. He loved sports and wandered over to Shibe Park one day in 1909 and asked Connie Mack if he could be a bat boy. Mack took an instant liking to Van Zelst and agreed. In the early part of the century, hunchbacks were considered to be good luck, and players would rub the hump for luck. He became a favorite of the A's players and fans, and the next year, 1910, Mack hired him for all home games and had a uniform made for him. As luck would have it, the A's won their first world championship that year, repeated in 1911 and 1913, and won the American League Pennant in 1914. He was taken on at least one road trip per year beginning in 1911 and to spring training in 1912. He had a sunny disposition and was an accomplished mimic who did a hysterical imitation of Eddie Plank in the batter's box. In the five years he was with the A's, they won

Here lies the Philadelphia Athletics first mascot, players used to rub his hunchback for good luck.

four pennants and three World Series. In the winter of 1915, he was diagnosed with Bright's disease and died in March. Connie Mack and the team were crestfallen, and the A's next pennant didn't come until 1929.

There are four Congressional Medal of Honor recipients buried at Holy Cross. William Shipman, George Crawford Platt, and William Densmore all received their Medals of Honor for bravery in the Civil War. Philip Gaughan received his Medal of Honor for his courageous action in the Spanish-American War.

Frank Hardart of the famous Horn and Hardart restaurants is also buried in Holy Cross. In 1902, they opened the first American automat in Philadelphia. Hot entrees, cold sandwiches, bowls of soup, and slices of pie awaited behind the small glass doors, which opened when the right number of nickels were inserted. He died in 1918.

Also there are two Hall of Fame Boxers and the youngest US Open Golf Champion of all time. The boxers are light Heavyweight Champion Thomas Loughran who is regarded as one of the most skilled fighters of all time and died in 1982 and Joseph (Philadelphia Jack) Hagen who was also the World Light Heavyweight Champion from 1905-1912. Hagen died in 1942. The golfer John McDermott was the first US born golfer to win the US Open and the youngest ever at 19 years 10 months in 1911 (see *Keystone Tombstones - Philadelphia Region*).

19

Rhoads "Opera House" Fire

171 VICTIMS

County: Berks
City: Boyertown, Pennsylvania
Cemetery: Fairview
Address: 317 W Philadelphia Ave

Though it was referred to as an "opera house" after the tragedy in Dr. Thomas J. B. Rhoads' building at the corner of Philadelphia Avenue and Washington Street in the center of Boyertown, Pennsylvania, it was not a grandiose theater as imagined. Rather, the three-story building included a meeting hall on the second floor which could be rented to groups. This venue contained a small stage and was large enough to convene several hundred people. It was the chosen location by the local St. Johns Lutheran Church for a performance of "The Scottish Reformation," a play depicting the death of Queen Mary, performed primarily by young parishioners on January 13, 1908. By the next morning, the bodies of 170 people, about ten percent of the town's population, were being removed to a nearby makeshift morgue and a firefighter had lost his life.

This did not have to happen. The room only had one exit and the doors opened in. The fire escape was not well-marked and could only be accessed by crawling out of the windows, which were over three feet above the floor. The fire could have been easily contained, if not for some errors in judgment. And, the crowd panicked, including the gentlemen, who if they had been more heroic, would likely have saved most of the victims. Instead, what happened was a mad rush for the doors, which appeared to be locked or jammed, scores dying from the smoke and flames.

Boyertown, Pennsylvania, in Edwardian times, was like many smaller cities in the region, bustling with economic activity and growing populations. The Model T had yet to be produced when the fire occurred,

Photo of the burnt interior of the Rhoads building including some victims.

making it very likely the vast majority of attendees arrived by trolley, horse-drawn carriage, or on foot, automobiles being relatively rare and expensive. In those days, the men wore derbies and jackets and ties. The ladies wore wide-brimmed hats and long-train dresses.

There were two performances scheduled for the play authored by Mrs. Harriet Earhart Monroe. The first was Monday evening, January 8. Another was booked for the following night. A total of 312 tickets were sold for the opening performance. It was estimated there were also over 60 people involved in the performance, including actors and stagehands from the church and local area. Mrs. Monroe was not present, but her sister, Mrs. Della Mayers, directed the play and had led the rehearsals. Monroe also provided the scripts, props, and costumes. The church and Mrs. Monroe planned to split the profits.

The initial two acts and first intermission went off without a hitch. During the second intermission, a young man, Harry Fisher, was working the stereopticon to project slides for a lecture by Mrs. Mayers about the historical background for the play. Said Fisher, an inexperienced projectionist, in the *New York Times* a few days later, "I must have turned the wrong valve. There was a long drawn out hissing sound that frightened the women and children. Several of them jumped up and screamed and ran toward the stage. The curtain was down. I don't know what happened next."

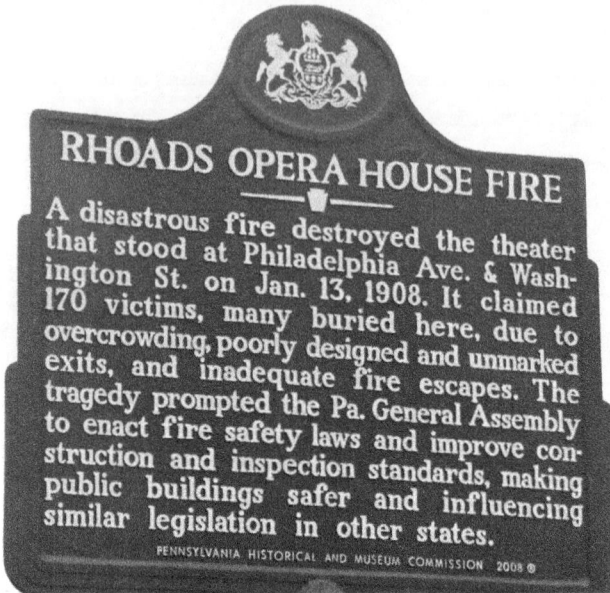

State historical marker in Boyertown at the cemetery.

Plaque on the wall of the rebuilt Rhoads building.

The commotion in the audience caused several of the actors to peek from behind the muslin curtain to see what was going on. While doing so, someone inadvertently knocked over a kerosene lamp which had been sitting on the piano. This spilled flaming oil onto the front of the stage. Men in the crowd quickly reacted, and most in the room waited anxiously, as the fire on the stage was being put out. However, a couple men, including the pastor, Reverand Adam M. Weber, attempted to move a tank of kerosene used to fuel the footlights away from the fire. This buckled the framework of the lights and caused more fuel to spill on the stage, reigniting the fire. Weber was severely burned by the mishap but called out to everyone urging "patience and unity." No one listened.

The inferno spread rapidly, first to the curtains, then to the wooden ceiling and wainscoting along the walls. Next, the gases emitted from the malfunctioning stereopticon caught fire. Everyone panicked and rushed for the exit, only to find the doors stuck due to the number of people pushing against them in the wrong direction. Parents grabbed their young children and tucked them under their arms as they darted about to find a way out.

"There was a wild rush for the exits. Everybody seemed to have lost control," recalled survivor Reubon Stover in the *Cranbury Press* a few days later. "The flames came towards the crowd like a great wave . . . once the crowd began to fight its way towards the doors no power on earth could have saved all the lives."

In the ensuing chaos, people smashed windows, some finding the fire escape while others jumped two stories to the ground. Reverand Weber called out to his family, who were in the crowd, like many who had lost track of loved ones. The women's long dresses hampered their movements and were also very flammable.

Finally, one of the doors was splintered, resulting in a cascade of stampeding patrons who fell to their deaths or stumbled down the stairs. Rescuers were later horrified to find dead bodies piled five or six deep at the head of the narrow four-foot wide staircase. "It was a terrible sight, and I shall carry the recollection as long as I live," continued Stover, ". . . but I believe that, if the men had not lost control of themselves, the loss of life would have been very small."

The rebuilt Rhoads building in downtown Boyertown, Pennsylvania.

"It was a battle in which only the strong had a chance to escape," Frank Cullen would later recall.

More than half of those in the building made it out. Reverand Weber was among the survivors but lost one of his young daughters. In some cases, entire families were lost. John Graver, a firefighter, was killed while responding to the incident. Della Earhart Mayers also died in the conflagration.

In his official report, the coroner would state that the victims included 110 females, forty-three males, and twelve whose sex was not distinguishable. The coroner noted that only the upper portions of the victims' bodies had been incinerated by the flames. The lower portions of the deceased had remained intact, clear evidence that fire had swept over the bunched-up victims, killing them while trapped against one another.

In the *New York Times* on January 14, 1908, Burgess Daniel Kohler of Boyertown stated, "Many of the men who perished in the fire were employed in the Boyertown Casket Company. The majority were carpenters employed in the making of coffins. Many a poor fellow unconsciously labored over the coffin in which he will be buried." In total, 171 perished and 75 were seriously injured.

Large monument at the mass grave of the unidentified victims of the fire.

Fire companies from Boyertown and surrounding areas responded to the blaze, but it took many hours to get it under control. Finally, the next morning, the grim work of removing bodies began. The basement of a nearby saloon served as a morgue. Two other morgues were required given the number of dead. Reports of missing persons were coordinated with identification activities.

News of the fire, the worst in Pennsylvania's history, spread to nearby towns, to Philadelphia, and across the nation. In the days immediately following the disaster, relief funds were received and 107 new graves were dug at nearby Fairview Cemetery, including a mass grave for the 25 who were unknown. Over 15,000 people attended the funerals at Fairview Cemetery on one day. Others were buried in various cemeteries around the area, some as far away as Philadelphia and Lancaster.

By early 1909, the Pennsylvania legislature, with the signature of Governor Edwin Stuart, signed into law new standards for fire safety including standards for exit signs, doors, lighting, extinguishers, and fire escapes.

Mrs. Monroe was the subject of lawsuits and was subpoenaed to appear before an official inquest, but declined to attend. She was exonerated

Grave of two victims named Boyer.

from any blame. Monroe retired her play and lived until 1927, when she passed away in Washington, D.C. She and her sister were the paternal aunts of Amelia Earhart, the aviatrix.

Dr. Thomas Rhoads was arrested for criminal neglect but was later freed. He received insurance proceeds from the fire and had his building rebuilt on the spot only two years after the fire. This new building, which stands to this day, has slightly different features and interior design.

In 2008, honoring the 100th anniversary, Boyertown remembered the victims and this tragic event throughout the year. Historical markers can now be found at the building and cemetery telling the tale of that fateful evening in 1908.

If You Go
The Boyertown Area Historical Society at 45 South Chestnut Street, contains an ongoing exhibit about the fire including many gruesome photographs. It is a short walk, around the corner, from the site of the fire. They are open on Tuesdays from 5 P.M. to 9 P.M. and Wednesdays from 9 A.M. to 4 P.M.

Durango's Saloon at 120 East Philadelphia Avenue is a couple doors down from the former Rhoads building. The basement was used as one of the morgues following the fire. They serve steaks, seafood, burgers, salads, and a variety of beers. The Book Nook is a used bookstore on the first floor of 130 East Philadelphia Avenue, the location of the fire. Visiting the bookstore will allow you access to the interior of the building which replaced the building involved in the fire. The upper floors have apartments for rent.

If eating steaks above a former morgue for burn victims isn't your thing, the authors highly recommend a short drive to the historic Yellow House Hotel near Douglasville, Pennsylvania, about seven miles west of Boyertown, at the intersection of routes 662 and 562. This charming inn serves high-quality food in an early Federal period setting.

Grave of Stella Kolb, a victim of the fire.

20

"Murder at Madison Square Garden"

HARRY KENDALL THAW

County: Allegheny
Town: Pittsburgh
Cemetery: Allegheny
Address: 4734 Butler Street

On June 25, 1906, the man with the large moustache was seated in the privileged section of the dining theater on the roof of Madison Square Garden. He was there to see the opening of a new play called "Mam'zelle Champagne." He was very well known in New York City and was considered to be the most distinguished architect of his time. As a matter of fact, he was sitting on the roof of a building he had designed. His name was Stanford White.

Another man was attending the play that night. Despite the fact that it was summer and quite warm, he wore a black overcoat. Earlier the hat check girl had attempted to check the coat, but her offer was refused. During the performance of a song titled "I Could Love a Million Girls" the man approached White's table. He reached into the overcoat and produced a pistol and at point blank range shot White three times in the face. The architect fell to the floor, mortally wounded. The killer calmly moved toward the exit holding the murder weapon over his head. His name was Harry Thaw.

Thaw was born on February 12, 1871. His father, William Thaw, had made a fortune through both the coal and the railroad business. Even when he was very young, Thaw exhibited a violent nature. He did poorly at a number of private schools in Pittsburgh, and his teachers described him as a troublemaker. He gained admission, probably with the help of his father, to the University of Pittsburgh where he planned to study law. A few years later, again using his social status, he was admitted to

Harry Kendall Thaw

Harvard. Thaw later said that his main field of study at Harvard was poker. He also did a lot of drinking and was finally expelled after he was arrested for chasing a cab driver through Cambridge with a shotgun. It is believed that around this time Thaw created the speedball which involved the injection of Morphine or heroin and cocaine.

After leaving Harvard, Thaw began hanging out in New York City. He made it a habit to inject himself with both morphine and cocaine. He enjoyed Broadway shows largely because of the chorus girls. It was during this time that he first met Stanford White who also had a keen interest in chorus girls. One of these girls would play a key part in the lives of both men. Her name was Evelyn Nesbitt.

In the early 1900s Nesbitt was one of the most sought after models in New York. She appeared on the cover of *Vanity Fair*, *Cosmopolitan* and *Harper's Bazaar*. She eventually tired of modeling and decided to move into theatre. In July of 1901, Nesbit joined the chorus line in a popular play called "Florodora." It was here where she was first noticed by Stanford White. He was 47 years old and a known womanizer when he met Nesbit who was 16 at the time.

White kept a loft apartment on West Twenty-fourth Street. When Nesbitt first visited the apartment, she was impressed by the furnishings and fine paintings. She was given a glass of champagne and escorted upstairs to a studio that contained a red velvet swing. Nesbitt would later testify in court that White found sexual pleasure in pushing naked or very nearly naked young women in the swing. On a subsequent visit to the apartment, the two had dinner and multiple glasses of champagne. She was given a tour of the apartment and more champagne. She tried on a yellow satin kimono for White and then in her own words "passed out." When she awoke she was in bed nearly naked, and White was beside her. When she entered the room, she was a virgin, but she did not leave as one. Having completed the conquest, White moved on and pursued other young women.

Around this time Thaw became enamored with Nesbitt. White, who had warned other showgirls to stay away from Thaw, gave Nesbitt the same advice. At first she heeded the warning and made it a point to avoid Thaw. Thaw took advantage of the situation when Nesbitt was admitted to a hospital due to appendicitis. He visited often showering her with gifts and praising her amazing talents. White had her moved to a sanatorium in upstate New York, but Thaw continued to visit her there.

Upon her release from the sanatorium, Thaw invited Nesbitt and her mother to visit Paris with him. While on this trip Thaw proposed to Nesbitt, but she turned him down. While in Paris he continued his practice of giving Nesbitt lavish gifts. Thaw also continued to ask her to marry him, and she confessed that White had taken her virginity, and therefore she wasn't worthy of marrying Thaw. The news built up the hatred Thaw already had with regard to White. After he sent Nesbitt's

Evelyn Nesbitt

mother back to New York, he took the daughter to an isolated castle in Germany. It was here that Thaw forced himself sexually on Nesbitt and began beating her repeatedly with a dog whip. Finally, she convinced Thaw to return to New York.

Back in New York Thaw, continued in his pursuit to marry Nesbitt. He also harassed her about her relationship with White. Thaw began referring to White as "the beast." Thaw's mother went to see Nesbitt and urged her to marry her son. Nesbitt gave in and married Thaw who seemed to lose interest in her after they became man and wife. At the same time, Thaw's obsession with White seemed to grow. Nesbitt later recalled that on a voyage to Europe Thaw tied her to a bed and began beating her to force her to confess to every sexual act she had engaged in with White.

As detailed earlier in this chapter, Thaw eventually got his revenge with regard to White. At the time of the shooting, witnesses said they heard Thaw say, "You ruined my life." Others reported that he said "You ruined my wife." Whatever was said after the shooting, Thaw walked to the elevator where Nesbitt was waiting, and when she saw the gun in his hand she exclaimed, "Oh Harry, what have you done"?

Thaw was arrested, charged with murder and placed in the Tombs prison. His prison life was far from ordinary. He didn't eat prison food; instead his meals were catered by Delmonico's then one of New York's finest restaurants. He also had whiskey brought to him and was permitted to have visitors day and night. Meanwhile his mother was assembling a defense team that would be led by Delphin Delmas known as one of the finest defense attorneys in the country. The District Attorney at the time was William Travers Jerome who had declared Thaw a fiend and stated, "No matter how rich a man is, he cannot get away with murder."

It would take six months for what the press was calling "The Trial of the Century" to begin. The trial would last for seven months. The prosecution attempted to make the case that Thaw had committed premeditated murder. The defense claimed that Thaw was insane and that he had murdered White after being directed to do so by the spirits of the dead. The defense had doctor's testify that, in their opinion, Thaw was insane. The defense even produced a medium who claimed that during a séance a spirit spoke through her and confessed that it had forced Thaw to kill White. Nesbitt also testified providing details on her seduction by White and of their sexual relations. Thaw's mother had convinced Nesbitt to testify by promising her a divorce and payment of one million dollars. After the trial she got the divorce but not one cent of the money.

The jury was unable to return a verdict: seven jurors believed Thaw was guilty, but the other five judged him to be insane. Nine months later Thaw was retried, and this jury found him not guilty by reason of insanity. The judge ordered that Thaw be placed in an asylum. Thaw made the trip to the asylum in a private train car loaded with friends. On the way, they drank whiskey and champagne and enjoyed a meal. Nesbitt did not accompany her husband on the trip. In 1913 Thaw walked out of the asylum and was driven to Canada. He was arrested in Canada and deported back to the United States where, in 1915, a judge found him to be sane and ordered his release.

In 1916, Thaw was accused of sexually assaulting and beating Fred Gump, a high school student. After he was indicted, he left New York and went to Philadelphia. When he was found in Philadelphia, he had slashed his own throat, but the wound had not killed him. He was once again found to be insane and returned to an asylum. Seven years later he was again declared sane and released.

After his release in 1924, Thaw purchased a home in Clearbrook, Virginia. His neighbors viewed him as being eccentric, but he managed to stay out of trouble with the law. He spent the rest of his life travelling to various locations around the world, and he was generally accompanied by attractive young girls. On February 22, 1947, while in Miami, Thaw died as a result of a heart attack; he was 76 years old. In his will, he left $10,000 to Evelyn Nesbitt, an amount that represented less than 1% of his wealth. Thaw's body was returned to Pittsburgh and was buried in Allegheny Cemetery.

While Thaw was in the asylum, Nesbitt gave birth to a son who she named Russell Thaw. Thaw, however, denied that the child was his.

Here is the family plot where the notorious Harry Thaw was laid to rest.

Without Thaw's financial support Nesbitt was forced to return to the Vaudeville stage. Despite another short marriage to a man named Jack Clifford, she was always billed as Mrs. Harry K. Thaw. Nesbitt moved to Northfield, New Jersey, where she battled an addiction to morphine and alcoholism. In 1955 she was a technical advisor for the movie *The Girl in the Red Velvet Swing*. The movie was a highly fictionalized story of the famous love triangle between her, Thaw and White. The 1975 novel and later the film *Ragtime* also tells the story of the three lovers. Late in life she declared that Stanford White was the only man she ever loved. She died in 1967, at the age of 82 in a nursing home in Santa Monica, California.

If You Go:

Allegheny Cemetery is a historical treasure. The famed singer and actress Lillian Russell was laid to rest here. Hall of Fame baseball player Josh Gibson, who hit 800 home runs in a 17-year career, is buried in Allegheny Cemetery. Gibson was a major star in the Negro League, and many who saw him play claimed he was as good if not better than Babe Ruth.

Two Civil War Medal of Honor recipients, Archibald H. Rowand Jr. and Alfred L. Pearson, are buried here as well. After the war, Pearson commanded the National Guardsmen who were sent to Luzerne County to quell riots in the coal region. He ordered his men to open fire on the rioters and killed a number of them. As a result he was arrested and charged with murder, but a grand jury failed to indict him, and he was set free.

In addition, you may want to visit the Arsenal Monument on the cemetery's grounds. The monument honors 43 woman buried here after an explosion at the nearby Allegheny Arsenal took their lives. The explosion was the worst industrial accident associated with the Civil War.

Not far from the cemetery there is a great restaurant called Piccolo Forno. It is located at 3801 Butler Street. The eatery offers great service and terrific Italian food that is very reasonably priced. It's definitely worth checking out.

21

TITANIC VICTIMS AND SURVIVORS

41°43.5' N 49°56.8' W
15 April 1912

For more than 100 years, the story of the sinking of the RMS *Titanic* has fascinated people all over the world. On the night of April 14 and the morning of April 15, 1912, four days into her maiden voyage, the largest passenger liner in the world hit an iceberg and sunk in the icy North Atlantic Ocean. Two hours and forty minutes after hitting the iceberg, she disappeared beneath the sea. She was carrying an estimated 2,224 people from Southampton, England to New York City, 1,500 of whom lost their lives in the tragedy, making it one of the deadliest peacetime maritime disasters in history.

Once the British passenger liner hit the iceberg and started taking on water, much chaos ensued and many controversies have endured for over a century. The evacuation was chaotic and controversial. Those who survived were rescued by the RMS *Carpathia*, which arrived about an hour and a half after the sinking. Less than a third of those aboard survived the disaster. Some survivors died shortly afterwards from injuries or the effects of exposure. Statistics compiled after the disaster show that 49% of the children and 26% of the female passengers died. The percentages for male passengers and crew were 82% and 78%, respectively. However, the figures show stark differences in the survival rates of the different classes. Only 3% of first-class women were lost, but 54% of those in third class died. Similarly, five of six first-class and all second-class children survived, but 52 of the 79 in third class perished. The figures for men show one-third of first-class men were saved but only 8% and 16% of second- and third-class men survived, respectively.

As the great ship went down, over a thousand passengers and crew members were still on board. Hundreds more were left dying in the icy 28°F sea, due to insufficient lifeboats and an inefficient, chaotic

RMS Titanic sea trials, April 2, 1912.

evacuation. Most lifeboats had empty seats. As the occupants sat and watched the horror around them, they could hear those freezing to death in the water as they yelled, screamed and pled for their lives.

Only a few of those in the water survived. Occupants of the lifeboats debated and argued about attempting to help those in the water. In all but two of the boats the occupants decided against trying to help, fearing that they would be capsized by the desperate, panicked swimmers. After about 20 minutes, the cries for help began to fade as the swimmers lapsed into unconsciousness and died. One of the *Titanic*'s officers in Lifeboat No. 14 gathered together five of the lifeboats and transferred the occupants between them to free up space and headed back to the site of the sinking. Almost all of those in the water were already dead. They found four men still alive, one of whom died shortly afterwards. The *Carpathia* took the survivors to New York where the full scope of the disaster was just becoming known.

For years after, controversies and investigations would ensue. Issues like the speed and course of the *Titanic*, the failure to heed six warnings, the insufficient number of lifeboats, the chaotic evacuation, poor radio communication between ships at sea, and the survival of J. Bruce Ismay, managing director of the White Star Line (owner of the *Titanic*) who was aboard, were just a few of the subjects that came under close scrutiny following the disaster.

Pennsylvania, while welcoming home its share of *Titanic* survivors, also shared in the grief and sorrow of this horrible event. These are the remarkable stories of several such Pennsylvanians.[1]

Austin Van Billiard (35)
James Van Billiard (10)
Walter Van Billiard (9)
County: Montgomery – *Town:* Flourtown
Cemetery: Union Cemetery of Whitemarsh
Address 654 Bethlehem Pike

Imagine the shock and despair of James Van Billiard and his wife, who learned in several days after the accident that their son Austin Van Billiard and two of their grandsons—James (age 10) and Walter (age 9)—were passengers on the *Titanic* and were missing.

Austin had been working in the diamond mining industry in South Africa for 10 years, living there with his wife and four children. During that time he was not able to see his brother or parents, who lived in Pennsylvania (North Wales Borough, Montgomery County). After much success, Austin decided to return to the U.S. to be a diamond

---

1. A number in parenthesis after an individual's name in each heading indicates that person's age at the time he or she perished on April 14-15, 1912. If no number is present after a person's name, that indicates the person survived the disaster.

merchant there. The family left South Africa and on their way to America they stopped to visit his wife's parents who lived in London. Austin then decided to take his two eldest sons with him ahead of the rest of the family for a surprise visit. He took with him at least 12 uncut diamonds—diamonds which would soon be found on his body when it was recovered from the icy Atlantic.

This monument marks the final resting place of two Titanic *victims the Van Billiards Austin, and his son James. Another son named Walter also perished but his body was never found.*

The senior Van Billiards received a cablegram from their daughter-in-law informing them that Austin and the boys were on the *Titanic*. It was the first they knew of it.

Austin's body and that of his son Walter were recovered. James' body was never found (or, if it was recovered, was never identified). The family speculates that the boys would not have left their father to get on a lifeboat. The bodies of Austin and Walter are buried in Union Cemetery in Whitemarsh, Montgomery County. The headstone also lists James.

William Loch Coutts
County: Allegheny – *Town:* Penn Hills
Cemetery: Sunset View (a/k/a, Riverview Memorial Park)
Address 2023 Lincoln Road

Unlike the Van Billiards, the situation was different for two other little boys who accompanied a parent aboard the *Titanic*. Mrs. Winnie "Minnie" Coutts and her two sons, William (age 9) and Neville (age 3) were third-class passengers on the *Titanic* heading to be reunited with her husband who was working in Brooklyn as an engraver. He had been sending money to Winnie for a year to pay for the trip.

The night of the disaster, she was awakened by the commotion outside her stern cabin. She dressed her boys but found only two life preservers in her cabin. She put them on her boys and entered the hallway. She quickly found herself lost but soon encountered a crewman who gave her his life preserver and directed her up to the lifeboats, all the while asking her to pray for him if she was saved. After finding their way to the boat deck, Winnie and her sons encountered a problem: the officer in charge of the lifeboat refused to let Willie board because he looked too old. Apparently the straw hat he was wearing made him look older. Nevertheless, Winnie finally persuaded the officers to let the 9-year old join her and Neville in Lifeboat No. 2. All three Coutts were picked up by the *Carpathia*. There were only 17 in the lifeboat, which was designed to hold at least 40-60 people.

Life as *Titanic* Survivors: The family moved to Pittsburgh in 1920, and Mrs. Coutts and Neville moved to California about 20 years later. William became a professional musician, got married, and had two daughters. On Christmas Day 1957, he was found dead in the street in Steubenville, Ohio. His death was attributed to natural causes. He is buried at Sunset View Cemetery in Penn Hills Township near Pittsburgh. He was 55 years old.

His mother, Winnie, died in New Jersey in 1960, at the age of 84.

On December 16, 1958, his brother Neville was one of a dozen or so *Titanic* survivors who attended the New York City premiere of the movie "A Night to Remember" (a 1958 British drama film adaptation of Walter Lord's 1955 book *A Night to Remember*, which recounts the *Titanic's* fateful final night). Neville died in Florida in 1977, at the age of 78.

Victorine Chaudanson
County: Delaware – *Town:* Springfield
Cemetery: Saints Peter and Paul
Address 1600 South Sproul Road

At the Philadelphia premiere of *A Night to Remember*, a woman named Victorine Chaudanson was honored. Miss Chaudanson was a maid for the Ryersons, a wealthy Philadelphia family, and was traveling with them on the *Titanic*. Arthur Ryerson, along with his wife (Emily) and their children (Emily, John and Suzette), were hurrying back to the U.S. after learning of the death of their son, Arthur Jr., who died in a car accident at the age of 20. Mr. Ryerson gave Victorine his life preserver when he saw that she had none. She and Mrs. Ryerson and the children were rescued in Lifeboat No. 5. Mr. Ryerson was lost in the sinking.

The grave of Victorine Chaudanson a woman who survived the sinking.

Life as a *Titanic* Survivor: Victorine Chaudanson later became Mrs. Henry Perkins and lived in Ridley Park, Pennsylvania. She died on August 13, 1962 (age 87), and is buried as Victorine Perkins at Saints Peter and Paul Cemetery in Springfield, Delaware County.

Sophie Halaut Abraham
County: Westmoreland – *Town:* Greensburg
Cemetery: Westmoreland County Memorial Park
Address 150 Eastside Drive and West Newton Road (Route 136)

Another survivor, 18-year old Sophie Halaut Abraham, was returning from Syria where she was visiting family, witnessed some panic. When she arrived near the lifeboats, men were fighting for an opportunity to get in. Several of the ships' officers had to command them to stand back and make way for the women and children. The first sailor who tried to help Mrs. Abraham into the lifeboat lost his grip on her, and she was tossed into the sea. She was lucky enough to be taken into a crowded lifeboat, but those fortunes quickly changed when that lifeboat was upset by a big wave, dumping everyone on board into the water. Yet another lifeboat picked Mrs. Abraham and a few others out of the water. Four sailors in her lifeboat rowed away from the *Titanic* to safety.

Life as a *Titanic* Survivor: Sophie returned to Greensburg, Pennsylvania, where she lived until her death in December 1976, at the age of 82. She is buried in Westmoreland County Memorial Park in Greensburg.

Lily Potter
Olive (Potter) Earnshaw
County: Philadelphia – *Town:* Philadelphia
Cemetery: Laurel Hill
Address 3822 Ridge Avenue

Things went relatively smoothly for Lily Potter and the two passengers who accompanied her aboard the *Titanic*: her daughter (Olive Earnshaw); and her friend (Margaret Hays). Olive was going through a divorce and Lily, now a widow, thought a vacation would be good for her. They invited Margaret to join them. After touring Italy and the Middle East, they booked passage home on another ship. However, after hearing about the *Titanic* and how grand it would be to sail on her, they changed their reservations. Following the collision with the iceberg, Olive and Margaret went to see what had happened. They returned to their cabin and reported to Lily that a steward had told them not to worry and to go back to bed. Lily was upset and did not believe the steward. They dressed quickly and warmly and were put on the first lifeboat launched. All three survived in Lifeboat No. 7.

Life as *Titanic* Survivors: Lily and Olive spent the rest of their lives as huge supporters of the Red Cross. Lily helped found the Southeastern Pennsylvania Chapter of the American Red Cross. She received the Gimbel Award as Philadelphia's outstanding woman in 1939 and gave the $1,000 prize to the Red Cross. She died in January 1954, at the age of 98. Olive remarried and had two sons. She was a Red Cross volunteer for the rest of her life, which ended when she died of cancer in 1958 (age 69). Olive and Lily are buried together at Laurel Hill Cemetery in Philadelphia.

Benjamin Guggenheim (46)
Died at sea
Atlantic Ocean (375 miles South of
Newfoundland, and 963 miles northeast of New York City)
Aboard RMS *Titanic*
Body never recovered

Benjamin Guggenheim

"Women and children first!" was the order, but as the situation became more obvious and more desperate, there was some not-so-noble behavior. Many men, however, did act heroic-ally in the face of death. One such notable person was Benjamin Guggenheim, a fabu-lously wealthy industrialist from Philadelphia. He was traveling with his mistress, a French singer named Leontine Aubart. He went to the boat deck and helped Aubart and her maid into Lifeboat No. 9 (both of whom survived), and then helped other women and children into lifeboats. Once they were loaded, Guggenheim and his valet, Victor Giglio, returned to their cabin and changed into evening wear. Guggenheim was heard to say "we've dressed up in our best and are prepared to go down like gentlemen." He then told a steward:

"If anything should happen to me, tell my wife in New York that I've done my best in doing my duty. No woman shall be left aboard because Ben Guggenheim was a coward."

Guggenheim and Giglio were last seen seated in deck chairs in the foyer of the Grand Staircase, sipping brandy and smoking cigars. The steward survived and delivered the message to Mrs. Guggenheim.

Benjamin Guggenheim and Victor Giglio went down with the ship. Their bodies were never recovered. Guggenheim was one of the most prominent Americans lost in the disaster and has been depicted in numerous movies about the *Titanic*.

William C. Dulles (39)
County: Philadelphia – *Town:* Philadelphia
Cemetery: Laurel Hill
Address 3822 Ridge Avenue

Another prominent Philadelphian who perished in the disaster was William C. Dulles, a relative of long time CIA director John Foster Dulles, and a prominent Philadelphia lawyer in his own right. Dulles, a bachelor, had been traveling with his mother in Europe. His body was recovered by the Cable Ship (CS) *MacKay-Bennett*, and he was buried at Laurel Hill Cemetery. He was 39.

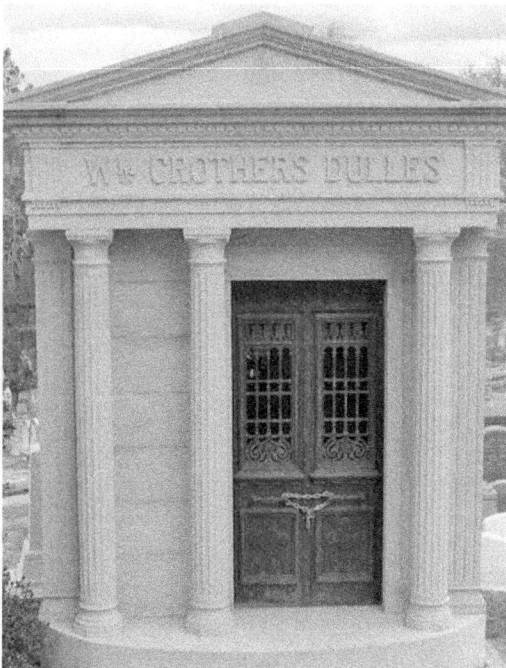

Final resting place of William Dulles who died when the great ship went down.

Henry Blank
County: Delaware – *Town:* Drexel Hill
Cemetery: Arlington
Address 2900 State Road

Mr. Henry Blank, a successful jeweler from New Jersey, was also 39 as he sat aboard the *Titanic* en route for New York. He was traveling alone, returning from a business trip to Europe. On the night of the tragedy at the moment when the *Titanic* hit the iceberg, Blank was playing cards with two men he had befriended on the ship. Someone yelled that the ship had hit an iceberg and all three went up to the Promenade Deck to catch a look at an iceberg, but the berg had passed and was not in sight. The men returned to their game.

We will never know how lucky Blank was at cards that night, but he was extremely lucky at life. The *Titanic* came to a stop shortly after the men resumed their game and curiosity got to them. They went below to look for trouble and saw seawater entering the squash court. They hurried to prepare to evacuate. Blank was among the first to arrive on the starboard Boat Deck. He and his friends and the women they were traveling with were assisted into Lifeboat No. 7. It was the first lifeboat lowered into the water. Here, Blank was extremely lucky.

The Captain's order of put "women and children in and lower away" was interpreted differently by *Titanic* Officers Charles Lightoller and William Murdoch, who each took charge of a side (Lightoller the port side; Murdoch the starboard side). Lightoller took the Captain's order to mean women and children *only*; Murdoch took it to mean women and children *first*. Initially, few passengers were willing to board lifeboats.

Here is the grave of Henry Blank, a Titanic survivor, who found a place in a lifeboat because women who were offered seating refused to leave their husbands.

Many women refused to leave the *Titanic* without their husbands and male companions. In an effort to move the evacuation along, Murdoch allowed several men into Lifeboat No. 7. It was lowered with 28 passengers on board despite a capacity of 65. Neither officer knew the capacity of the lifeboats nor that there weren't enough lifeboats for everyone.

Blank helped row away from the sinking ship. After a while, revolver shots could be heard coming from the *Titanic*. As the massive ship began to sink, the lifeboat occupants could hear the screams and cries from those left on board.

Several hours later, Blank and the other occupants of Lifeboat No. 7 were pulled from the icy Atlantic by the *Carpathia*.

Life as a *Titanic* Survivor: Blank returned to his business and prospered for many years. He died from pneumonia on St. Patrick's Day 1949, at the age of 76. He is buried in the family plot in Arlington Cemetery, in Drexel Hill, Pennsylvania.

Richard Williams
Charles Duane Williams (51)
County: Chester – *Town:* Wayne
Cemetery: Old St. David's Churchyard
Address 763 South Valley Forge Road

Mr. Charles Williams and his son, Richard, weren't quite so lucky. Charles (sometimes referred to as "C. Duane") was a lawyer originally from Radnor, Pennsylvania, and a direct descendant of Benjamin Franklin. Richard, a 21-year-old accomplished tennis player, had won the Swiss Championship while being tutored privately at a Swiss boarding school, and after playing in some summer tournaments in the U.S., would be entering Harvard in the Fall. The two men were traveling from Geneva back to the U.S.

After the collision, both men left their stateroom and encountered a steward trying to open the door of a cabin behind which a panicking passenger was trapped. The younger Williams broke through the door with his shoulder. The steward threatened to report him for damaging White Star Line property. This event inspired a scene in the 1997 film "*Titanic*."

Final resting place of Richard Williams a Titanic survivor who became a tennis champion.

The two men wandered the decks as the ship sank under them. They went to the bar and the elder Williams tried to get a steward to fill his flask with whiskey. The steward refused, stating that the bar was closed and it would be against the rules. Charles handed the flask to Richard, which remains a Williams' family heirloom.

As the *Titanic* sunk, Richard and Charles found themselves in the water—swimming for their lives. There was a loud cracking sound, and Richard turned to see his father crushed by the forward smokestack as it crashed down. It almost got Richard too. The resulting wave pushed him towards a lifeboat referred to as "Collapsible A," which was upright but partly flooded as its sides had not been properly raised. Richard clung to the side for some time, as the occupants were being very careful not to take on any more water. Even after being hauled aboard, the occupants had to sit in a foot of freezing water. Many died of hypothermia during the night.

The *Carpathia* arrived near dawn. Richard Williams and those still alive in Collapsible A were lifted aboard. When a doctor on board examined Richard, the doctor recommended amputation of both legs, fearing gangrene. Williams refused permission and instead walked every two hours around the clock, hoping to save his legs.

The decision worked out well for Williams. Three days later when the Carpathia arrived in New York, he walked off the ship. Three months later at the Philadelphia Cricket Club, he won the U.S. Mixed Doubles Tennis Championship.

Life as a *Titanic* Survivor: "Dick" Williams (as he was sometimes referred to) continued his tennis career and entered Harvard as planned. He went on to win the U.S. Singles Championship in 1914 and again in 1916, the U.S. Men's Doubles Championship twice (1925 and 1926), and the Wimbledon Men's Championship in 1920. In 1914, he played with another *Titanic* survivor, Karl Behr (rescued on Lifeboat No. 5) on the U.S. Davis Cup team. He subsequently captained the Davis Cup team from 1921 through 1925. At the 1924 Olympics in Paris, Williams and Hazel Wightman won the gold medal in mixed doubles.

Richard Williams served with distinction in the U.S. Army during World War I and was awarded the Croix de Guerre for heroism as well as the Chevalier de la Legion d'Honneur (Legion of Honor), two of France's highest military honors.

Williams went on to be a successful investment banker in Philadelphia and for 20 years served as President of the Historical Society of Pennsylvania. He died of emphysema in 1968, at the age of 77. He is buried in Old St. David Church Cemetery in Wayne, Pennsylvania. Next to his grave is a memorial marker for his father, C. Duane Williams, whose body was never recovered.

George Dunton Widener (50)
Harry Elkins Widener (27)
Eleanor Elkins (Widener) Rice
County: Philadelphia – *Town:* Philadelphia
Cemetery: Laurel Hill
Address 3822 Ridge Avenue

Reports say that one of the people seen with C. Duane Williams during the last moments of the *Titanic* was 50-year-old George Dunton Widener, one of the wealthiest men in Philadelphia. George and his wife (Eleanor) and son (Harry) were returning from a trip to Paris, where they had gone with the intention of finding a chef for George's new Philadelphia hotel, The Ritz Carlton.

Their fate was more in line with what was expected. After the evacuation began, George and Harry escorted Eleanor to Lifeboat No. 4 and helped her in. John Jacob Astor IV, who was one of the richest men in the world, did the same with his wife. The men were refused entry themselves by Officer Lightoller, who launched the boat with 20 of the 60 seats unoccupied.

George and Harry died, and Eleanor was rescued by the *Carpathia*. Harry's body was never recovered. George's body was recovered by the *MacKay-Bennett*, but its condition was such that it was buried at sea. A memorial service for the two of them was held at St. Paul's Episcopal Church in Elkins Park, Pennsylvania, where stained-glass windows were dedicated in their memory.

Life as a *Titanic* Survivor: Eleanor presented Harvard University with a two million dollar library in memory of her son Harry, a 1907 Harvard graduate. She also rebuilt St. Paul's Episcopal Church as a

The Widener mausoleum honors both George and Harry Widener, Father and son, who perished on the voyage. The wife and mother Eleanor who was a survivor was laid to rest here.

memorial to her husband, and in 1929 gave $300,000 to the Hill School at Pottstown for a general science building in memory of Harry, a 1903 Hill School graduate.

In 1915, Mrs. Widener married explorer Dr. Alexander Hamilton Rice and traveled extensively in South America, Europe and India. In July 1937, while shopping in a Paris store, she died of a heart attack, at the age of 76.

Eleanor Elkins Rice is buried in the Widener mausoleum in Philadelphia's Laurel Hill Cemetery. Her crypt makes no mention of the *Titanic*. Harry and George Widener have cenotaphs in the mausoleum, both of which reference the ship.

William Ernest Carter
Lucile Polk Carter Brooke

Counties: Montgomery, Berks – *Towns:* Bala Cynwyd, Birdsboro
Cemeteries: West Laurel Hill, St. Michael's[2]
Addresses: 227 Belmont Avenue, Mill and Church Streets

William Thornton Carter
Lucile Carter Reeves

County: Montgomery – *Towns:* Bala Cynwyd, King of Prussia
Cemeteries: West Laurel Hill, Valley Forge Memorial Gardens
Addresses: 227 Belmont Avenue, 352 South Gulph Road

Things turned out differently for the Carter clan from Philadelphia, who ironically on the night of the accident were together with the Wideners at a dinner party in honor of the ship's Captain. William Carter, 36 years old, was traveling with his wife, Lucile (also 36), and his children (11-year-old son, William, and 13-year-old daughter, Lucile). Also traveling with them were their maid (Auguste Serreplan), Mr. Carter's servant (Alexander Cairns) and his chauffeur (Charles Aldworth).

The original story was that Cairns, Aldworth, and Mr. Carter escorted his wife, two children and maid to Lifeboat No. 4. The three men

---

2. Now known as the New First Baptist Church of Birdsboro

Grave of William Ernest Carter and his son William Carter both of whom survived the sinking.

then left, accompanied by George Widener, John Astor and John Thayer. Mrs. Carter, her son and daughter, and the maid were all rescued. The men all died, *except for Mr. Carter.* Carter escaped on the Collapsible "C" lifeboat, along with Bruce Ismay. Ismay was the President of White Star Lines, the company that owned the *Titanic*. In the tragedy's aftermath, Ismay was savaged by both the American and British Press for deserting the ship while women and children were still on board. Some papers called him the "Coward of the *Titanic*." There are accounts that Ismay and the elder Carter stepped into Collapsible C at the last minute. By other accounts, Carter was swimming in the water and then picked up by the lifeboat. Whatever happened, Carter actually ended up on board the *Carpathia* before his family members. More than two hours after his arrival, his wife and children reached the *Carpathia* in Lifeboat No. 4, which Mrs. Carter had helped row.

Two years later, Mrs. Carter sued for divorce and testified that her husband had left her and their children to fend for themselves. She said that after the *Titanic* hit the iceberg at 11:40 P.M., Mr. Carter came to the stateroom, told her to get up, get herself and the children dressed, and then he essentially . . . vanished. According to her, from that moment until the time she arrived at the *Carpathia* around 8:00 A.M. the next morning, she did not once see Mr. Carter.

Life as Titanic Survivors: After the divorce, Lucile married George Brooke in 1914. She died in 1934 at the age of 58 and is buried in St. Michael's Cemetery in Birdsboro, Pennsylvania. Her tombstone reads: "Lucile Polk Brooke."

William Ernest Carter died in 1940, at the age of 65. He was buried in a huge mausoleum in West Laurel Hill Cemetery. His son, William Thornton Carter, died in 1985, at the age of 84. He was buried alongside his father.

The daughter, Lucile, married a man named Samuel J. Reeves. She died in 1962, at the age of 64. Lucile Carter Reeves is reportedly buried in Valley Forge Memorial Gardens, but when the authors visited there, the staff could not find any record of her being there.

John Borland Thayer, Jr. (49)
Marian Thayer
John B. ("Jack") Thayer III
County: Montgomery – *Town:* Bryn Mawr
Cemetery: Church of the Redeemer
Address 230 Pennswood Road

Also at that dinner party hosted by the Wideners were John and Marian Thayer of Philadelphia, along with their 17-year-old son, Jack. Mr. Thayer was the second Vice President of the Pennsylvania Railroad. They were preparing for bed when the collision occurred. Jack at first went to investigate and returned to put on warm clothes and alert his parents. They went up to the "A" Deck where things were crowded and noisy. Jack and his parents were separated in the confusion, but John saw Marian safely into Lifeboat No. 4.

Jack encountered a friend he had met earlier that evening over coffee, Milton Long, and tried to board a lifeboat, but they were turned away because they were men. They discussed jumping overboard and swimming to a lifeboat, but decided against it for the moment.

Memorial to Marian and John Thayer who were both passengers on the great ship. Only Marian survived the voyage.

John watched as Lifeboat No. 4 was lowered and his wife, Marian, helped row away from the *Titanic*. He then joined his friends, Charles Duane Williams, George Widener, and George's son, Harry, to await their fate. His body was never recovered.

Jack and Milton had watched the last lifeboats being lowered and realized they were not full. They now felt that jumping and swimming to a boat was their best chance. At 2:15 A.M.—just minutes before the *Titanic* slipped beneath the ocean's surface—the two men along with hundreds of other passengers made their way towards the stern of the ship. As the water rushed up the sinking deck, Long and Thayer stood at the starboard rail near the second smokestack, shook hands and prepared to jump into the water, now just 12 to 15 feet below them. It was the last time the two of them would ever see each other.

It was fortunate that Jack Thayer was a stronger swimmer. He struggled in the numbing cold but ultimately did manage to successfully swim against the suction of the sinking liner. Long did not fare as well. In subsequent interviews, Jack said that although he never actually saw Long again after the two of them jumped, it was his belief that Long had "been sucked into the deck below" and drowned.

Jack swam until he reached the Collapsible "B" lifeboat, which was overturned as a result of having been improperly launched. About 35 men were clinging precariously to the hull of the capsized boat. A few of

Grave of Titanic survivor Jack Thayer who later committed suicide.

those men helped pull Jack (who by that time was too exhausted to help himself) from the frigid water. Realizing the danger to the boat of being swamped by the mass of swimmers trying to reach them, the men who had found refuge on Collapsible B slowly paddled away from them.

They drifted all night, trying to remain motionless so as not to slip off into the icy water. After daylight, Lifeboat Nos. 4 and 12 came to their aid. Thayer was so distracted trying to get into boat 12 that he did not notice his mother in boat 4 nearby. Likewise, his mother was so numbed by the cold that she did not see him either. When Lifeboat No. 12 finally was rescued by the *Carpathia*, Jack and his mother were reunited and discovered that the senior Thayer, John, had not made it.

Life as *Titanic* Survivors: Marian Thayer never remarried. She died on April 14, 1944, the 32nd anniversary of the disaster, at the age of 72. She is buried in the Church of the Redeemer Cemetery in Bryn Mawr, Pennsylvania.

Jack Thayer went on to graduate from the University of Pennsylvania, served as a captain in the artillery during World War I, got married and had five children, and had a career in banking and finance. In 1940, he described his experiences with the *Titanic's* sinking in vivid detail in a self-published pamphlet printed for family and friends. This paper was published again in 2012 as "A Survivor's Tale: The *Titanic* by John B. Thayer."

Both of Jack's sons, Edward and John the IV, enlisted in the armed forces during World War II. In October 1943, Edward was killed in action in the Pacific. Jack had survived the *Titanic*, but he could not survive the death of a son. He committed suicide on September 20, 1945. He was found in an automobile at 48th and Parkside Avenue with his wrists and throat cut. He was 50 years old. He too is buried at the Church of the Redeemer Cemetery.

Charlotte Cardeza
Thomas Cardeza
County: Montgomery – *Town:* Bala Cynwyd
Cemetery: West Laurel Hill
Address 227 Belmont Avenue

Another Pennsylvanian who survived the disaster was Mrs. Charlotte Cardeza. Her father, Thomas Drake, was a co-founder of Fidelity Insurance. Mrs. Cardeza—a lover of big-game hunting—was returning home to Germantown, Pennsylvania with her 36-year-old son (Thomas), after an African safari and a visit to Thomas' hunting reserve in Hungary. They were accompanied on board the *Titanic* by Mrs. Cardeza's personal maid (Anna Ward) and Thomas' servant (Gustave Lesueur). The Cardeza entourage brought fourteen trunks, four suitcases, and three crates of baggage. They stayed in the most expensive suite on the *Titanic*, which featured two bedrooms, a sitting room, and a private 50-foot promenade.

In a strange twist of fate, all four members of their party—including two males—were allowed to board Lifeboat No. 3, and all four were rescued by the *Carpathia*.

Life as *Titanic* Survivors: Mrs. Cardeza died on August 1, 1939, at the age of 75. She is buried in a mausoleum in West Laurel Hill Cemetery. Thomas went on to be a director of his grandfather's company, Fidelity Insurance, from 1922-1951. Thomas died in June 1952, at the age of 77, and is buried with his mother in West Laurel Hill Cemetery.

Anna Ward, who had a premonition that something bad was going to happen, had to be persuaded to make the trip by her mother. She went on to marry Mrs. Cardeza's gardener, William Moynahan. She died on

Christmas Day 1955, at the age of 81, and is buried with her husband in West Laurel Hill Cemetery.

Fortunately for chocolate lovers all over the world, Milton Hershey and his wife, Kitty, who had put a $300 deposit down for tickets on the *Titanic*, did not make the journey. The Hersheys were on a lengthy trip to Nice, France, and had planned months in advance to make their return voyage home aboard the supposedly-unsinkable luxury vessel. However, urgent (and ultimately, life-saving!) business matters arose in the U.S. for which Mr. Hershey was needed. He and Kitty thus had to cancel their

Milton Hershey c. 1905

Titanic reservations and return to America a few days earlier than planned, ironically aboard the German ship, *Amerika*. They arrived back home several days before the *Titanic* sunk.

The check for the transaction, made out to White Star Lines, is still in the Hershey Community Archives.

If You Go:

We have said many times in our various volumes what treasures Laurel Hill Cemetery and West Laurel Hill Cemetery are. They contain hundreds of graves of interesting and important historical figures, many of whom are mentioned in our books.

Some other graves of interest in other cemeteries mentioned in this chapter are:

At Old Saint David Church Cemetery, you will find one of the graves of Anthony Wayne, a Revolutionary War hero who is buried in two places.

Also at Old Saint David Church Cemetery is the grave of William Atterbury, who was vice president of the Pennsylvania Railroad when he was abruptly commissioned a Brigadier

General in the United States Army during World War I. He was appointed Director General of Transportation for the Armed Services in Europe. His reorganization of the European Railroad Network contributed to the victory for the Allies. He was nicknamed "The Railroad General" and received medals from many nations, including the Distinguished Service Medal and the French Legion of Honor.

The Church of the Redeemer Cemetery has the grave of artist Mary Cassatt, who became the sole American artist at the forefront of the Impressionist movement. She is widely recognized as one of the most important figures in the development of American culture and an inspiration to a generation of women in the arts. You will also find the grave of George Earle, the Governor of Pennsylvania from 1935-1939, and a confidant and advisor to President Franklin D. Roosevelt.

Three interesting sports figures can be found at Saints Peter and Paul *Cemetery:*

Danny Murtaugh, who was a major league baseball player and manager. He was named National League Manager of the Year in 1944 with the Pittsburgh Pirates. He later led the Pirates to the famous upset of the heavily-favored New York Yankees in the 1960 World Series, and won the championship again in the 1971 World Series versus the Baltimore Orioles.

John Facenda, who was a sports newscaster for WCAU-TV in Philadelphia for 25 years and the voice of NFL Films for two decades.

Jack "Blackjack" Ferrante, who played for eight seasons as a wide receiver for the Philadelphia Eagles in the 1940s, despite never having attended college. He was discovered in the sandlots of Philadelphia and wound up being named an All-Pro two times and scored 31 touchdowns over his career.

At Arlington Cemetery are the graves of:.

Morris "Morrie" Rath, who was a major league baseball player for the Philadelphia Athletics (1909-10), the Cleveland

Naps (1910), Chicago White Sox (1912-13) and Cincinnati Reds (1919-1920). Batting leadoff for the Reds in the 1919 World Series, Rath became a key figure in the ensuing "Black Sox" scandal when he was hit by White Sox pitcher Eddie Cicotte with the second pitch of the Series. This was believed to be a signal to gamblers that the White Sox had agreed to throw the series.

Theodore Smith, who was an Indian Wars Medal of Honor recipient.

RATH-CHICAGO-AMER.

Morrie Rath baseball card

22

"The Triangle Shirtwaist Factory Fire"

84 GARMENT WORKERS

Counties: Queens, Kings, Richmond
Towns: Maspeth, Brooklyn, Staten Island
Cemeteries: Mount Zion, The Evergreens, Mt. Richmond
Addresses: 59-63 54th Avenue, 1630 Bushwick Avenue, 420 Clarke Avenue

It was near closing time, 4:45 PM, on a quiet spring afternoon on March 25, 1911, when a fire started at the Triangle Shirtwaist Company located on the 8th, 9th, and 10th floors of the Asch Building at 23-29 Washington Place in Manhattan (now known as the Brown Building, part of New York University). The fire was the deadliest industrial disaster in the history of the city and one of the deadliest in U.S. history. It caused the deaths of 146 garment workers. Most of them were recent Jewish and Italian immigrant women between 16 and 23 years old. The youngest victim was just 14 years old. The details of this tragedy shocked a nation and brought widespread attention to the dangerous sweatshop conditions of factories. It led to the development of a series of laws and regulations that better protected the safety of workers.

Owned by Max Blanck and Isaac Harris, the company produced women's blouses known as "shirtwaists." The workers, around 500 of them, worked nine hours a day on weekdays, plus seven hours on Saturdays, earning between $7.00 and

Monument remembering the victims.

Local firefighters respond during the tragedy.

$12.00 a week. They worked in cramped space at lines of sewing machines. The building had four elevators with access to the factory floors, but only one was operational, and it was down a long narrow corridor. There were two stairways down to the street, but one was locked from the outside to prevent stealing and the other only opened inward.

Only a year before the deadly fire, New York's garment workers had begun agitating for shorter hours, better pay, safer shops and unions. To the horror of Blanck and Harris, the young women of the Triangle factory joined the crusade and called for a strike. They became leaders in the largest women's strike in American history. More than 50 of the smallest factories gave in to their workers' demands. The Triangle bosses organized other owners and refused to give in.

After eleven weeks, the Triangle owners finally agreed to higher wages and shorter hours but drew the line at a union. Thus, back on the job, the Triangle workers still lacked any power to improve the worst conditions on the factory floor: inadequate ventilation, lack of safety precautions and fire drills, and locked doors. The danger of fire in factories like the Triangle Shirtwaist was well-known, but corruption in the garment industry (and in government,

Tombstone of a victim of the fire.

Bodies of young women who threw themselves to their death to escape the flames.

generally) insured that no safety measures were enacted. Blanck and Harris already had a history of four suspicious factory fires and had collected on large fire insurance policies. They had become known as New York's "Shirtwaist Kings," and each owned fully-staffed brownstones on Manhattan's Upper West Side.

When a tossed match or lit cigarette ignited a fire on the 8th floor of the building on that day in March, 1911, flames spread quickly. The manager attempted to use the fire hose to extinguish it, but was unsuccessful, as the hose was rotted and its valve was rusted shut. As the fire grew, panic ensued. Blanck and Harris received warnings by phone and escaped, but the 240 workers on the 9th floor continued stitching, oblivious to the flames gathering force on the floor below. When they finally did see the smoke, the women panicked. Some rushed toward the open stairwell, but columns of flames already blocked their path. They then tried to exit the building via the

Grave of another victim.

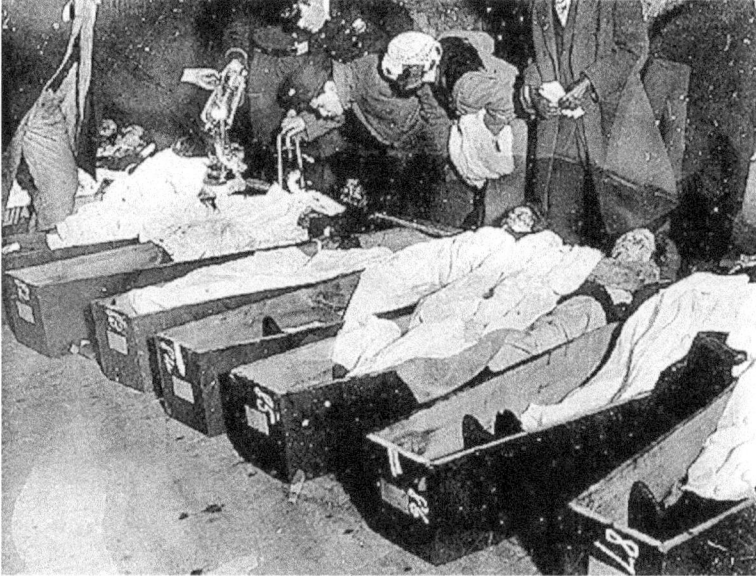

Bodies lined up waiting to be identified.

elevator, but it could hold only twelve people, and the operator was able to make just four trips before it broke down amid the heat and flames.

The door to the other stairway descending to Washington Place was locked to prevent theft by the workers. A bookkeeper on the 8th floor warned employees on the 10th by telephone, but there was no audible alarm and no way to contact staff on the 9th floor. Some on the 10th floor escaped by going up the Greene Street stairway onto the roof and then to another building, before the stairway became unusable in both directions. The foreman, who held the key to the locked stairway door, had already escaped and listened to the cries for help from the street.

Terrified employees crowded onto the single exterior fire escape. It was a flimsy and poorly anchored iron structure which may have been broken before the fire. It twisted and collapsed from the heat and overload, spilling about twenty people to their deaths on the concrete below.

Tombstone of a young father who lost his life.

Victims of the tragic fire.

Once the firefighters did arrive, their ladders were only long enough to reach as high as the 6th or 7th floors. A large crowd of bystanders gathered on the street and watched one after another of the girls jumping to their deaths on the concrete over 100 feet below. Sometimes the girls jumped three or four at a time. A total of 62 jumped or fell to their deaths. The bodies of teenage girls lined the street below. Blankets that rescuers used to catch the jumpers ripped from the weight and speed at which the bodies were falling. Some girls tried to jump to the ladders, but were unsuccessful.

William Gunn Shepherd, a reporter at the fire, would later say that, "I learned a new sound that day, a sound more horrible than description can picture, the thud of a speeding living body on a stone sidewalk." A man named Louis Waldman was in the crowd of bystanders and described the scene this way:

"Horrified and helpless, the crowds—I among them—looked up at the burning building, saw girl after girl appear at the reddened windows, pause for a terrified moment, and then leap to the pavement below, to land as mangled, bloody pulp. This went on for

Tombstone of a 20-year-old woman who lost her life.

Fruitless attempts to rescue trapped victims.

what seemed a ghastly eternity. Occasionally, a girl who had hesitated too long was licked by pursuing flames and, screaming with clothing and hair ablaze, plunged like a living torch to the street. Life nets held by the firemen were torn by the impact of the falling bodies."

When it was finally over, a total of 146 people were dead: 123 women and 23 men. The oldest victim was Providenza Panno, 43, and the youngest were 14-year-olds Kate Leone and Sara Rosaria Maltese. The bodies of the victims were taken to Charities Pier, located at 26th Street and the East River, for identification by friends and family.

Immediately after the fire, Triangle owners Blanck and Harris declared in interviews that their building was fireproof and that it had just been approved by the Department of Buildings. Yet the call for bringing

Employees before the fire.

those responsible to justice, and reports that the doors of the factory were locked at the time of the fire, prompted the District Attorney's office to seek an indictment against the owners. On April 11, 1911, a grand jury indicted Harris and Blanck on seven counts, charging them with second-degree manslaughter.

The trial started on December 4, 1911, and despite the testimony of 103 witnesses, the jury acquitted Blanck and Harris on December 27. The task of the jurors had been to determine whether the owners knew that the doors were locked at the time of the fire. Assistant District Attorney Charles Bostwick relied heavily on the testimony of survivor Kate Alterman, who spoke English as a second language, and when she testified, her story sounded rehearsed. She was not allowed to testify in her native language, Yiddish. The jurors believed that the door was locked, but defense attorney Max Steuer planted enough doubt in the jurors' minds

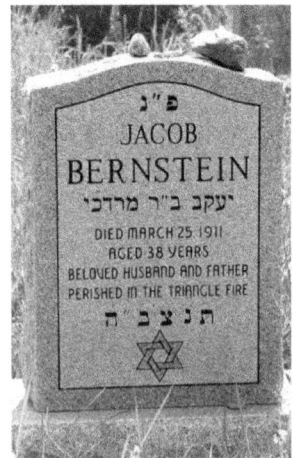

Tombstone of husband and gather who perished in the blaze.

Monument over graves of unidentified victims.

that they could not conclude that the owners were aware of this fact or were responsible.

A subsequent civil suit was filed in 1913, and on March 11, 1914, Harris and Blanck settled. They paid $75 per deceased victim. The

Staten Island Cemetery that is the final resting place of several victims.

insurance company paid Blanck and Harris about $60,000 more than the reported losses, or about $400 per casualty. In 1913, Blanck was once again arrested for locking the door in his factory during working hours. He was fined $20.

The Triangle Factory fire is widely considered a pivotal moment in history since, as a result of the fire, the New York State legislature created the Factory Investigating Commission to "investigate factory conditions in this and other cities and to report remedial measures of legislation to prevent hazard or loss of life among employees through fire, unsanitary conditions, and occupational diseases." The Commission was chaired by Robert Wagner, the Majority Leader of the State Senate, and co-chaired by Al Smith, the Majority Leader of the State Assembly. They held a series of widely-publicized investigations around the state, interviewing 222 witnesses and taking 3,500 pages of testimony. They hired field agents to do on-site inspections of factories. They started with the issue of fire safety and moved on to broader issues of the risks of injury in the factory environment.

New York City's Fire Chief, John Kenlon, told the investigators that his department had identified more than 200 factories where condi-tions made a fire, like the one at the Triangle Factory, possible. The State

Commission's reports and recommendations helped modernize the state's labor laws, making New York State one of the most progressive states in terms of labor reform.

From 1911 to 1914, a total of 36 new laws reforming the state labor code were enacted. They mandated better building access and egress, fireproofing requirements, the availability of fire extinguishers, the installation of alarm systems and automatic sprinklers, better eating and toilet facilities for workers, and placed limits on the number of hours that women and children could work. Two other significant developments were the creation of the Fire Prevention division as part of the Fire Department and the founding of the American Society of Safety Engineers on October 14, 1911.

Once the New York legislature enacted safety laws, other states in the U.S. followed suit. Workers also began to look towards

Tombstone of a 17-year-old female victim.

unions to voice their concerns over safety and pay. Robert Wagner went on to the United States Senate, where he spearheaded the passage of the National Labor Relations Act, which gave organizing rights to workers. Another Commission member, Frances Perkins, served as President Roosevelt's Labor Secretary from 1933 to 1945, becoming the first woman appointed to the U.S. Cabinet. In that job, she helped craft federal laws that limited working hours nationally and the age children could work, set minimum wages and inaugurated the social security system.

The last living survivor of the fire was Rose Freedman, who died in Beverly Hills, California, in 2001 at the age of 107. She was two days away from her 18th birthday at the time of the fire, which she survived by following the company's executives and being rescued from the roof. The building, at 23-29 Washington Place, has been designated a National Historic Landmark as well as a New York City Landmark.

Victims of the fire were interred in sixteen different cemeteries. At Mount Zion Cemetery in Maspeth, Queens, there are 44 victims buried. There is a monument inside the Workman's Circle section of the cemetery. There is also a monument at The Evergreens Cemetery in Brooklyn dedicated to what once were eight victims who were burned so badly that relatives could not identify them. Six remained unknown for over a century and then, in 2011, their identities become known and a headstone with their names was added. A researcher named Michael Hirsch nailed down their identities for an HBO documentary, *Triangle: Remembering the Fire*.

Twenty-two victims of the fire were buried by the Hebrew Free Burial Association in a special section at Mt. Richmond Cemetery on Staten Island.

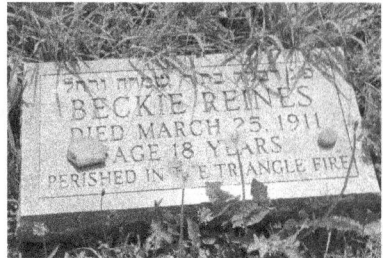

The Remember the Triangle Fire Coalition is an alliance of more than 200 organizations and individuals formed in 2008 to encourage and co-ordinate activities commemorating the fire and to create a permanent public art memorial to honor its victims. This project is still underway. In December 2015, New York Governor Andrew Cuomo announced that $1.5 million in state funds would be earmarked for the memorial.

If You Go:

Along with these three cemeteries, Calvary Cemetery in Queens has 34 victims of the Triangle Fire interred there, including the fire's oldest victim, Providenza Panno, as well as its two youngest victims, Kate Leone (buried in the family plot, but only her father and a brother are memorialized on the headstone) and Rosaria Maltese (buried there with her 36-year old mother, Catherine, and 20-year old sister, Lucy—co-workers at the Triangle factory who also died in the fire).

The Evergreens is the final resting place for Bill "Mr. Bojangles" Robinson and Amy Vanderbilt (1908-1974).

Mt. Zion is a large, congested cemetery that contains the graves of composer Marvin Hamlisch (1944-2012) and author Nathaniel West (1903-1940).

One of the many monuments contained in several cemetery's where the victims were laid to rest.

23

"Mad Anthony"

ANTHONY WAYNE

County: Delaware
Town: Wayne
Cemetery: Old St. David's Church
Address: 763 South Valley Forge Road

Anthony Wayne was a United States Army general in the American Revolutionary War and a statesman who is buried in two places. Had he not died suddenly at the age of 51, he might have given John Adams or Thomas Jefferson a real challenge for the Presidency in 1796 and 1800.

Wayne was born on New Years Day 1745 in Chester County, Pennsylvania, and attended a private school in Philadelphia operated by his uncle. He eventually became an excellent surveyor and in 1765 was sent to Nova Scotia as a financial agent and surveyor in the service of a real estate company on the recommendation of Benjamin Franklin. He returned to the United States in 1767, married, and continued in his profession as well as serving in several local offices. In 1774, his father Isaac died and Anthony inherited his father's prosperous tannery business. Also that year, he was chosen as one of the provincial representatives to consider the relations between the colonies and Great Britain, and was a member of the Pennsylvania convention that was held in Philadelphia to discuss this matter.

Wayne served in the Pennsylvania legislature in 1775. He was fond of military affairs. He began studying works on the art of war, and at the onset of the Revolutionary War raised a militia. In 1776, Wayne became colonel of the 4th Pennsylvania regiment. He and his regiment were part of the Continental Army's failed invasion of Canada. He attacked the British at the Battle of Three Rivers and although wounded and defeated, withdrew his troops creditably and then was ordered to assume command at Fort Ticonderoga.

Anthony Wayne

In February 1777, Wayne was commissioned a brigadier general. Prior to the war, Wayne had no military experience and other more experienced officers resented his quick advancement. He became known for his bravado and ill-advised attacks. He earned the nickname "Mad" Anthony Wayne because of his impulsive actions on the battlefield. Wayne was known for his fiery temper and would rather attack the enemy than avoid them.

Later in 1777, he assisted George Washington in the failed defense of the nation's capitol, Philadelphia. He commanded troops at Brandywine, Germantown and Paoli. The British surprise attack at Paoli on September 20, 1777, was a dark moment for Wayne. He lost a lot of men, and some of his officers thought he handled it poorly. Wayne's temper took hold, and he demanded first an official inquiry and then a full court martial.

General Anthony Wayne, after portrait by Charles Willson Peale. The General's portrait was painted c. 1783 with him in full Revolutionary War uniform.

The court martial unanimously exonerated Wayne and acquitted him "with the highest honor." Washington heartily approved.

Washington relied heavily on Wayne throughout the war. Before making strategic decisions, it was Washington's habit to have his top generals write out their suggestions. He could always count on Wayne to propose aggressive and well thought-out plans.

During the winter of 1777-78, Wayne did much to supply the American camp at Valley Forge. In March, he made a successful raid into British lines, capturing hor-ses, cattle and other needed supplies. In June of 1778, he led the American attack at the Battle of Monmouth. It was the first time Americans held their own in toe-to-toe battle with the British troops.

The highlight of Wayne's Revolutionary War service was his victory at Stony Point, New York on July 16, 1779. Washington had asked Wayne to form and command an elite "American Light Corps" (the equivalent of to-day's Special Forces). Wayne led his troops in a carefully planned, night-time, surprise attack against a heavily fortified stronghold on top of a steep Hudson River palisade. The assault was successful and Wayne's troops captured the fort and its occupants. Before dawn, Wayne sent Washington a message that read: "The fort and garrison with Colonel Johnston are ours. Our officers and men behaved like men who are determined to be free."

The assault at Stony Point was widely recognized as one of the most brilliant maneuvers of the war. Congress unanimously passed resolutions praising Wayne and awarded him a gold medal commemorative. The Continental Army had experienced few successes. This victory, led personally by General Wayne, substantially improved the soldiers' morale.

In 1780, Wayne helped put down a mutiny of 1,300 Pennsylvania men who had not received payment from the government. He did so by serving as the men's advocate before the Confederation Congress, where he arranged an agreement to the advantage of the government and the satisfaction of the men.

In the summer of 1781 just before the Battle of Yorktown, Wayne saved a Continental Army force led by the Marquis de Lafayette from a trap set by the commander of the British Army, Lieutenant General Lord Cornwallis, near Williamsburg, Virginia. Wayne's small contingent of 800 Pennsylvanians was the vanguard of the continental forces. They were crossing over a swamp by a narrow causeway when they were am-bushed by over 4,000 British. Instead of retreating, Wayne charged. The unexpected maneuver so surprised the enemy that they fell back confused allowing the rest of Lafayette's command to avoid the trap.

After the British surrender at Yorktown on October 19, 1781, Wayne went further south and severed the British alliance with Native American tribes in Georgia. He negotiated peace treaties with both the Creek and Cherokee, for which Georgia rewarded him with the gift of a large rice plantation. In October 1783 he was promoted to major general and re-tired from the Continental Army.

Wayne returned to Pennsylvania and resumed his civilian life. In 1784, he was elected to the general assembly from Chester County and served in the convention that ratified the Constitution of the United States. He then moved to Georgia and was elected to the Second United States Congress in 1791. He lost that seat during a debate over his residency qualifications and declined to run for reelection.

President Washington showed his high regard for Wayne once again in 1792 when he recalled him from civilian life and appointed Wayne as the commanding general of the newly-formed "Legion of the United States." At the end of the Revolutionary War, Great Britain agreed that the Mississippi River would be the Western boundary of the United States and that the Great Lakes would be the northern border. Presumably this meant British troops would withdraw from these areas into Canada. In fact, they did not. They encouraged and supplied a Western Indian Confederacy led by Blue Jacket of the Shawnees and Little Turtle of the Miamis. The Indians had achieved major victories over U.S. forces in 1790 under command of General Josiah Harmar and in 1791 under

The blockhouse where Wayne died and he was originally buried.

command of General Arthur St. Clair. More than 700 Americans died in the fighting.

Wayne recruited troops from the Pittsburgh area and established a basic training facility at Legionville to prepare the men of the "Legion of the United States" for battle. Located in Beaver County, Legionville was the first facility ever established to provide basic training for U.S. Army recruits.

In August 1794, Wayne mounted an assault on the Indian confederacy at the Battle of Fallen Timbers near Toledo, Ohio. It was a decisive victory for the U.S. forces and ended for all time the power of the British on American soil.

Wayne then negotiated the Treaty of Greenville between the Indian tribes and the United States. The treaty was signed in August 1795 and gave most of what is now Ohio to the United States. He returned home to a hero's welcome in the Philadelphia area.

In June 1796, Wayne was back in the frontier overseeing the surrender of British forts to the U.S. In a visit to Fort Presque Isle in Erie, Pennsylvania, he suffered a serious gout attack. There were no physicians at the fort and calls went out to Pittsburgh and the Army hospitals. Unfortunately, help arrived too late, and Anthony Wayne died on December 15, 1796.

A year earlier at Fort Presque Isle, to assist in defending against attacks from Native Americans, 200 Federal troops from Wayne's army under the direction of Captain John Grubb built a blockhouse on a bluff there known as Garrison Hill. Wayne had requested that upon his death he be buried there. When he died, his body was placed in a plain oak coffin, his initials and date of death were driven into the wood using round-headed brass tacks, and his request was honored: he was buried at the foot of the blockhouse's flagstaff on Garrison Hill.

Twelve years later, Wayne's son, Isaac, rode to Erie in a small, two-wheeled carriage called a "sulky." He came (at the urging of his sister Peggy) to bring his father's remains back to be buried in the family plot at St. David's Church about 400 miles away outside of Philadelphia. Young Wayne enlisted the help of Dr. J.G. Wallace, who had been with Mad Anthony at the Battle of Fallen Timbers and at his side when he died.

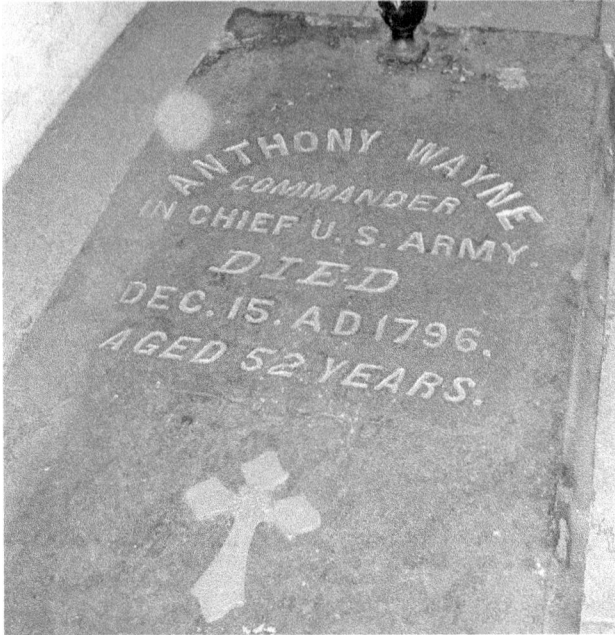

The original grave site of "Mad" Anthony Wayne.

When Wallace opened Wayne's coffin, he found little decay except in the lower portion of one leg. This caused a dilemma, as Isaac did not have enough space to transport the entire body. He expected to put bones in boxes on his sulky. Dr. Wallace used a custom common to American Indians to solve the dilemma. He dismembered the body and boiled it in a large iron kettle until the flesh dropped off. He cleaned the bones and packed them into Isaac's boxes. The task was so distasteful that Dr. Wallace threw the remaining tissue and his instruments into the coffin and closed the grave. Isaac Wayne made the long journey across Pennsylvania with his father's bones in the back of his sulky. The bones were interred at Old St. David's Church Cemetery with funeral rites celebrated on July 4, 1809. A huge crowd attended.

General Anthony Wayne is well-memorialized. He has a long list of cities, towns and municipalities named after him, including 15 states that have a Wayne County. In Pennsylvania, there is a Wayne County as well as a Waynesboro and a Waynesburg. He has schools, bridges, a university (Wayne State University in Detroit), a brewing company (Mad Anthony Brewing Co. in Fort Wayne, Indiana), an ale (Mad Anthony

Memorial marks one of the gravesites that hold the remains of a hero of the American Revolution Mad Anthony Wayne.

Ale, a product of Erie Brewing Co.), a hotel (General Wayne Inn in Merion, Pa.), parks, hospitals and even a barber shop named in his honor. There is a large statue in Fort Wayne, Indiana, as well as a gilded bronze equestrian statue at the Philadelphia Museum of Art and one at Valley Forge. In 1929, the U.S. Post Office issued a stamp honoring Wayne and commemorating the 150th anniversary of the Battle of Fallen Timbers.

If You Go:

Anthony Wayne's strange interment has given rise to a popular ghost story. It was a long, tough trip from Erie to Wayne over 380 miles of unpaved roads of what is now Route 322. The story goes that Isaac had many prob-lems along the way and that the trunk kept falling off and breaking open, losing bones along the way. Some claim that on each New Year's Day (Wayne's birthday), his ghost rises from his grave in Wayne and rides across the state searching for his missing bones. The kettle used to boil Wayne's body and the dis-section instruments used by Dr. Wallace are on display at the Erie County History Center on State Street in Erie.

Very nearby is Erie Cemetery, which contains the graves of a number of interesting people, including famous Civil War General Strong Vincent, who was a hero at the Battle of Gettysburg where he died; Harry Burleigh, the internationally known African-American baritone and composer who composed such spirituals as "Swing Low Sweet Chariot" and "Nobody Knows the Trouble I've Seen;" Andrew Forbeck, a Congressional Medal of Honor recipient from the Philippine Insurrection; and Samuel Jethroe, who was the oldest man to win baseball's Rookie of the Year award in 1950 at the age of 32.

About 15 miles outside of Erie is the small town of Girard, which is home to the Battles Bank Gallery. Battles was a bank until the late 1980s but its owner, Charlotte Elizabeth Battles, brought much attention to Girard when she defied President Roosevelt's order to close in 1933. She sent a note to FDR saying "Mr. President, we're minding our business, you do the same. Since I do not presume to tell you how to run the country, please do not presume to tell me how to run my bank." Ms. Battles, who died in 1952, is buried in Girard Cemetery.

The Girard Borough Building contains a statue of a dog that is an interesting grave story. For over 100 years the statue of a dog named "Shep" had stood vigilantly over the grave of his master, H.C. Davis, who died in 1881. Shep died of poisoning in 1884 and was buried in the same plot. Mrs. Davis commissioned the statue in 1889 using a photograph to sculpt a life-sized figure of Shep sitting in a captain's chair. The statue was placed to mark the family plot in 1890. On September 30, 1993, the statue of Shep suddenly disappeared, the victim of an apparent theft. The town was stunned and angered. A reward fund was organized and flyers bearing a picture of the statue were distributed nationwide. Despite these efforts, local police went years without a lead in the case.

This is the caldron of death where Wayne's son boiled the body down to the bare bones.

In 1997, Girard police received a phone call from an antique dealer in New Haven, Connecticut. The dealer had recently purchased a statue matching the description on the flyer. The police invest-igated and found the statue had traveled through antique dealers in Pennsylvania, Ohio, New York, Maine and Connecticut. The police never solved the case as the first buyer of the statue had passed away in 1995. The dealer graciously agreed to return the statue to Girard and many in town were delighted. Once back in his hometown, Shep was donated by the descendants of the dog's owner to the Borough of Girard. Today, Shep remains on display in the lobby of the Girard Borough Municipal Building.

There are also interesting people buried at Old St. David's Church Cemetery (sometimes referred to today as St. David's Episcopal Church or simply "Old Saint David's") in the town of Wayne. Two of note are William Wallace Atterbury and Richard Norris Williams.

Known as the "Railroad General" in World War I, Atterbury was operating vice-president of the Pennsylvania Railroad at the outbreak of the war and reorganized the European railroad network to create rapid movement of allied troops and equipment that contributed greatly to victory. He was awarded medals by the United States, France, England, Serbia and Romania. He appeared on the cover of Time Magazine in February 1933.

R. Norris Williams (as he was generally known) was a champion tennis player, a *Titanic* survivor, and the great-great-grandson of Benjamin Franklin. He won two U.S. Open singles championships in 1914 and 1916. He also was on the victorious American Davis Cup teams in 1925 and 1926, and at the 1924 Olympics in Paris he won a gold medal in mixed doubles. All of this came after surviving the *Titanic* disaster, where his father with whom he was traveling died. Williams was inducted into the International Tennis Hall of Fame in 1957.

24

"Cold Blooded Murder"

JOSEPH "JOCK" YABLONSKI
(1910–1969)

County: Washington
City: Washington
Cemetery: Washington Cemetery
Address: 498 Park Avenue

In 1963 a cantankerous bully served as president of the United Mine Workers of America. W.A. "Tough Tony" Boyle rose to the presidency that year with the endorsement of legendary John L. Lewis, lord of the UMW for over 50 years. Boyle ran the union like a mob boss and was viewed as corrupt, isolated and cozy with mine owners. Boyle—along with UMWvice-president George Titler and secretary-treasurer John Owens—were taking unjustifiably large sums from the union as salary and benefits.

Boyle's daughter and brother and Owens' two sons had high paying staff jobs. The officers were chauffeured around town in Cadillacs and the union paid for Owens' residence in the Sheraton Carlton Hotel in Washington, D.C. The leadership was out of touch with ordinary miners and they hadn't been in a mine in years.

On November 20, 1968, 99 men entered the Consolidated Coal Company's No. 9 Mine in Farmington, West Virginia. Some of the men had been worried about too much coal dust and too much methane gas in the mine, either of which could cause an explosion. They did not know that a safety alarm on one of the ventilation fans had been disabled. The lack of fresh air allowed methane to build up in the mine and at around 5:30 A.M. an explosion occurred. Some died where they stood. Others lived to suffocate in the toxic fumes. Seventy-eight men died in all.

The Yablonski funeral.

Jock Yablonski was no radical. He had been a Lewis loyalist since 1934, a district president from 1958–1965 and a member of the Union's Executive Board from 1942-1969. He realized slowly that Boyle was no John Lewis and the union's mild response to the Farmington accident pushed him to break with its leadership. On May 29, 1969, Yablonski announced he was running against Boyle for union president. He had been encouraged to run by Ralph Nader, who assured him of legal and financial help.

"If I do run, Ralph, they'll try to murder me," Yablonski said.

"Oh they wouldn't dare," Nader replied.

Yablonski was born in Pittsburgh on March 1910. His parents were Polish immigrants. He began working in Pittsburgh-area mines as a boy and in 1925 he joined the union at age 15. Eight years later, when his father died in a mine explosion, he vowed to fight for the well-being of miners. He was elected a local union rep. in 1934, then to the UMW International executive board in 1940, and in 1958 he was elected president of UMW District 5.

When Tony Boyle became president of the UMW in 1963, he and Yablonski began to clash. In 1965, Boyle removed Yablonski as president of District 5, using new rules that made district presidents appointed not elected. This contentious relationship would reach its peak in the struggle for control of the union. On December 9, 1969, in an election widely seen as corrupt, Boyle beat Yablonski by a vote of 80,577–46,073. Yablonski felt the election was fixed and said so. He asked the U.S. Department of Labor to investigate the election for fraud and filed five lawsuits against the UMWA in federal court.

On New Years Eve 1969, three small-time hoods sat in a car on a lonely road in Clarksville, Pennsylvania, drinking beer and whiskey and waiting for the lights to go out in an old, brick farmhouse they were watching nearby. Around 1:00 A.M. the house went dark. The three men, Paul Gilly, Aubran Martin and Claude Vealey, approached the house, flattened the tires on two cars in the driveway, cut the house's telephone wires and then entered through a back door.

They crept upstairs where Yablonski, his wife Margaret, and his 25-year old daughter Charlotte, slept. Charlotte was killed first, shot twice in the head by Martin while she slept. Margaret was awakened by the shots and screamed when she saw Gilly and Vealey and was killed next. As Jock Yablonski made a move for a shotgun he kept near his bed, he was cut down by five bullets.

The killers quickly left the house and sped away. The bodies weren't discovered until January 5 when Yablonski's son, Kenneth, went to the house to check on them. Yablonski had actually met his killers weeks before his death, when they knocked on his door intending to kill him. They failed to carry out their plan that day, making up a story about how they were miners looking for work. Yablonski was suspicious of these men, however, and jotted down their license plate number on a yellow pad that the police later found on his desk. Authorities traced

"Tough" Tony Boyle

the car to Paul Gilly, a Cleveland house painter. They were intrigued to learn that Gilly's father-in-law was a UMW official in Tennessee named Silous Huddleston. Less than a month after the murders, the three gunmen were identified. They would become known in the press as the "Hillbilly Hit Men."

The day after the Yablonskis' bodies were found, 20,000 miners in West Virginia walked off the job in a one-day strike, convinced Boyle was responsible for the murders. The murders also sparked federal action. On January 8, 1970,

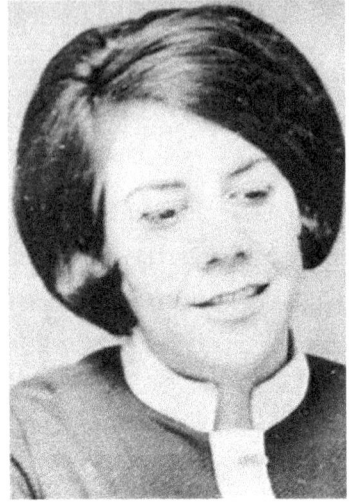

Charlotte Yablonski

Yablonski's attorney requested an investigation into the election by the Department of Labor. The Department had done nothing on Yablonski's complaints while he lived but after his murder Labor Secretary George Shultz assigned 230 investigators to the case.

Investigators discovered a diabolical plot and soon arrested Paul Gilly's wife, Annette, and her father, Silous Huddleston, who was president of a UMW Local in LaFollette, Tennessee where Boyle had defeated Yablonski 61–0. Huddleston, investigators discovered, was asked by two UMW bosses—Albert Pass and William Prater—to have Yablonski killed. He was promised $20,000. The money was embezzled from the union's funds. Huddleston asked his son-in-law Gilly to do the job, promising $5,000. He promised up to $1 million for legal aid if he got caught and a no-show job if he didn't. Gilly proceeded to hire Vealey and Martin to do the job.

The local Washington County (Pa.) District Attorney was Jess Costa. Costa realized that the defendants in this case would have experienced, tested trial lawyers. He realized his small staff of assistants in sleepy Washington, Pa. could be outmatched. He and his assistants were part-time employees. Costa didn't hesitate. He called on Richard Sprague, the first assistant District Attorney in Philadelphia—an experienced, hardened and well-known prosecutor—to oversee the investigation, arrest and prosecution.

Sprague accepted the assignment and it was announced in a press conference on February 28, 1970. On May 6, 1970, a county grand jury in Washington returned murder indictments against the five suspects (the three gunmen, plus Annette Gilly and Silous Huddleston), clearing the way for extradition proceedings to begin.

Vealey was the first to crack as he pled guilty and agreed to testify against the others, hoping to avoid the death penalty. He did testify and both Martin and Gilly were convicted and sentenced to death in November 1971 and March 1972.

While awaiting their trials in the Spring of 1972, Annette Gilly and Huddleston pled guilty to recruiting Paul Gilly, Martin and Vealey to commit the Yablonski murders. They also testified they were acting under the orders of UMW officials Prater and Pass. As a result, both Prater and Pass were indicted on murder charges in July 1972. Prater was convicted in March 1973 of three counts of murder. The next day he confessed and agreed to testify against Pass.

Meanwhile, the Department of Labor filed suit in federal court to overturn the 1969 UMWA International election. On May 1, 1972, Judge William Bryant threw out the results of the election and scheduled a new election to be held during the first eight days of December 1972. He also ordered that the Labor Department oversee the election. On May 28, 1972, the Miners for Democracy nominated Arnold Miller, a miner from West Virginia, to run against "Tough Tony" Boyle. The election took place as ordered. Miller was declared the winner on December 15 and certified by the Labor Department a week later. The vote was 70,373 for Miller and 56,334 for Boyle.

Pass's trial lasted only 15 days and on June 19, 1973 he was convicted of three counts of first-degree murder. He was the only defendant who did not agree to help the prosecutors make their case against Tony Boyle.

On September 6, 1973, Tony Boyle was charged with three murders. Before he could be extradited to Pennsylvania for trial, he swallowed an overdose of sedatives and nearly died. He recovered in a District of Columbia prison hospital. His trial began in late March 1974 in Delaware County, Pennsylvania. He was convicted on April 11 and sentenced to three consecutive terms of life in prison.

The Yablonski grave in Washington, Pa.

On January 28, 1977, the Supreme Court of Pennsylvania overturned Boyle's conviction and ordered that he be given a new trial. The court found that the trial judge had improperly refused to allow a government auditor to testify. Boyle was tried a second time and again found guilty in February 1978. Boyle filed a third appeal to overturn his conviction in July 1979, but the motion was denied. He served his sentence at the state correctional institution in Dallas, Pennsylvania. He suffered from a number of ailments in his final years and was repeatedly hospitalized. In 1983, he suffered a stroke. He died in custody at a Wilkes-Barre hospital on May 31, 1985 at age 80.

Little is known about Annette Gilly and Silous Huddleston after they were placed in a witness protection program. Martin, Vealey, Prater, and Pass all died in prison while serving their sentences. Paul Gilly was still alive and in prison at the time of this writing.

The Yablonski's are buried in Washington Cemetery and the grave is prominent yet plain. There have been a number of books written about the murders including *A Man Named Tony: The True Story of the Yablonski Murders*, by Stuart Brown and *Act of Vengeance* by Trevor Armbrister.

In 1995, the Pennsylvania Historical and Museum Commission installed a historical marker in California, Pennsylvania noting Yablonski's historical importance. The murders were also portrayed in a 1986

HBO movie, *Act of Vengeance*. Charles Bronson portrayed Yablonski, and Wilford Brimley played Boyle. It also starred Ellen Burstyn and Keanu Reeves.

If You Go:

Washington, Pa. is a nice college town, home to Washington & Jefferson College. Washington Cemetery also contains the grave of Hugh Patterson Boon (1834–1908), an Army Captain during the Civil War who was awarded the Medal of Honor for his bravery at the Battle of Sailor's Creek, Virginia, on April 6, 1865.

INDEX

www.ingramcontent.com/pod-product-compliance
Lightning Source LLC
Chambersburg PA
CBHW021221090426
42740CB00006B/317